The Church as the Family of God and the Care for Creation

Copyright 2018 Maximian Khisi

All rights reserved. No part of this publication may be reproduced, stored in a retrieval system, or transmitted in any from or by any means, electronic, mechanical, photocopying, recording or otherwise without prior permission from the publishers.

Published by
Mzuni Press
P/Bag 201 Luwinga
Mzuzu 2

ISBN 978-99960-60-62-5
eISBN 978-99960-60-63-2

The Mzuni Press is represented outside Africa by:
African Books Collective Oxford (orders@africanbookscollective.com)

www.mzunipress.blogspot.com
www.africanbookscollective.com

Editorial assistance and cover: Daniel Neumann
Cover picture: Daniel Neumann (View from Sengha Hill towards Lake Malawi)

The Church as the Family of God and the Care for Creation

Maximian Khisi

Mzuni Press

Mzuni Books no. 36

Mzuzu

2018

Acronyms and Abbreviations

ACWECA	Association of Consecrated Women in Eastern and central Africa
ADCOM	Association of Diocesan Clergy in Malawi
AMECEA	Association of Member Episcopal Conferences in Eastern Africa
CADECOM	Catholic Development Commission
CCJP	Catholic Commission for Justice and Peace
CFM	Christian Family Movement
CICLSAL	Congregation for Institutes of Consecrated Life and Societies of Apostolic Life
ECM	Episcopal Conference of Malawi
IUSG	International Union of Superiors General
SCC	Small Christian Community

In this book the Bible version used is the New International Version (NIV), © 1973, 1978, 1984, 2011 International Bible Society, unless indicated otherwise.

Contents

Introduction	6
Chapter 1: Use of Models in Ecclesiology	10
Chapter 2: Historical Development of the Model of Church as God's Family	30
Chapter 3: Biblical and Socio-anthropological Foundations of the African Ecclesiology	70
Chapter 4: Challenging Issues with the African Concept of Family	97
Chapter 5: Applications of the Model of Church as Family of God in the Archdiocese of Lilongwe	108
Chapter 6: Challenging Issues with the Metaphor of Family for the Church	133
Chapter 7: Biblical and Theological Basis for Human Stewardship of the Environment	150
Chapter 8: Expressions of Church as God's Family and their Practices in Saving the Environment	192
Chapter 9: Church as New Creation, a New Concept for Saving the Environment	232
Bibliography	265
Index	277

Introduction

Of late there has grown in African Catholicism the concept of Church as the Family of God, *Familia Dei,* which has enhanced greater social cohesion among the members of the Church and strengthened interpersonal relationships among them. This was in tandem with the design of God who willed to make men and women holy and save them, not as individuals without any bond or link between them, but rather wanted to make them into a people who would acknowledge him and serve him in holiness.[1] The modern understanding of this concept emerged from the Vatican II ecclesiology of communion with its consequent theology of the local Church (1962-1965). It received impetus and adoption in the African Synod (1994) as a model of being Church particularly appropriate for Africa.[2] The understanding of Church as Family of God in Africa was based on rich biblical and African anthropological and sociological foundations. The being of Church as Family in Africa led to the development of the Small Christian Communities (SCCs), *Miphakati,* which eventually became the privileged loci for the living of the ecclesiology of Church as God's Family.[3]

Pastorally, the concept was to remind the faithful that through faith and baptism they had one Father (God himself) and through their spiritual regeneration they were made brothers and sisters. As such they had the task of creating a new humanity in which everyone would be considered an authentic human being and in which there would be no room for racial, tribal, and gender discrimination.[4] However the

---

[1] Vatican II, *Lumen Gentium: The Dogmatic Constitution on the Church*, no. 9.

[2] John Paul II, *Ecclesia in Africa, Apostolic Exhortation on the Church in Africa*, Nairobi: Paulines, 1995, no. 63, pp. 47-48.

[3] Joseph G. Healey, *Building the Church as Family of God: Evaluation of the Small Christian Communities in Eastern Africa*, Nairobi: CUEA Press, 2012.

[4] Francis Appiah-Kubi, "The Church, Family of God: Relevance and Pastoral Challenges of a metaphor from an African perspective", part of Doctoral Dissertation, in Thomas Knieps (et al), *The Household of God and the Local*

application of this concept, which had become a model of being Church, in the Archdiocese of Lilongwe was found wanting in the dire need for human responsibility over the natural environment. It was discovered to be too anthropocentric and tended to focus more on the protection of human life found in the ideals of togetherness, fellowship, participation, and solidarity. The model did not awaken among the faithful of Christ the sense of universal fraternity with God's creation which should have called for their environmental commitments amidst the challenge of ecological and environmental crises.

There was little, sporadic and insignificant involvement of the parish communities with environmental issues either through environmental commitments or through provision of environmental education to its members. The diocese of Lilongwe covers seven of the nine districts of Central Malawi; Kasungu, Nkhotakota, Salima, Ntchisi, Dowa, Mchinji, and Lilongwe. This was an area that was once upon a time greatly endowed and graced with the things of nature. Yet it was suffering from environmental degradation seen in: pollution of its water, air, land, soil, growing deforestation, poor waste management and escalation of the throwaway culture, loss of biodiversity, and depletion of the natural resources. Together with the global community this area was also bearing the negative effects of the environmental and ecological crisis evidenced in: droughts, intermittent rains, dry spells, climate change, global warming, floods, and the reduction in the quality of human life among others.

Given the complexity of the environmental and ecological crises efforts towards mitigation were not to be left only in the hands of science and education. There was not only one way to the solution of the problem. Every form of art and wisdom, including religion and theology, were to be involved towards providing answers and solutions to the problem of the environmental and ecological crisis.

This book is an endeavour to offer a path towards the solution of the problem of environmental crisis through the theological discipline of

---

Households: Revisiting the Domestic Church, Bibliotheca Ephemeridum Theologicarum Lovaniensium (CCLIV), Leuven: Peeters, 2013, pp. 72-76.

ecclesiology. Using the Catholic Archdiocese of Lilongwe's understanding of Church as the Family of God, the book concludes that the application of the concept of Church as family of God brought great social cohesion among the people but did not manage to de-hyphenate the human relationship to the world. It has broadened the human feeling of superiority over the natural environment. The application of this concept joined the rank of other authentic Christian theological concepts which were but wrongly understood and applied by some sections of the Church which contributed to the abuse and misuse of nature like; the theological concept of *creatio ex-nihilo* (creation out of nothing), *imago Dei* (human creation in the image and likeness of God), and the *scala natura* (scale of nature), and the understanding of dominion over nature.[5]

There was need for a renewal of the concept of being Church for it worked on the premise that certain mindsets were really capable of influencing human behaviour. Since Malawi is mostly Christian (approximately 80% of the population) of which 20% are Roman Catholic, there would be a contribution towards environmental mitigation if there was a renewal in the self-understanding of the Church. The book provides an ecclesiological complementarity which promotes universal fraternity among people and the things of nature, and one that could offer ample motivation for environmental and ecological commitments. It recommends an ecclesiological concept of Church as New Creation, *Nova creatio*. This concept and its newness would be a call for human beings to an ecological conversion, leading new lifestyles, change in their models of nature-worldviews, and change in the models of production and consumption. With it should come an environmental information, catechesis and education aimed at creating an "ecological citizenry."[6] This information and self-understanding as New Creation is to be aimed at instilling a sense of universal fraternity with God's creation and good habits in relating to and dealing with the things of nature. It is to lead the Church and

---

[5] www.uvm.edu/gflomenh/ENV-NGO-PA395/articles/Lynn-white/ [30.9.2015].

[6] Pope Francis, *Laudato Si*, pp. 115-116.

people of good will to find it noble to care for creation through little daily actions and changes in lifestyle. This would develop an ecological spirituality of protecting the world grounded in the convictions of their faith of Church as the community of the new creation.[7] The protection of the world by human beings was to be with a feeling of being its stewards, with God as creation's everlasting proprietor. The ecological conversion and ecclesiological renewal of being new creation needs to effect among the believers an evident new way of relationship with the world around them.

---

[7] David Kirchhoffer, *Saving Our World: Approaches to Ecology*, Johannesburg: Lumko, 2002.

Chapter 1: Use of Models in Ecclesiology

The Catholic Church adopted the model of the Church as God's Family to be the guiding idea for evangelism in Africa. The 1994 African Synod[8] Fathers approved it as the ecclesiological model appropriate for Africa.[9] In ecclesiology, a model is a typology metaphor which has a staying power. The use of models as an expression of the Church's nature was not totally new. What was new was that the Fathers laid the development of this model for the Church in Africa on the solid foundations of the African cultures with their emphasis on family and solidarity. The model of Church as Family had grown within the wider tradition of the Church of seeking to understand itself through the use of models.

Justification for the Use of Models in Ecclesiology

The use of models in understanding what the Church was, and what made the Church the Church, grew because it was not easy to capture the definition of the Church with finite human minds and intellect. Usage of models for the Church was felt to be an important intellectual tool in understanding a reality that was not easy to define and conceive.

Christian Theology, as faith seeking understanding, has, among the others, the task of interpreting faith, revelation and other realities using faith and reason. From the foundations of the theological

---

[8] The word synod comes from the Greek *synodos* which means assembly or meeting. The Greek word '*synodos*' with the sense of assembly or meeting is synonymous with the Latin word 'Concilium'. A synod is historically a council of a Church, usually convened to decide issues of doctrine, discipline, administration or its application. Synods held at the diocesan level offer a way the Church can renew itself, encouraging ongoing institutional and personal renewal. Through them, members learn to walk together: the people, the bishops and the pope.

[9] Pope John Paul II, *Ecclesia in Africa: Post-Synodal Apostolic Exhortation on the Church in Africa*, Nairobi: Paulines Publications, 1995, no. 63, pp. 47-48.

enterprise of seeking understanding of what the Church is, it became definitely clear that the reality of the Church was something that was too difficult to capture, grasp and exhaust in one word, language, phrase, or definition. The Church is a mystery because essentially it is a transcendent reality. No single human language could capture the richness of this transcendent reality. The Bible described the Church through different images, typologies and metaphors. The Scripture and theologians sought to describe this transcendental cum phenomenological reality, called Church, by the use of models.[10] Different Ecclesial communities have tried to describe this reality by using concepts, images, metaphors and expressions which they felt could facilitate the conceptualization of the Church's transcendent reality which were relevant to their contexts. In this daunting task ecclesiological theology had to engage various methods.

The self-understanding of the Church searched for the models (metaphors or images) that had essentially included its source and finality (salvific destiny). It had to include its identity (which makes it constant) and mission. The Church's mission in different contextual backgrounds necessitated the task of making the Church relevant to the situation of the time (which made it developing).

Definition and Use of Models in Ecclesiology

In different disciplines people have used models as intellectual tools in an attempt to say something about the unfamiliar in terms of the familiar, and to speak about what we do not know in terms of what we know. Images had the potential to make visible what was invisible.[11] As such the metaphor had the character of is and was not. The difference between a metaphor and a model was that the model was a metaphor with staying power. It was a metaphor that has gained stability and scope to present a pattern for relatively comprehensive and coherent explanation. It is through models that those pursuing to

---

[10] Dennis M. Doyle, *The Church Emerging from the Vatican II: A Popular Approach to Contemporary Catholicism*, Connecticut: XXIII, 1992, pp. 27-35.

[11] Martin Ott, *African Theology in Images*, Zomba: Kachere, 1999, pp. 13-16.

understand what the Church is were given some insight into the reality.

The extent to which these mediums of interpretation could function adequately was still questionable on some grounds. Not all interested in the field were convinced of the effectiveness of these models. These images and metaphors were mental constructs and as such they could impair the objectivity of the interpretation. Typologies and models were limited in giving concrete descriptions of reality. They were mere heuristic devices and may not give the correct representation of unstatic and evolving realties like culture, relationships, societies, Church, and human persons in their mundane and eternal pursuits. These dynamic and evolving realities could be difficult to capture in one typology and model. In this sense then, no metaphor always fits and exactly fits.

Theological or Biblical Models

Ecclesiology undoubtedly occupied a central place in the theological debates of the twentieth century. The major disagreement in the debate was over the nature of the Church perhaps because one of the most common biblical categories for describing the Church was that of "mystery." The way biblical images of the Church worked together was said to be characterized by a fair degree of flexibility, so that figures from relatively unrelated areas could fold into each other, as in the case of the body and temple metaphors in 1 Corinthians 6:19. In some cases there was a certain degree of ambiguity concerning the metaphorical or literal nature of the images. This happened for instance in the image of the Christians seen as members of the body of Christ (1 Cor 12), as well as in those of the Church seen as the family or as the people of God. Many of the models were basically theological, products of faith's reflection upon ideas drawn from the New Testament.

Models from the New Testament

The word Church (Latin Ecclesia, from Greek *ek-kalein*, to call out of) meant convocation or an assembly. It designated the assemblies of the people, usually for a religious purpose. In the Old Testament it frequently referred to the assembly of the chosen people of God before God, above all on Mt Sinai where Israel received the Law and was established as his holy people: "After they set out from Rephidim, they entered the Desert of Sinai, and Israel camped there in the desert in front of the mountain" (Ex 19:2). By calling itself 'Church' the first community of Christian believers recognized itself as heir to that assembly of the people of God.

In the Scriptures, there is a host of interrelated images and figures which the divine revelation spoke about the inexhaustible nature of the Church. In the New Testament all these images found a new centre because Jesus Christ had become the head of the people of God. Around this centre were grouped images taken from the life of the shepherd or from the agricultural life of the people and the cultivation of the land, from the art of building or from the social life of the people exhibited through family and marriage.[12]

In the New Testament the Church is among other images referred to as the flock of God which forms a sheepfold (Jn 10:16-17; 10:11, 12; 21:15-17). Peter exhorted the elders of the Church to take good care of the Church and the language he used in reference to the Church is from the life of shepherds (1 Pet 5:3). In reference to Jesus Christ as the good shepherd and prince of shepherds he stated: "And when the chief shepherd appears, you will receive the crown of glory that will never fade away" (1 Pet 5:4).

Another Biblical image of the Church drawn from the New Testament is that of the Church as the building of God. Often the Church was called the building of God. The Lord Jesus compared himself to the stone which the builders rejected, but which was made into the corner stone (Mt 21:42). The Church was like the house of God in which his family dwells, the household of God in the Spirit, the dwelling place of God among people and it is the holy temple of God.[13] Paul spoke of

---

[12] Vatican II, *The Dogmatic Constitution on the Church, Lumen Gentium*, No. 6.

[13] John Paul II, *The Catechism of the Catholic Church*, no. 756, p. 206.

Jesus Christ as the firm foundation of the Church (1 Cor 3:11-13). He referred to the community of the Christians as the temple of God (1 Cor 3:16, 17), and God's household and temple of God (Eph 2:19-20), being built together to become a dwelling in which God lives by his Spirit (Eph 2:21-22). The Church is also referred to as God's house or dwelling among people (Rev 21:3). The Church as building of God is likened to a city construction (Rev 21:2).

The nature and mission of the Church is also described in terms of the human body. The different images of the Church found their centrality in the New Testament in the person of Christ who had become the head of the people of God. Christ, as the head of the people of God, made the Church as his body.[14] The Church as the body of Christ expressed the intimate communion between him and his Church. From the beginning, Jesus associated his disciples with his own life. He revealed the mystery of the kingdom to them and gave them a share in his mission, joy and sufferings (Mk 1:17; Jn 15:4, 5; Lk 10:3). As his companions, he revealed to the disciples the mystery of the kingdom (Mt 13:11).

After the resurrection, by communicating his Spirit, Christ mystically constituted as his body those brothers and sisters of him who were called together from every nation. The comparison of the Church with the body casts light on the intimate bond between Christ and his Church. Not only was the Church gathered around Jesus, it was also united with him, in his body. There were three aspects of the model of Church as the body of Christ which needed to be specifically noted; the unity of all the members of the Church with each other as a result of their union with Jesus Christ; Christ as the head of the Body; and the Church as the bride of Christ.[15] As the head of this body, he is the principal of creation and redemption (Col 1:18).

In an attempt to increase the understanding of the mystery of the Church, another model is used, and of the Church as the Bride of

---

[14] Vatican II, *The Dogmatic Constitution of the Church, Lumen Gentium*, no. 9.

[15] Ibid.

Christ. The Lord referred to himself as the bridegroom (Mk 2:19). The apostles spoke of the whole Church and of each of the faithful as members of his body, as a bride betrothed to Christ the Lord so as to become but one spirit with him. They likened the kingdom of God to a wedding feast (Mt 22:2). The Church was like a bride of Christ (2 Cor 11:2). Christians are encouraged to take care of their bodies not to defile them through sexual immoral activities and that they should remember their bodies belong to Christ (1 Cor 6:15). The Church, the Holy City, the New Jerusalem, is being prepared like a bride adorned for her husband. Christ united himself to the Church by an unbreakable bond and alliance, which he constantly nourishes and cherishes.[16] In this understanding and likening of the relationship of Christ and his Church to marriage (Eph 5:22-23), Jesus Christ joined the Church with himself in an everlasting covenant, and he never stopped caring for it as for his own body.[17]

Models from the Theological Tradition of the Church

It was also reasonable to contend that much confusion on the multitude of models to work in our understanding of Church could be avoided if the ecclesiological model for which we are looking was constructed from outside of the limited data of biblical revelation. It suggested a perichoretic model of the church.[18] This could be a valuable instrument for investigating ecclesiological systems in general, but particularly those developed on a Trinitarian basis without excluding recourse to biblical metaphors of the Church. Such models which developed from the theological tradition of the Church included the models of Church as institution, sacrament, herald, and servant.

---

[16] John Paul II, *The Catechism of the Catholic Church*, no. 757, p. 207.

[17] Henrich Fries, *Aspects of the Church*, Dublin: Gill and Sons, 1965, pp. 29-62.

[18] Reality is on all levels engaged in dynamism of relatedness. The word perichoretic comes from Greek *perichoresis*, meaning rotation, a term referring to the relationship of the three persons of the triune God. All the images of the Church are related in their pursuit to explain the nature and mission of the Church. None exhausts the whole reality of the Church.

As an institution, the Church was essentially a society—a perfect society in the sense that it was subordinate to no other and lacked nothing required for its own institutional whole or completeness. It is a society as visible and palpable community that had a constitution, set of rules, a governing body, a set of actual and real members who accepted this constitution and rules as binding on them. This notion of Church as society tended to highlight the structure of government as the formal element in the society and it led to the institutional vision of the Church. This institutional element of the Church was the view that defined the Church primarily in terms of its visible structures, especially the rights and powers of its officers.[19] The Church of Christ could not perform its function without some stable organizational structures.

Another theological model of the Church that developed very close to the typical New Testament models was that of Church as a sacrament. The Church was also understood as the universal sacrament of salvation in terms of its nature and mission. The word sacrament (Latin *sacramentum*, sign of a hidden reality) denoted a visible sign of the hidden reality of salvation. The Church, in Christ, was a sacrament i.e. a sign and instrument, that is, of communion with God and of unity among all people. As sacrament, the Church was Christ's instrument. It was taken up by Christ as the instrument for the salvation of all, the universal sacrament of salvation by which Christ was at once manifesting and actualizing the mystery of God's love for people.[20]

The Church as Herald model made the Word primary. It saw the Church as gathered and formed by the Word of God. The mission of the Church was to proclaim that which it had heard, believed and been commissioned to proclaim. This model laid emphasis too on faith and proclamation of the Word of God to the whole world. It had to proclaim it with integrity and persistence. The Church could not hold

---

[19] Avery Dulles, *Models of the Church*, p. 31.

[20] Vatican II, *The Pastoral Constitution on the Church in the Modern World, Gaudium et Spes*, 45.1. Also, *Lumen Gentium*, no. 48.2, and *Lumen Gentium*, no. 9.2.

itself responsible for the failure of people sometimes, or often times, to accept it as God's Word. It only has to proclaim it (2 Cor 5:18). The Word of God and the Church were inseparable. It was called together by the Word of God and it is sustained and nourished by the word of God.[21]

The Church was also seen as a servant. All the other models considered so far, both from the New Testament and from the theological tradition of the Church, give a primary and privileged position to the Church. But since the Enlightenment the world has increasingly become active and independent of the Church. It has become emancipated, as it were, from the control of the Church. In such a world enjoying its freedom from the Church, the fact remained that it was still a vulnerable world with many problems and challenges that affected humankind. It was a world that is being torn apart by the human activities. To such a world the Church realized that it needed to become a servant. Just as Jesus came into the world not to be served but to serve, so the Church, carrying on the mission of Christ, sought to serve the world by fostering fraternity of all people.[22] In carrying out its servant role the Church brought about the actualization of the Kingdom of God. The Church announced the coming of the Kingdom of God not only in word, through preaching and proclamation, but more particularly in work, in her ministry of reconciliation, of binding up wounds between peoples and nations.[23] The Church needed be attentive to the needs and challenges of the time and hence be a servant at the service of justice, peace and reconciliation. The Church needed to share in the secular problems of ordinary human life, not dominating, but helping and serving. The Church did not need to dominate the world but move together with it and offering it the light of the gospel.[24] To make this servant role of the Church very concrete,

---

[21] Avery Dulles, *Models of the Church*, 1974, p. 71.

[22] Vatican II, *The Pastoral Constitution on the Church in the Modern World, Gaudium et Spes*, no. 3, and no. 92.

[23] Avery Dulles, *Models of the Church*, 1974, p. 86.

[24] Agbonkhianmeghe E. Orobator (ed), *Reconciliation, Justice and Peace: The Second African Synod*, Nairobi: Acton Publishers, 2011, pp. 1- 10.

the individual Christian had to be a person for others. As the Lord was a man for others[25] so the Church had to be a community for other.

Other Models of the Church

In the discussion of the models of the Church, another important question that needed to be asked was whether there were other models of the Church than the so called New Testament models and those drawn from the theological tradition of the Church, or not. Yes, there were other models drawn from philosophy, political science, sociology, anthropology and from managerial or organizational theories. These other models of the Church presented different perspectives of the Church. They have been actively employed in interpreting Roman Catholic theology of the Church (Catholic ecclesiology). There was uncertainty in the influence of such systems of models, whether they helped or frustrated the future realization of more biblical and pastorally responsive models of the Church.[26]

Models from the Articulation of a Specific Worldview (Philosophy)

"Philosophy" is the articulation of a specific world view. Philosophy is the ontological expression of the way a particular time thinks; it distils, expresses, structures the image of the person and the world which emerges from a culture. Philosophy fashioned ecclesiology by offering structures (not immediately biblical) for ecclesial life and worship which themselves depended upon a particular understanding of being and existence. These philosophical models are not images or symbols but are structures which reveal and arrange reality. These philosophical models can be discovered by tracing the origins of Church structures. These structures can be institutional as well as architectural for architecture too participates in the cultural epoch. Architecture has at

---

[25] This theme is taken up in: Rodney Schofield, *Jesus – the Man for others*, Mzuzu: Luviri Press, 2018.

[26] Thomas Franklin O'Meara OP, "Philosophical Models in Ecclesiology", in *Theological Studies* 39 (1978), Santa Clara (California): SCUP, pp. 3-4.

times frozen the philosophical form into stone, for example, the ecclesiology of the Roman Catholic Church from the time of Cyprian to the time of Gregory the Great is rendered concrete and tangible in the construction and deployment of the basilica, that of Pseudo-Dionysius in a Gothic façade.[27]

There has been a philosophical origin and weight on the way of being Church and this remained imposing. The philosophical models in ecclesiology were concrete, not abstract as the word philosophy could sometimes connote. This meant that the influence and effect of a form of philosophy on the Church was real and concrete.[28] Each of these philosophical models had its own vocabulary, values, way of thinking, as well as its problems and weaknesses.

There are five different philosophical frameworks which have been found in ecclesiology operative in the Catholic Church: Neoplatonic, Aristotelian, Nominalist, Idealist, and Phenomenological-historical. Each of them exemplified the strong presence of ontological thought forms in the theology of the Catholic Church and each displayed the characteristics of its own world. All these models illustrated the power of philosophy in ecclesiology, although each fashioned its own unique theology of the Church. They described the influence of philosophy in the history of ecclesiology.

In the Neoplatonic model the Church was seen as illuminating hierarchy. Neoplatonism was a philosophy that was founded in the third century by Plotinus who lived between 204 – 270 CE. Plotinus' system was governed by two principle features: its pantheism and its opposition to materialism. The principle of its ontological hierarchy is the One, which is at the same time being, the Good and the Deity. All things emanated from the One: first, the world of the spirit, of ideas, and secondly, the soul, the vivifier and animator of the entire world and of individual souls. These retained a trace of the oneness of the

---

[27] Thomas O'Meara OP quoting D.R. Wall, "Church Architecture", in *New Catholic Encyclopedia* 3, New York: McGraw-Hill, 1967, pp. 785.
[28] Thomas Franklin O'Meara OP, *Philosophical Models in Ecclesiology*, pp. 7-8.

world soul, which is, as it were, their source. The lowest level of being was matter, which was almost non-being: that which is multiple, which barely exists or exists only in the furthest reaches of the process of emanation. The One illumined with knowledge the further and further outer beings of the process of emanation. There were similarities between Neoplatonic doctrine and several Christian themes and this explained the great influence of Neoplatonism on the Fathers of the Church and on mediaeval Christian thinkers and mystics.[29]

One influence of Neoplatonism on ecclesiology was seen in the area of grace. The basic framework of the *Summa Theologiae* of Thomas Aquinas was the Plotinian *exitus-reditus*. Thomas Aquinas viewed the Church as a communion to nourish faith, hope and love. Yves Congar found the influence of Platonism in Thomas Aquinas' ecclesiology of grace in which all grace flowed to the members of the mystical body from Christ, the head. In the world of grace, a kind of Platonism is valid, for Christ contained in himself the fullness of the species of grace in a similar way to that in which the archetype of Man, in Plato, contained the fullness of the human species so that if other individuals were to receive grace, too, they may only do so in dependence upon Christ. From the liturgical perspective, the influence of Neoplatonism was evident, among others, in the Episcopal power which has as its goals the purification, illumination and leading to perfection of the ranks of the Church members below it. The grace of Christ rebounded as from the head to the members in different degrees, so that the body of Christ might be perfect. The liturgy of the ordination of a bishop showed symbolically that the bishop participated in the power of the total hierarchy by illuminating all beneath him. With this conception of the hierarchy the Episcopal activity became the imparting of grace and truth. The Middle Ages loved *ordo* (order), the arrangement of beings. Since ancient times there was in the Church's liturgy spoken about the order of bishops (Latin, *ordo episcoporum*), order of priests (Latin, *ordo presbyterorum*), and order of deacons (Latin, *ordo diaconorum*). In the understanding of the Catholic Church the bishops possessed the fullness of the priesthood which was then imparted to

---

[29] Julian Marias, *History of Philosophy*, New York: Dover, pp. 98-101.

ordinary priests and deacons through the laying on of hands.[30] While this could be based upon the Aristotelian logic proceeding from the general to the specific, it was often a Neoplatonic arrangement proceeding from the specific to the general.[31] Visually expressed, this is like a pyramid. Concrete expressions of this Dionysian ecclesiology still occur, often determining the life of the Church. The Church was visualized as a hierarchy, containing an inner, vertical and downward movement. The higher levels, whether of beings, angels, ecclesial offices, or social states of life, fashioned and controlled the lower levels.

Another philosophical paradigm which influenced Roman Catholic ecclesiology was called the Aristotelian model. The Aristotelian philosophy of the four causes had influenced the development of ecclesiology especially in explaining the origin, nature and mission of the Church. Owing to their ecclesiastical background and training, many church leaders and scholars tended to define things and realities, including the Church, in the Aristotelian manner, an approach that enabled them to categorize different realities.[32] This metaphysical paradigm was less, surprisingly, present than it would have been expected in the thought system of the Middle Ages. Traces of Aristotelianism were found in the medieval theology of ordination in descriptions of grace in the Church through efficient and formal causality.[33] But this Aristotelian model found wider influence in the Neo-scholastic revival of the hundred years prior to the convocation of the Second Vatican Council. There were different doctrines of Aristotelian physics and metaphysics which were used as the background for the theology of the Church. Aristotelianism was

---

[30] John Paul II, *The Catechism of the Catholic Church*, Nairobi: Paulines Publications Africa, 1994, pp. 378-381.

[31] Thomas Franklin O'Meara OP, *Philosophical Models in Ecclesiology*, p. 10.

[32] Jude Thaddeus Ruwaichi, "The Newness and Pastoral Implications of the Church as Family", in Cecil Mac Garry et al (eds), *New Strategies for a New Evangelization in Africa*, Nairobi: Paulines Publications Africa, 2002, pp. 23-24.

[33] Julian Marias, *History of Philosophy*, New York: Dover, pp. 59-85.

concerned with the analysis of an empirical (visible) and metaphysical reality (being) and that the inner structure of each being was bestowed by a material and a formal element. For him full scientific knowledge of something came through knowing its causes. He considered four realms of causality; efficient cause, formal cause, ultimate purpose, and material substratum that provided the potential for its process of becoming and existing.[34]

The strength of the Aristotelian model on the Church was the emphasis on the visible nature of the Church, its intelligibility (knowability), its capacity of being captured in a definition. Ecclesiology then became the metaphysics of the Church. With this impact, stress was placed on the juridical elements, since they were the most visible. The idea of the invisible was hardly accepted not only because of its association with the Reformation but that it would render ecclesial analysis impossible. Thus, from this perspective, according to the four causes, the Church was defined as One, Holy, Catholic and Apostolic. All the activities of the Church were directed, as towards their end, to the sanctification of people in Christ and the glorification of God.[35] In this Aristotelian ecclesiology there was also the dualism of matter and form, body and soul so much so that the hierarchy was viewed as the form, soul, spiritual, and graced filled, while the laity were the matter, material and body part of the Church.

The third philosophical model that influenced the history of ecclesiology was the Nominalist model which denied the existence of universals and abstract objects but affirmed the existence of general terms and predicates. There were at least two main versions of Nominalism. One version denied the existence of universals – things that could be instantiated or exemplified by many particular things. The other version specifically denied the existence of abstract objects – objects that did not exist in space and time.[36] With this philosophy of nominalism that mainly developed from the eleventh CE, it was the

---

[34] Thomas Franklin O'Meara, *Philosophical Models in Ecclesiology*, pp. 12-13.
[35] John Paul II, *The Catechism of the Catholic Church*, pp. 224-225.
[36] www.wikipedia/wiki/nominalism/ [26.11.2016].

individuals or particular things that existed. There was nothing in nature that was universal. The universals only existed in the mind, as something posterior to the things, and they were expressed in words.[37] The nominalist model described a general approach to reality, not really articulated by particular theologians. Its influence on ecclesiology had been the separation of mental systems from the real world, exposition of the superiority of the will over the mind, and the elevation of codes of language over charism of the Spirit which is evident from the council of Trent to Vatican II. It had seen the Church defining the limits of its own power and authority as power over the deposits (treasuries) of the divine, with power over the Bible and sacraments. With it the Church moved from the position of servant to being lord.[38]

The fourth philosophical model that influenced the Church was the Idealist model which defined the Church as the unfolding of the self. Idealism was concerned with a total explanation of reality. This explanation began not with individual entities or beings but with the active consciousness of the mind. Consciousness, spirit, has a history which is self-unfolding into the various levels of the world around humanity.[39] In an Idealist ecclesiology the Church was seen as a collective self and this self was transcendental, and surrounded with the Spirit of God. There were degrees of belonging to the collective self, stages in that community's realization of its own essence in historical forms to the extent that other churches, religions and movements partook in it and resembled the center of the collective self, and they were similar to the Church. Ministry and mission of the Church did not proceed from a hierarchy downwards to the needy members, and no ministry could exhaust the charism and services potential in the spirit.[40]

---

[37] Julian Marias, *History of Philosophy*, New York: Dover, pp. 133-136.
[38] Thomas Franklin O'Meara OP, *Philosophical Models in Ecclesiology*, p. 14.
[39] Julian Marias, *History of Philosophy*, pp. 284-296.
[40] Thomas Franklin O'Meara OP, *Philosophical Models in Ecclesiology*, p. 20.

Another philosophical model that has influenced the Church in recent times is the phenomenological model, and with this the Church has been viewed as partially disclosed in history. It is phenomenological because it refused to deduce a formal structure from a given essence of the Church, seeing it as an emerging and only partially disclosed nature or entity. It was historical because no longer expecting perfect definition or eternal essence; the Church unveiled an enduring reality by means of the formal arrangement of the old and new characteristics. The partial disclosure took place in time. Only in history could the essence appear, and it appeared only partially. Full reality was never apprehended. With this the Church was a historical being whose public life was shaped through the forms of a particular time calling forth an ecclesiology for this or that particular time or epoch.

From the application of this model it was not possible to separate the essence of the Church from its historical forms. A glimpse of the real Church could only be gotten if the essence was seen as existing in its historical forms, rather than as existing beyond and above them. Every age stood before God in its own particular way. The Church was not ready-made only to be mapped. It was made taking into account the phenomenon of the time or epoch and historical context. In this vein the Church was a sociological being (entity) and could be more correctly viewed as a social construct. As such the form of the Church was always exposed to the process of mutation, change, being constantly modified by the way in which the members of the Church externalized their own experience.[41]

Models from Social and Behavioural Sciences

Other models of the Church came from the social and behavioural sciences: from society, from political science, from managerial and organizational theories. Social science is a major category in academic disciplines, concerned with society and the relationships among individuals in the society. It in turn has many branches, each of which is considered a social science. They deal with the institutions and functions of the human society and with interpersonal relationships of

---

[41] Thomas Franklin O'Meara OP, *Philosophical Models in Ecclesiology*, p. 23.

the individuals as members of society. The major disciplines include political science, economics, demography, psychology, and sociology. In a wider sense, social science includes some fields in the humanities such as anthropology, archaeology, jurisprudence, history and linguistics.[42]

On the other hand, behavioural science encompasses all the disciplines that explore the activities of and interactions among organisms in the natural world. It involves the systematic analysis and investigation of human and other animal behaviour through controlled and naturalistic observation, and disciplined scientific experimentation. It attempts to establish legitimate, objective conclusions through rigorous formulations and observations. Examples of behavioural sciences include psychology, psychobiology and cognitive science.[43] The application of behavioural sciences includes disciplines like organizational behaviour, political science, operative research, organizational research and media psychology.

There has been the discovery of the influence and usage of insights and themes from social and behavioural sciences in understanding, defining, and structuring the Church. The reason for this had been the understanding that, despite the transcendental origins of the Church, the Church was a human reality and it was also a human society.[44] Throughout the history of the Christian community there has always been a tension between the doctrinal or eschatological Church and the Church that is here-and-now, the invisible Church and the visible Church, and between the Spiritual Church and the Church as institution. The Church, though the mystical body of Christ, was also an organized human community in actuality. This, however, did not solve the problem of understanding the reality of the Church for it still remained a complex reality.

---

[42] https://www.wikipedia/wiki/social_science/ [7.11.2016].

[43] https://en.wikipedia.org/wiki/Behavioural_sciences/ [4.11.2016].

[44] Clare Watkins, "Organizing the People of God: Social Science theories of Organization in Ecclesiology", in *Theological Studies* 52 (1991), Santa Clara: SCUP, pp. 689-690.

However, the sociality model bound the mystery of the Church with the actual historical reality of the Church as composed of humans, living and with relationships. It opened up ecclesiology to sociology in such a way as to concretely offer the possibility of looking at the Church as a social system, composed of human beings and living in relationships. Their belonging to the Church invited the members of the Church to have a new way of looking at and relating to other believers as brothers and sisters in the Lord, and together invited to a mission towards those that do not yet belong.

In the same vein of the interdisciplinary possibility of looking at the nature of the Church, ecclesiologically and sociologically, there was growing awareness that the Church was also organized in a democratic manner even from the perspective of its universal leadership. The universal Church was governed by the college of bishops, who in the teaching of the Church were understood as the successor of the Apostolic College. The college of bishops through councils, synods and symposiums taught, shepherded, and governed the entire membership of the Church. Even within the hierarchical structure of the Church there was a constant give and take (dialogue) between pope and bishops. Since Vatican II solemn definitions of doctrine were pronounced only after consultation with the entire episcopate or college of bishops. The governance of the Church by a college entailed some kind of democratic model running in the Church.[45]

This meant the increased participation of the ordinary members in the life of the Church, different from the way it was in the past. There was a long tradition of popular participation in the Christian community, from the Acts of the Apostles to the commendable development of the Church in the neighbourhood, the Small Christian Communities, where all Christians are actively involved in the way of being Church. There were reforms in the Catholic Church, aimed at doing away with the clericalization of the Church, which saw the increased participation of the laity in government matters and decision making. At the grass-

---

[45] Karl Rahner & Joseph Ratzinger, *The Episcopate and the Primacy*, London: Burns & Oates, 1962, pp. 83-102.

roots level of the Church this involvement of the laity was, for example, witnessed with the elections of local leaders of the councils at the various levels of the local Church structure right from the SCC, outstation, zone, parish, deanery[46] to the diocesan councils. There was more and more involvement of the people (*laos*) and power sharing in the Church. The Church constantly got bombarded with the winds of the social environment and it had to constantly respond to the wider society. It also changed in relation to the changes in the environment. Such changes depended on a complex system of communication in which information from outside was brought into contact with the norms and authorities of the organization. The output of the organizational decisions and policies depended, in some way at least, on the input from the environment which was the raw material of authoritative decision. The central component in this communication system was the feedback loop by which members in the organization could respond to the organizational decision, so as to reform or renew it in some way or other. The lay people were involved in communicating environmental information to the organization as a whole. This communication of the lay people was essential for the Church to be relevant and to survive. It was from this perspective that the ideas of participation and democracy were deduced. Participation, democracy, collaboration and involvement of the grassroots people were good management tools.[47] Though they had a lot of strengths, they also had gotten their weaknesses like the inevitable tendency of the majority to empathy, which allowed the energetic few under the semblance of democracy to dominate. Sometimes too the management of the organization might well adopt structures of participation so as to reduce the probability of conflict and satisfy the members' needs,

---

[46] A deanery is a cluster of parishes which share geographical proximity. In this kind of ecclesiastical organization there are at all levels leaders who are meant to animate the faithful in the life of the Church. Over the deanery there is a priest called Dean who has supervisory responsibility over the parishes in the deanery.

[47] William Pickett, *A Concise Guide to Pastoral Planning*, Notre Dame: Ave Maria Press, pp. 31-41.

while remaining in control themselves. The management could thus still carry the day through use of democratic structures.[48]

Another model coming from the social and behavioural sciences in trying to understand the nature of the Church was the administration model. To be relevant, dynamic and effective, the leadership styles in the Church too needed to evolve with the changing times.[49] Administrative and leadership work was also central to the ecclesiastical administration. Though pastoral work was often valued as the real work of the Christian ministers, in contrast to administration, there was need to also assert the dignity and importance of administration in the Church as in any other human organization. There were different organizational theories, leadership styles and administrative approaches all of which needed to be employed in the Church due to the complexity of the Church and the complex realities of human social life. Pastoral leadership styles, borrowed from the organizational theories and sciences, now existed and were in use in the Church. Such styles included servant, empowering, transactional, strategic, visionary, innovative, moral, transformational, and entrepreneurial leadership styles. All these were deployed to respond to the needs of the community, the different and changing contexts of the Church. The Church needed surely to be different if it had to be relevant, dynamic and truly in touch with the whole people of God at all times.[50]

Conclusion

This chapter has presented the reason why there was the tendency to define the Church through models, namely because of the difficulty to conceive it, and the different types of models that were in use in ecclesiology and these were largely based on their concepts' origins. Biblical models included: the Church as the people of God, flock of God, building of God, household of God, temple of the Holy Spirit,

---

[48] Clare Watkins, "Organizing the People of God", pp. 697-700.

[49] Fr. P.T. Joseph SJ, *Pastoral Leadership Styles and Emotional Intelligence*, Mumbai: St. Paul's Publications, 2010, pp. 7-11.

[50] Ibid., pp. 51-217.

Body of Christ, and as the bride of Christ. There were also models that developed from the theological tradition of the Church and as such were fruits of the believing community's reflection on their faith. Such understood the Church as: institution, sacrament, mystical communion, herald, and servant.

A number of other ecclesiological models developed as a result of the influence of philosophy (as articulation of a specific worldview) on the history of the Church, while others developed owing to social and behavioural sciences. Philosophical models were based on the Church strong ontological thought forms in the theology of the Church. On the other hand, social and behavioural sciences' insights and themes influenced the understanding, defining, and structuring of the Church. In spite of its transcendental origins, the Church was viewed as a human reality and also a human society.

Chapter 2: Historical Development of the Model of Church as God's Family

The model of Church as God's Family which was felt appropriate for Africa and applied in the Archdiocese of Lilongwe, has a long history that needs unpacking. Such a historical development of this model is full of ecclesiological frameworks (models) which were there in use before the arrival and usage of this current ecclesiology of Church as God's Family. The models were not just appreciated, but there were also arguments for the usage of such a model as appropriate generally for the universal Church and specifically for Africa.

This chapter presents the periods and arguments of the self-understanding of the Church before the Council of Trent, after the Council and by the time of the first Vatican Council. It also deals with the first formal mention of the concept of Church as Family of God at Vatican II and other images of the Church which were used in the documents of the Second Vatican Council. In addition, it retrieves how the concept was adopted through the African Synods taking into account the influence of other movements such as decolonization upon African ecclesiology. Finally, the chapter explores the development of the Small Christian Communities (SCCs) in general, the privileged *loci* for living the new ecclesiology of Family of God, and the specific historical development of the SCCs in the Archdiocese of Lilongwe.

The pre-Tridentine Church Model

Before the Council of Trent, the Church saw itself as a visible reality of an invisible one, and then as essentially having an institutional-hierarchical nature. It was such ecclesiology that ran and was perpetuated through its pre-Vatican II councils. The Catholic ecclesiology was influenced by two events in Church history: the publication of the final and most significant work of Augustine of Hippo, *The City of God*, and the publication of the *Catholic Catechism of the Council of*

Trent which followed the Reformation.[1] In this work, *The City of God,* Augustine of Hippo shared his reflection on the effects of original sin on human beings, their eventual history and the consequent plan of salvation. Augustine visualized the world as divided into two cities: the human city and the city of God. The human city was inhabited by those who followed their human inclinations and passions and were thus self-indulgent. These had chosen and opted to turn away from God. It was a city where temporary and material affairs dominated. The second city, the city of God, was inhabited by those chosen by God and destined for salvation. For him this was a city someway connected to the visible Church, which, though in the world was not of the world, and was separated and distinct from the world.[2]

This portrayal and understanding of the world and the Church implied that "the Church and the world, the spiritual and the temporal, the sacred and the profane, the holy and the ordinary, comprised two fundamentally different, even if related, aspects of history and, hence, of human experience." With this understanding, the Church was so to speak in opposition to the world. The events of the 16th Century Reformation, on the other hand, had led the Catholic Church to take a defensive stance and an apologetic ecclesiology (self-understanding of the Church). The Church saw itself as a visible reality, sacred and spiritual, of an invisible (supernatural) one which would not allow itself to be contaminated by the temporal, secular and profane world.[3]

---

[1] The Roman Catechism of Trent was published in 1566 and commissioned during the Catholic-Counter Reformation by the Council of Trent. It enjoyed an authority within the Catholic Church equaled by no other Catechism until the 1992 publication of the Catechism of the Catholic Church, cf. http://en.wikipedia.org/wiki/Roman_Catechism/ [16.10.15].

[2] St. Augustine, *The City of God,* (translated by Gerald G. Walsh et al), New York: Image, 1958, pp. 21-33, 323-507.

[3] Gabriel Afagbegee SVD, *Building Small Christian Communities: Foundation and Step-by-Step Approach to Building SCCs*, Germiston: Lumko, 2007, pp. 1-23.

The Church by the First Vatican Council (1869 – 1870)

By the time of the First Vatican Council (1869 – 1870) the dominant ecclesiology of the Catholic Church, in its universality, was very stringent and apologetic. This was because of the felt need of the Catholic Church to defend itself against Protestantism with its stress on the invisible and inward character of the Church. Such stress seemed like rejection of the Church's fundamental visible nature i.e. its sacramental, institutional and hierarchical nature with its mediatory powers. Another reason for the stringent and apologetic character of the Church's ecclesiology were the cultural forces and nationalistic ideologies of the time. These were calling into question the legitimacy and primacy of papal power. In response the First Vatican Council Fathers voted for papal primacy and papal infallibility. The Petrine (papal) office was regarded as constitutive of the very essence of the Church, which was a perfect society (sufficient onto itself), an institution in which all jurisdiction came from above.

The ecclesiology of the entire Catholic Church this time was one that saw the Church as an institution with a hierarchy. Though this institutional-hierarchical nature of the Church was the dominant ecclesiology, this time there were some renewal movements in the Catholic Church, such as Study of the Scripture and Liturgical Renewal, which emphasized the mystical nature of the Church. In addition there were works of theological scholars, like Johann Adam Mohler, which proposed that, "the starting point of any reflection on the Church should not consist in an elucidation of the juridical and structural aspects of the Church but on the Holy Spirit, who constitutes the fundamental and dynamic 'Principle' underlying these structures."[4] This new understanding of the Church developed and crystallized in the teachings of Vatican II, and especially in *Lumen Gentium*, the Dogmatic Constitution on the Church.

---

[4] www.en.wikipedia.org/wiki/Johann_Adam_Mohler/ [4.9.2015].

The First Formal Mention of the Concept of the Church as Family of God

The first formal mention of the concept of the Church as Family of God was a result of the intervention of a Bishop from Vietnam in the Second Vatican Council. In July 1963, the Most Reverend Simon Hoa Nguyen-Van Hien, bishop of Dalat, during the 37th to the 39th sessions of the Conciliar discussions, argued apologetically that the Pauline image of the Church as the Body of Christ, though very Scriptural, was a Western image which was too abstract and too organic for the people of Vietnam to come to terms with the reality and nature of the Church.[5] He proposed the image of the Church as Family of God. This he strongly defended with a lot of reference from Scripture as well. For him this paradigm of Church as Family of God corresponded very well with God's plan of salvation. Among others he quoted John 11:52[6] in defense of his position that God the Father sent his Son Jesus Christ to gather all the scattered children of God into one big family. In all of the sixteen documents of the council the metaphor of Church as *Family of God* finds a place in some way, either explicitly, or implicitly.

In the history of the Roman Catholic Church, the Second Vatican Council was the 21st Ecumenical Council which Pope John XXIII convoked. It met in four sessions from 9 October 1962 to 8 December 1965.[7] John XXIII had three main aims as he called for an ecumenical

---

[5] Francis Appiah-Kubi, "The Church, Family of God: Relevance and Pastoral Challenges of a metaphor from an African Perspective," part of his doctoral dissertation in Systematic Theology with Specialization on Ecclesiology in Thomas Knieps (et al), *The Household of God and the Local Household: Revisiting the Domestic Church*, Bibliotheca Ephemeridum Theologicarum Lovaniensium (CCLIV), Leuven: Peeters, 2013, pp. 71-774.

[6] "and not only for that nation but also for the scattered children of God, to bring them together and make them one" (John 11:52 NIV).

[7] The Second Vatican Council (Vatican II) was a meeting of Catholic Bishops from throughout the world that took place intermittently between 1962 and 1965. This council was one of the most significant events in the history of the

council. He wanted the Church to experience a spiritual renewal inspired by the Word of God, and the Church to update itself to meet the demands of the modern age. He called it "*aggiornamento*" which in Italian means "renewal or updating." This was certainly going to lead the Church to renew its self-understanding in nature and mission. Lastly, he wanted the council to promote the unity and reunion of Christians through dialogue among the different Christian denominations but also with other faiths.[8]

The approach of the Vatican II was marked by a pastoral dimension and orientation. This meant the council was to be attentive to the spiritual needs and concrete situations of the people of the time. It strived to avoid the dogmatic nature that characterized many of the former ecumenical councils including its predecessor, Vatican I. It was not so much interested in the definition of dogmas. It also avoided the pessimistic attitude of the Church towards the modern world. John XXIII opened the council in October 1962 but eight months later he died on 3rd June 1963. He was succeeded by Paul VI. As the council unfolded throughout the four sessions the spiritual élan of its convener, John XXIII, persisted. The council was able to breathe new life into the Church and through it the windows of the Church were opened, as it were, for fresh air to come in. The council had a distinctive influence on the Church's self-knowledge and understanding in terms of its nature, mission, and method. At its conclusion the council produced sixteen documents and many of these are directly concerned with the Church's self-understanding and renewal. Generally, in the documents of the council, though a tension can still be noticed, an ecclesiological paradigm shift from the institutional-hierarchical model to the community (Latin '*communio*' and Greek '*koinonia*') model can be identified.

Catholic Church. Its purpose was to bring the church up to date by opening it to dialogue with the modern world.

[8] Dennis M. Doyle, *The Church Emerging from Vatican II: A Popular Approach to Contemporary Catholicism*, pp. 2-3.

It is important to understand that from an ecclesiological perspective, Vatican II, owing to its view of the Church as a mystery, did not offer a simple self-understanding of the Church. Even if the concept of Church as a family of God was referred to in the documents of the council, this concept was not the outstanding image of the Church in these documents.[9] But it had to be stressed that the Council, other than mentioning the image of family of God either explicitly or implicitly in its documents, had images which acted as genuine foundations of the post-Vatican II African Catholic Church with emphasis on the metaphor of 'family.' I now look at some of these images.

Images of the Church in Vatican II Documents

In the Vatican II documents, images of the Church which precipitated the emergence of model of Church as Family of God included the model of a community and the 'institutional-hierarchical' model.

The Model of a Community

The model of the Church as a Community strongly became prominent in Catholicism since Vatican II, in both ecclesiology and practical theology. A special synod of bishops held in Rome in 1985, 20 years after the conclusion of the council, said that the model of Church as a community—together with the concept of the Church as mystery of faith and sacrament of salvation for the world, was the central idea of the self-understanding of the Church at the council.[10] The community approach of the Church was indeed an emphasis that Vatican II reintroduced and which had been further developed in the post-Conciliar Church documents, theology, ecclesiology and pastoral practice. The word used, *communio*, was a notion that is very prevalent in New Testament writings and which means something of 'community life' and 'participation.'

---

[9] Asaah Awingya speaks about this fact that the image of family is not the most prominent in the documents of the Second Vatican Council, in http://books.googlecom/books/ [3.5.2015].

[10] www.adoremus.org/the-ecclesiology-of-communion/ [1.5.2015].

The Church is a community in more than one sense. It is a community of the faithful but also a community of local churches. The *koinonia* or *communio* aspect of the Church is revealed in a number of ways in *Lumen Gentium* which is the Second Vatican Council's dogmatic constitution on the Church. With this the character of the Church became 'we' and not 'I.' There was then no individual or particular group of individuals who could call themselves the church. There was nobody who could say, 'I am the church.' The term *communio* is not often mentioned explicitly, but the idea is strongly and, in many ways, present in the document.

The first section of *Lumen Gentium* speaks about the Church that is at the service of the unity of the whole world.[11] In the structure of this dogmatic constitution of the Church it is remarkable to note the Church is firstly mentioned as a mystery and as the people of God. It is only in the second place within the framework when this constitutional document deals with the institution and the hierarchy.

In the dogmatic constitution of the Church, *Lumen Gentium*, there are three biblical 'community' images which are put in a very striking way: the Church is seen as 'people of God,' 'body of Christ' and 'temple of the Holy Spirit.' These three biblical images in fact imply a Trinitarian foundation of the Church. Together they also contribute to the popular post-Vatican II image of the Church as *'communio'* (community), and consequently to the African model of Church as Family of God. This means the Church community participates in the dynamism and the life of the triune God, who is himself a community of the Father, the Son and the Holy Spirit. The Second Vatican Council summarized this vision aptly with a quotation from Cyprian of Carthage: the Church appears as "the united people, which takes part in the unity of the Father, the Son and the Holy Spirit."[12] So God as triune *'communio'* was the source and the model of the Church as community. To consider the Church as 'community,' was not a mere detail or coincidence but had to do with the Christian faith in the

---

[11] Vatican II, *Lumen Gentium*, no. 1.

[12] Vatican II, *Lumen Gentium*, no. 4.

triune God. It was the conviction of the Second Vatican Council itself that God was essentially a community (*communio*), interpersonal communication of love, the perfect community of life, which wanted people to be involved in its dynamism. Too many people, though, kept seeing God as a kind of super individual, a kind of Monarch, whereas in the Christian sense God was not a solitary Subject, but solidarity, and an open community of love. One could only think of love in terms of relationship. This self-understanding of the Church as community central in Vatican II was also foundational to the African ecclesiology of the Church as Family of God.

The breakthrough of a new Church's self-understanding at the Second Vatican Council could not be denied. But on the other hand, the texts of the council did not constitute a complete break with the past, which had never the intention of the council. The old patterns of thought were still at work during the council and mixed with the new self-understanding of the Church that manifested itself in it. Therefore, the ecclesiology of the Vatican II is more complex and less unambiguous than was suggested by the simple opposition between 'old' and 'new.' Thus, *Lumen Gentium*, is not free of internal tensions. Different accents had to be joined together at times, not only because the Church itself was a reality full of tensions, but also because divergent opinions were at work at the council and the ultimate aim was to bring all of them together in one and the same conclusive text—which actually also succeeded.[13]

It can therefore be concluded that *Lumen Gentium* still puts two models in a kind of juxtaposition next to each other. There is a sort of compromise between two Church visions which are in an irreconcilable tension: on the one hand the new 'community' model and on the other the 'institutional-hierarchical' model. Vatican II's *Lumen Gentium* in its second chapter speaks well about this 'community' model of the Church as it discusses the Church as the people of God saying:

> At all times and in every race, anyone who fears God and does what is right has been accepted to him. He has, however, willed to

---

[13] Vatican II, *Lumen Gentium*, no. 37.

> make men and women holy and save them, not as individuals without any bond or link between them, but rather to make them into a people who might acknowledge him and serve him in holiness.[14]

The Institutional-Hierarchical Model

The following chapter three of *Lumen Gentium* goes flat out on the institutional-hierarchical model when it says:

> In order to shepherd the people of God and to increase in numbers without cease, Christ the Lord set up in the Church a variety of offices which aim at the good of the whole body. The holders of office, who are invested with a sacred power, are in fact, dedicated to promoting the interests of their brethren, so that all belong to the people of God, and are consequently endowed with true Christian dignity, may, through their free and well-ordered efforts towards a common goal, attain to salvation.[15]

This was said in reference to the already taught model of the Church, in the previous councils, that it was also a hierarchical institution. The Church was and remained a paradoxical reality with many poles. However, suffice to say that the new self-vision of the Church as 'community' became a great watershed for the African Church's self-understanding of the Family of God.

Christian Family as the Domestic Church

Lumen Gentium,[16] in reference to this topic, speaks of the Christian family as the domestic Church.[17] By this, the council taught that it was in the context of the family that people first knew who God is and it was there in the family where they learn how to prayerfully seek his will. The family becomes a school of faith and prayer. The council thus exhorted families to bear in mind what they were and honour their

---

[14] Vatican II, *Lumen Gentium*, no. 9.
[15] Vatican II, *Lumen Gentium*, no. 18.
[16] Vatican II, *Lumen Gentium*, no. 11.
[17] www.vatican.va/archive/documents/ [3.5.2015].

mission of transmitting faith to the children and teaching them the fear of the Lord and what they had become through baptism. The council exhorted the Christian families to build these 'domestic churches.' The Pastoral Constitution on the Church in the Modern World, *Gaudium et Spes (GS)*, having probed more profoundly into the mystery of the Church, understands the Church as a community of the redeemed people through Jesus Christ and thus forms the family of God.[18] *Gaudium et Spes* in its first chapter speaks of the church in the family. Pope Paul VI, in his great apostolic exhortation, *Evangelii Nuntiandi*, quotes the Second Vatican council's description of the Christian family as a domestic church. For Paul VI, this meant that to truly become a domestic church, there was need to be in every Christian family the various aspects which are found in the Church. Since the Church was called to holiness, those in families needed to live their lives in ways that would help all in the family to grow in holiness.[19] Pope Francis said God had a magnificent plan for the family. In fact, from the time of creation, the human family had been at the center of God's plan for the world.

The history of salvation that unfolded in the pages of Scripture was a family drama—from the wedding of Adam and Eve in the beginning, through the story of Noah's family, to the wedding of Abraham, and his children, to the establishment of the kingdom of David and his dynasty. Finally, God sent his only Son.[20] Jesus chose to be born from a mother's womb and to be nurtured in a human family with his mother, Mary, and Joseph, her spouse. He performed the first 'sign' at a wedding feast. Jesus gave his Church the mission of creating what amounts to a worldwide family of families. He commissioned the church to proclaim his Gospel and men and women of every nation to live as children of God in his family, the Church. And in the Scriptures' final pages, it is revealed what God intended from the start—a great cosmic wedding feast and a vast family drawn from every nation, people, and tongue, all worshipping before God's heavenly throne:

---

[18] www.vatican.va/archive/documents/ [3.5.2015].
[19] www.knight of Columbus/domestic-church [7.5.2015].
[20] www.catholic.org/news/europe/story/ [8.5.2015].

"Then I heard what sounded like a great multitude, like the roar of rushing and like loud peals of thunder, shouting: Hallelujah! For our Lord God Almighty reigns. Let us rejoice and be glad and give him glory! For the wedding of the Lamb has come, and his bride has made herself ready" (Rev 19:6-7).[21]

The Catechism of the Catholic Church states that Christ chose to be born and grow up in the bosom of the holy family of Joseph and Mary and that the Church was nothing other than "the Family of God." From the beginning, the core of the Church was often constituted by those who had become believers 'together with their households:' "Crispus, the synagogue leader, and his entire household believed in the Lord; and many of the Corinthians who heard Paul believed and were baptized" (Ac 18:8). When many of the early Christians converted, they desired that their whole household should be saved. The jailer in the prison at Philippi asked Paul and Silas what he needed to do to be saved. They answered: "Believe in the Lord Jesus Christ, and you will be saved, you and your household" (Ac 16:31), and earlier on, an angel of the Lord had also spoken to Cornelius to send for a man named Simon Peter in Joppa and said: "He will bring you a message through which you and all your household will be saved" (Ac 11:14). The families and households which converted and became believers were islands of Christian life in an unbelieving world.[22]

Although the term 'family of God' is not explicitly mentioned and used in many of the Church documents, there are others like *Gaudium et Spes* in which this is closely mentioned. The Pastoral Constitution on the Church in the Modern World states that the Church is so to speak a family of God because God, who has fatherly concern for everyone, has willed that all should constitute one family and treat one another in a spirit of brotherhood. For having been created in the image of God, who from one person had created the whole human race and

---

[21] www.osv.com/artMID/articleID/the-ordinary-vocation-of-the-domestic-church/ [8.5.2015].

[22] John Paul II, *The Catechism of the Catholic Church*, no. 1655.

made them live over the face of the earth, all men and women were called to one and same goal, God himself.[23]

Vatican II's document on the Church in the Modern World is one of the most remarkable of the sixteen documents produced by the council. In many ways it is the fruit of the council itself since originally there had been no plans for such a document in the preparatory stages. The very title is a surprise. Just a hundred years before, Pius IX issued a document which basically denies that the Church can ever have anything to do with the modern world and its idea of democracy, individual dignity, the rights of people to follow their conscience, and the importance of history. The same document is not shy to imagine the church in the language of this world, the 'family.' The well-known quotation of this document talks about the solidarity of the Church with the whole human family:

> The joys and the hopes of, the grief's and the anxieties of the women and men of this age, especially those who are poor or in any way afflicted, these are the joys and hopes, the grief's and anxieties of the followers of Christ. Indeed, nothing genuinely human fails to raise an echo in their heart. That is why this community realizes that it is truly and intimately linked with humankind in its history.[24]

Many post-conciliar magisterial documents showed profound interest in the Church which was community and hence, a family. Popes who followed the Second Vatican Council called many congresses on the family. They even wrote apostolic exhortations and encyclicals, like *Familaris Consortio*, by John Paul II, which promotes this metaphor, concept and understanding of the Church as God's Family.

The model of Church as Family of God, developing from the afore-seen communitarian images in the Second Vatican Council has had profound impact in Africa. The sub-Saharan post Vatican II Church has

---

[23] Vatican II, *Gaudium et Spes*, no. 24.
[24] Vatican II, *Gaudium et Spes*, no. 1.

been transformed through this image. The metaphor has changed the way of being church on mission.[25]

The Adoption of the new Ecclesiology through the African Synods

The special assemblies of the synod of bishops for Africa added their own energy to the development of this contemporary African ecclesiology of the Church as God's Family. The Roman Catholic Church has the tradition of holding synods in its history.

The Holding of Synods on the African Continent

The continent of Africa came into contact with Christianity in the 1st Century CE and this was due to North Africa's inclusion within the Roman world and Christianity's outward growth from its Jewish roots. There were sizable-Jewish populations and God-fearers in many North African towns and cities and these became the seed bed of Christianity. The local populations also found Christian teaching very appealing to their religious expectations.[26] There were plenary assemblies of bishops representing the North African Church held in ancient times. These were commonly called African Synods or Carthaginian Synods because they were mostly held in the city of Carthage. There were six ecclesiastical provinces corresponding to the six political and civil provinces in North Africa and these ecclesiastical provinces lasted till after the Muslim invasion in the 7th Century.[27] In this region Carthage was the most prominent civil city. Consequently, the bishop of Carthage had control over the satellite provinces. The bishop of Carthage was in rank and privilege, though not in name, the Patriarch of the African Church. This is worth mentioning and noting because it was he, the bishop of Carthage, who convoked and presided over the general synods for Africa. He would eventually sign the

---

[25] www.academia.edu/The_Second_Vatican_Council/ [5.5.2015].

[26] Thomas Bokenkotter, *A Concise History of the Catholic Church*, New York: Image, 1979, pp. 88-95.

[27] www.christian classics Ethereal Library/html [17.5.2015].

decrees decided upon in the name of all the bishops of the region. Most of these synods, in the patristic era, were held, not in Rome, but in Carthage. A few of these synods were held outside Carthage. For instance, the African synod of 393 was held in the city of Hippo (modern day Annaba in Algeria) and the African Synod of 402 was held at Milevum (modern day Mila in Algeria). Even then they were still convoked by the bishop of Carthage and seen through under his presidency.

It is difficult to say how many African synods were held in the early history of the Church because of their frequency and the many changes that took place in their development. There was even a time when these assemblies of the leaders of the Church in Africa were held on a yearly basis until when this procedure had to be revisited and changed. During the time of Tertullian, there were no synods held in Africa. In 220, Agrippinus, bishop of Carthage, called together an assembly of 70 bishops from Preconsular Africa and Numidia. It was from the time of Cyprian of Carthage that general synods were seen as needed resources of Church administration. As a result of this feeling the synods became more frequent and regular in Africa than anywhere in Christendom. The letters of Cyprian say that African bishops met at least once a year. Seven synods were held under Cyprian's presidency in the ten-year period of his administration (from 249 – 258) in Carthage. More than fifteen (15) synods were held under Aurelius (391 – 429). Carthage was still the meeting place for these synods. This is why these ancient African synods, held in patristic times, were sometimes and correctly so, called Carthaginian Synods.[28]

The ancient African synods were convoked to deal with matters of local and regional discipline, doctrine and administration. However, it is important to mention that through these synods the African Church was able to contribute a lot to the ecclesiastical growth of the universal Church. The decrees made during these synods transcended their immediate and local scope and they helped to fix the discipline and define doctrine of the universal Church. It was at one of the

---

[28] www.theodora.com/encyclopedia/synods-of-Carthage/ [18.5.2015].

synods of Carthage, for instance, that a list of Holy Books (Canon) was drawn up defining what material was considered of Divine Revelation in contrast to religious books which were felt not to be divinely inspired.[29] This formed the basis of the Catholic canon. However, the Church in Africa, though contributing this much from Carthage, was humble enough to recognize the primary role of the bishop of Rome, as it said: "But let the Church beyond the sea (Rome) be consulted to confirm this Canon."[30] The wide scope these African synods focused upon included: discipline, doctrine, unity, administration and pastoral applications. They were a powerful tool in ecclesiastical governance and practice.[31] In all these synods the African ecclesiology that was being perpetuated was of the institutional church which is organized hierarchically.

The Establishment of the Synod of Bishops for the Universal Church

In modern times the old tradition of holding synods re-emerged and received impetus from the Second Vatican Council where the decision to establish the Synod of Bishops for the Universal Church sprung from. It was the intention of the Second Vatican Council to make use of the bishops' assistance in providing for the good of the universal Church through their close collaboration. On 15 September 1965, Pope Paul VI promulgated an apostolic letter called *Apostolica Sollicitudo* (a

---

[29] The Third Synod of Carthage was held in 397 AD and the document produced thereupon is a great treasure as it is the earliest document where the Canon of the New Testament (list of holy books to be considered and believed as Scripture) was approved. The first council or synod that accepted the present New Testament canon was the synod of Hippo, in North Africa, in 393 AD. The synod's acts are lost, but a brief summary of them was read and accepted by the third synod of Carthage in 397 AD. Certainly this was to exert an influence on the decision of Rome on the canonicity.

[30] www.ntcanon.org/Carthage.canon.shtml/ [19.5.2015].

[31] www.afrikaworld.net/synod/ [11.5.2015].

Motu Proprio),[32] in which he puts into effect the decision of the Council to establish the ecclesiastical organization of the Synod of Bishops for the Universal Church. He established it in the following words:

> And so, after carefully considering the whole matter, because of our esteem and regard for all the Catholic Bishops and with the aim of providing them with abundant means for greater and more effective participation in our concern for the Universal Church, on our own initiative and by our Apostolic Authority, we hereby erect and establish here in Rome a permanent council of bishops for the Universal Church, to be directly and immediately subject to our power. Its proper name is to be the "Synod of Bishops."[33]

Paul VI also established a permanent secretariat under the supervision of the Holy See to oversee the organizations and activities of the synods of bishops in the future history of the church. Every time a synod was to be convoked there was to be a special council on it to assist the general secretariat with the organization and execution of the synod. This institutionalization of the Synod of bishops, springing from Vatican II, gave a lot of impetus to the universal Church even in its local existences to hold synods which were a common occurrence in the early and ancient Church. There have been universal, regional and local synods held with more vigour since then. In the post-Vatican II African Church, two synods have been held.

The Adoption of the Model by the First African Synod in Modern Times

The image of Church as God's Family in African ecclesiology was officially adopted by the African Catholic Church during the first African Synod in modern times which was held in Rome in 1994. The synod was convoked on 6 January 1989 by Pope John Paul II. On this

---

[32] A *Motu Proprio* is a decree issued by the pope on his own initiative. This type of papal document decree administrative decisions and even alter church law. However, a *Motu proprio* cannot alter the doctrine of the church.

[33] Paul VI, *Apostolic Letter, Apostolica Sollicitudo*, 1965, p. 1.

day he announced his intention to convoke a Special Assembly of the Synod of Bishops for Africa. Through this assembly John Paul II wanted the African Church to strategize itself in her mission of evangelization as the world approached the 3rd Millennium. In July 1990, while on a pastoral visit in Africa, in Lome (Togo), John Paul II published the *Lineamenta* which led to the eventual publication of the *Instrumentum Laboris*,[34] in Kampala (Uganda), in February 1993. The pope gave the theme of the synod as: "The Church in Africa and her evangelizing mission towards the year 2000 'you will be my witnesses'" (cf. Ac 1:8).[35]

The long-awaited synod was opened on 10 April 1994 by John Paul II, in St. Peter's Basilica, in Rome, and was closed about a month later on 8 May 1994. There were 315 participants in the Synod and their discussions dwelt largely on the general mission of evangelization but according to five perspectives: Proclamation of the message, Inculturation, Dialogue, Justice and Peace, and Social Media.[36] There were representatives (bishops, priests, religious and laity) from all African countries of Africa and Madagascar except Rwanda. The bishops of Rwanda did not attend this historic event, because they were overwhelmed by the tragedy in their country and this was the assassination of the presidents of Burundi and Rwanda.

On 14 September 1995, Pope John Paul II delivered the fruits of the discussions of the African Synod in a Post-Synodal Apostolic Exhortation, called *Ecclesia in Africa*, on the African soil itself. This was during his 11th trip to Africa, and 67th international trip. This trip took

---

[34] An *instrumentum laboris* (Latin for "working instrument") is a type of papal document. It is a summary of responses to the *lineamenta* (which is an introduction and outline of the subject for discussion at an upcoming General Assembly of the Synod of Bishops) sent to all Episcopal Conferences of the Catholic Church, Eastern Church, Departments of the Curia and the Union of Superiors General. This document summarizes information returned to the General Secretariat in preparation for an ordinary assembly.

[35] www.news.va/va/news/vatican-the-first-synod-of-africa/ [13.5.2015].

[36] John Paul II, *Ecclesia in Africa*, pp. 3-6.

him to Cameroon (West Africa), Kenya (Eastern Africa) and South Africa (Southern Africa). There was also something historic about the delivery of the final message of the African Synod, *Ecclesia in Africa*, in that it was signed by the Pope on 14 September 1995, in Our Lady of Victories Cathedral in Yaoundé, Cameron. This was the first time a papal document, of whatever type, was signed outside the Vatican and outside Rome. It was a sign of honour and respect for the Church in Africa. Three days later, on 17 September 1995, there was the commemoration of the publication of *Ecclesia in Africa* in Southern Africa in Christ the King Cathedral, in Johannesburg. There was another commemoration of the delivery of the same message of the synod in Nairobi-Kenya in the Resurrection Garden on 20 September 1995.[37] *Ecclesia in Africa* had seven chapters: An historic moment of grace, the Church in Africa, evangelization and inculturation in the light of the third Christian millennium, you shall be my witnesses in Africa, building the kingdom of God, and you shall be my witnesses to the ends of the earth, apart from an introduction and a conclusion to the document.[38]

The convocation of the Synod specifically for the Church in Africa by the pope was a great honour and a vivid acknowledgement of the living Church of Africa by the universal Church. From the opening liturgy, through the discussions, to the concluding liturgy the joy of all the African participants could be seen for it was the first time in modern history that the Vatican had called for an assembly of the Catholic Church leaders of Africa to discuss its challenges and its mission of evangelization. There was freedom of speech exercised in the deliberations. The presence of the pope and other senior personnel of the Vatican further gladdened the African Church represented in the synod.

It was in this synod that the ecclesiology of Church as Family of God was adopted. Furthermore, it is important to understand that the African Catholic Church did not begin to live the ecclesiology of Church

---

[37] www.news.va/va/news/Vatican-the-first-synod-of-africa/ [13.5.2015].

[38] John Paul II, *Ecclesia in Africa*, pp. 8-39, 41-102.

as family of God from 1994 when it was adopted. The immediate pre-Vatican II African Church was already beginning to live this sense of family togetherness through the Small Christian Communities (SCCs) which had begun to appear in many places in Africa. The post-Vatican II African Church continued to live this self-understanding as family of God through further formation, promotion and sustenance of the SCCs. Therefore, what the synod fathers did in the 1994 African Synod by adopting this image was to officially stamp an ecclesiology and pastoral practice that was already in use in Africa. This was nevertheless needed to give the lived theology and practice of Church as God's family more impetus.

The Synod Fathers approved the use of the image of Church as God's family as an expression of the Church's nature which is particularly appropriate for Africa. They said this image emphasizes care for others, solidarity, warmth in human relationships, acceptance, dialogue and trust. The synod delegates said the new evangelization was to aim at building up the Church as Family, avoiding all ethnocentrism and excessive particularism, trying instead to encourage reconciliation and true communion between different ethnic groups.[39]

In the 1994 Synod of Bishops for Africa in Rome, several themes such as Inculturation, Dialogue, Justice and Peace related to the proclamation of the Good News, were studied. It was only after the relator-general, Cardinal H. Thiandoum, had presented the *Relatio ante Disceptationem* on the 11 April 1994,[40] that in addition to the main ideas, the Synod Fathers critically studied the ecclesiological model that would be more appropriate in expressing the nature and mystery of the Church as a communion to the African Christians. The concept "Family of God" finally emerged and was accepted after a heated

---

[39] John Paul II, *Ecclesia in Africa*, no. 63.

[40] A *Relatio ante Disceptationem* is an official address by the cardinal appointed as the moderator of a synod in which he highlights the major points on the agenda of the synodal meeting, with particular focus on some of the main issues that have emerged from the grassroots consultations which will have been done in preparation for a synod.

debate in an effort to describe and define the Church in Africa on an evangelistic mission.

During the first two weeks of the Synod, eleven bishops were quite reluctant to adopt the paradigm of "family" to define the Church because of certain ambiguities and uncertainties that threatened the African family. For instance, Archbishop Albert K. Obiefuna, bishop of Awka (Nigeria),[41]

expressed the fear that the notion "family" was liable to a restrictive and compromising understanding of the Church and thus might deny the universal character of the Church. In defense of his position he employed the African proverb "*blood is thicker than water*" to caution the other Synod Fathers. The adage connotes that the tribal and ethnic relations, which are natural links or bonds, may prevail strongly over the Christians' baptismal bond. At the same time, other prelates from West Africa, especially Archbishop A.T. Sanon, bishop of the Archdiocese of Bobo Dioulasso (Burkina Faso), a prominent protagonist of the image of "family of God," Archbishop E. Djitangar, bishop of Sarh in Chad, and Archbishop Jean-Noel Diouf, bishop of Tambacouda in Senegal, having deeply experienced ecclesial life in the Basic Christian Communities, persistently insisted on the relevance of the use of the paradigm "family of God" in describing and defining the nature of the Church in Africa.[42]

It was therefore not surprising that during the *Relatio Post Disceptationem*, when Cardinal H. Thiandoum, in presenting a synthesis of the most important ideas of the bishops' interventions, he re-affirmed the ecclesiology of the Church as Family of God. He said:

> The African family solidarity constitutes a solid base or source for an ecclesiology of the Church as family of God on earth... This concept of the Church-Family of God takes its roots from the Holy Scriptures, but it is solidly rooted in the African and Madagascar

---

[41] DC 2094, p. 476.
[42] DC 2094, p. 487.

cultures. All the baptized are born from heaven and constitute one family where God is Father and Great ancestor.[43]

The image of the Church as Family of God was officially and solemnly adopted for the evangelization in Africa during the final message of the Synod in which the synod fathers said "the Synod throws light on our belongingness to the Family of God. We are members of the Family of God."[44] In addition the final message of the Synod strongly recommended the creation of Small or Basic Christian Communities, which are cells of the Church-family of God. In such communities all were expected to live concretely and authentically the spirit of fraternity, gratuity, solidarity and share a common fate.

In *Ecclesia in Africa*, Pope John Paul II endorsed this image of Family of God. He described it not only as the main idea of the synod but also as an appropriate expression of the nature of the Church particularly for Africa. For him the metaphor stressed care for others, solidarity, warmth in human relationships, acceptance, dialogue and trust.[45] The new form of evangelization aimed at edifying the Church, family of God on earth, since the entire human race reflected somehow the family of God. This implied then that for the African the notion of the Church as communion became more meaningful and concretely expressed in the metaphor 'Family of God.'

The Reconfirmation of the Model

The Second Special Assembly for Africa of the Synod of Bishops which was held in 2009 re-confirmed the self-understanding of the Church in Africa as God's Family. This synod noted and reiterated that the exceptional ecclesial vitality and theological understanding of the Church as God's Family were the most visible results of the 1994 Synod. It was felt important to convoke this Second Synodal Assembly so as to provide a new impulse, filled with evangelical hope and

---

[43] M. Cheza, *Le Synode Africain: Historie et textes*, Paris: Karthala, 1996, p. 182

[44] M. Cheza, *Le Synode Africain: Historie et textes*, p. 224 (nos. 24-25).

[45] John Paul II, *Ecclesia in Africa*, no. 63.

charity, to the Church of God on the African continent and the neighbouring islands.[46] Eleven years after the First African Synod, Pope John Paul II announced, on 13 November 2004, his intention to convoke a Second Assembly for Africa of the Synod of Bishops. This aimed at doing an evaluation of the progress made by the Church on the African continent at the beginning of the third Christian millennium amidst the upcoming challenges. Events did not permit him to live that long to officially convoke the Second Synod for in the following year John Paul II died. His successor, Pope Benedict XVI, confirmed his predecessor's plan by announcing on 22 June 2005, in the presence of the special council for Africa of the general secretariat of the Synod of Bishops, his decision to convoke in Rome the Second Special Assembly for Africa of the Synod of Bishops. But it was also convoked in keeping with the desires of the episcopate of Africa who wanted another assembly to do an evaluation of the impact of the first synod and re-plan the activity of the future African church amidst the contemporary challenges. Benedict XVI convoked it to take place in Rome from 4 to 25 October 2009.

In the *Lineamenta* that was given, the theme for this second assembly was: "The Church in Africa in service of Reconciliation, Justice and Peace: you are salt of the earth and light of the world." The theme was coined from the gospel of Matthew speaking about the life of the followers (disciples) of Jesus Christ: "You are the salt of the earth ... you are the light of the world" (Mt 5:13-14). In 2009, the *Instrumentum Laboris* was published, and its chapters three and four dealt with the Church-Family of God at work in witness and perspectives, and as salt of the earth and light of the world, a model of being church grounded in a transfigured African culture.[47] This topic was continuing the great theme of evangelization in the third Christian millennium which the first assembly had initiated. It envisaged an evaluation of the accomplishments made and also took into consideration the changes which had taken place since the last synod. These changes

---

[46] Benedict XVI, *Post-Synodal Apostolic Exhortation, Africae Munus*, no. 3.

[47] www.vatican.va/roman_curia/synod/documents/rc_synod_documents/ [8.9.2015].

provided new challenges which needed a renewed evangelization effort and an in-depth-study of specific topics important for the future of the Catholic Church on the continent.[48]

In its evaluation of the accomplishments the Fathers of this second assembly of the Synod of Bishops noted that the Church in Africa, Family of God in pilgrimage in Africa, had witnessed tremendous growth throughout the continent, especially in membership, by the advent of the third Christian millennium. The 2004 statistics showed Africa had 148,817,000 faithful, 630 bishops, 31,259 priests (20,358 Diocesan and 10,901 Religious), 7,791 lay brothers, 57,475 consecrated women and 379,656 Catechists. Benedict XVI noted that there was a precious treasure in Africa, the Faith. He saw Africa as "a spiritual lung" for humanity that appeared to be in a crisis of faith and hope.[49] This was great news for the Church not only in Africa but also for the universal Church. But the evaluation also noted grey areas of life on the African continent among which the environmental crisis and ecological problems were mentioned. These problems and challenges could not be ignored, hence the theme of Reconciliation, Justice and Peace, was chosen for the Second African Synod.

Though in continuity with the first African Synod, the particular focus of this Second Special Assembly for Africa of the Synod of Bishops was on an *ad extra* (outward) dimension of the Church, its prophetic role in the society, whilst the first synod, in defining the Church as Family of God showed it was concerned more with the *ad intra* dimension of the Church. This *ad extra* dimension of the second synod is indicated in the full title of the synod: "The Church in Africa in Service to Reconciliation, Justice and Peace." Though knowing pretty well that the Church in Africa could not cure all political, social and economic ills on the continent, the Synod Fathers were concerned with the question of how the Church in Africa could be an authentic and effective agent of transformation ("salt and light") in the current situation in Africa. This was against the background that, as others were saying, the

---

[48] Benedict XVI, *Africae Munus*, no. 4-5.
[49] Benedict XVI, *Africae Munus*, no. 13.

Church had not done enough in this area of transformation. Archbishop Charles Gabriel Palmer-Buckle of Ghana, for instance, said "the Church in Africa has transformed neither society nor itself."[50] He argued the Church in Africa had not been true to its calling as the Family of God and that is why it had failed to be an agent of reconciliation.[51] The Church was called upon to a concerted commitment to those deprived of their freedom and peace, to bring back their rights as human beings. In the closing Eucharistic celebration for the Synod, Pope Benedict XVI called the Church in Africa, given its experience then of civil and tribal conflict and poverty, to become a community of reconciled persons who would eventually be able to become operators of justice and peace. The Church in Africa, as God's Family, was to be the salt and light among people and nations, bringing about transformation. Benedict XVI called the Church in Africa, God's family, to become a potent leaven of reconciliation in each country of this great continent.

The fruits of this assembly held from 4 to 25 October 2009, were finally given to the people of Africa by Benedict XVI through the Post-Synodal Apostolic Exhortation, *Africae Munus*, which he published on 19 November 2011. He signed this document on the African soil, at Quida, Benin, presenting the fruits that emerged from the Second Special Assembly for Africa of the Synod of Bishops. In its structure, *Africae Munus* has an introduction, two parts and a conclusion. The first part of the papal exhortation has two chapters: In Service of Reconciliation, Justice and Peace, and Paths towards Reconciliation,

---

[50] www.ncronline.org/news/vatican/ghanaian/bishop/palmer/ [15.5.2015].

[51] The Ghanaian Archbishop of Accra, Charles Gabriel Palmer-Buckle took part in the Second Special Assembly for Africa of the Synod of Bishops in Rome, not in his ordinary right as an African bishop, but as a papal appointee. He has been a leader in peace efforts in Ghana and a veteran of the international Catholic scene through his work with groups such as *Caritas internationalis* and Catholic Relief Service. He is widely considered to be among the heavyweights of his generation in the African hierarchy. He has also been appointed by Pope Francis to represent Ghana on the Synod 'on the family' in October 2015.

Justice and Peace. The second part has three chapters: Members of the Church, Major Areas of the Apostolate, and Stand up, take your mat and walk (Jn 5:8). In this document the Church, the Family of God in Africa, against the turbulent present history of Africa, is called to help build a reconciled Africa by pursuing paths of truth and justice, love and peace.

Africae Munus seeks to re-enforce the ecclesial dynamism, outline a programme of pastoral activity for evangelization for the coming decades and in this it underlines the need for reconciliation, justice and peace in Africa. The Second Synod and its exhortation, *Africae Munus*, were to be seen in ecclesiology as a continuation of the first, *Ecclesia in Africa*.[52] The papal document, *Africae Munus*, notes that *Ecclesia in Africa* gives great impetus to the growth of the Church in Africa, and in this it seeks to develop further the idea of Church as Family of God. The Church is the Family of God and Jesus Christ is the first-born among many brethren: "For those God foreknew he also predestined to be conformed to the likeness of his Son, that he might be the firstborn among many brothers" (Rom 8:29), and he, by means of his cross, reconciled all people with God the Father: "And in his one body to reconcile both of them to God through the cross, by which he put to death their hostility" (Eph 2:16). He, by his resurrection, bestowed the Holy Spirit. After the resurrection he breathed on them and said: "Receive the Holy Spirit" (Jn 20:22). The Second African Synod crystallized the African ecclesiology of the Church as God's Family when it said that exceptional ecclesial vitality and a theological understanding of the Church as God's Family were the most visible results of the 1994 Synod.[53] The Exhortation reiterated that *Ecclesia in Africa* made its own the idea of the Church as God's family which the Synod Fathers acknowledged as an expression of the Church's nature particularly appropriate for Africa. For this image emphasized care for

---

[52] Agbonkhianmeghe E. Orobator (ed), *Reconciliation, Justice, and Peace: The Second Synod*, pp. 1-10.

[53] Benedict XVI, *Africae Munus*, no. 3.

others, solidarity, warmth in human relationships, acceptance, dialogue and trust.[54]

It was the intention of the Synod Fathers to develop further the ecclesiology adopted during the first Synod of Church as God's Family. However, there were some scholars who, when doing comparative studies of the two documents (*Ecclesia in Africa* and *Africae Munus*) from the ecclesiological perspective, argued that there is an evident paradigm shift, whether consciously or unconsciously, in *Africae Munus*. Such scholars argued that there was an internal shift from the ecclesiological model of Church as Family of God in the *Ecclesia in Africa* to the ecclesiological model of Church as Servant (a Church at the service of reconciliation, justice and peace). Nevertheless, the aspect of the Church at work (service) and doing service came out in the Second Special Assembly for Africa but not in such a way as to mark a departure from the ecclesiology of Church as God's Family. After all the Church-Family of God, was not to be an idle Church. The Church had always been called to service. The Second African Synod's theme "the Church in Africa in service to reconciliation, justice and peace" did not mark a paradigm shift and departure from the ecclesiology of Church as family of God adopted in *Ecclesia in Africa*. It rather cemented this self-understanding of the Church in Africa as God's Family.

Decolonization and the African Ecclesiology

The Church of Africa of the 1960s was influenced by two major movements. It was a Church that was emerging from the ecclesiology of communion developed during the Second Vatican Council and from the political movement of decolonization. The ecclesiology of communion developed during the Second Vatican Council also bred the theology of the local church through which the people at the grassroots were to see themselves as the Church. This theology had great impact on the way of being Church in Africa after the council.

---

[54] John Paul II, *Ecclesia in Africa*, no. 63.

During the same years surrounding the Second Vatican Council, the continent of Africa was going through a lot of changes. The 1960s contained promising prospects for the people of Africa and this wind of change was to have an impact on the life of the Church. The struggle for independence in African countries and the desire for self-rule, participation and self-expression, had begun earlier but heightened in the 1950s.[55] "The Report on the Experiences of the Church in the Work of Evangelization in Africa," prepared by Bishop J. Sangu for presentation at the 1974 Synod of Bishops in Rome, reflects that decolonization had a corresponding influence on the Church and this was the localization of the Church. The people's mindset had shifted from thinking of the missionaries (the hierarchy) as the Church to thinking of themselves as the Church. The lay faithful were taking more responsibility, ownership and leadership in the Church. Many Africans were becoming bishops of the local churches, priests, religious sisters and brothers.[56]

This independence of the African countries during these decades did not come on a silver platter. It had to be fought for and consequently it came at a cost. The success story of their independence came upon the rediscovery and use of the African values of solidarity, communion, identity, freedom, dignity, and participation. The ecclesial practice that developed in Africa just before, during and following the two movements (decolonization and localization) did emphasize the same ideals. The communitarian concept of the Church was developing with emphasis on the people at the grassroots as the Church. This was different from the pyramidal ecclesiology which had characterized the Church in the pre-Vatican II era.

---

[55] Adrian Hastings, *African Catholicism: Essays in Discovery*, London: SCM, 1989, pp. 122-123.

[56] Report on the Experiences of the Church in Africa in the Work of Evangelization in Africa. The African Continent's report for the 1974 Synod of Bishops on 'The Evangelization in the Modern World', pp. 15-16. A mimeographed text distributed to Bishops for Africa, delegates to the Bishops' Synod.

Development and Life of the Small Christian Communities

In African Catholic Ecclesiology the basic form of expression of the Church as a Family of God had been the development and life of the modern day Small Christian Communities (SCCs) which became the privileged *loci* where the model of Church as Family of God was lived. There were two schools of thought on the development of the Small Christian Communities in Africa. One school of thought said they developed from the ecclesiology of *'communio'* central in Vatican II and the theology of the local church developed with clarity in the same council. The other school of thought said the SCCs did not emerge from Vatican II. The modern day SCCs leitmotif in Africa, they said, was an ecclesiological tool and model borrowed from the Basic Ecclesial Communities in Latin America which developed in the 1950s where they were commonly referred to as *Comunidades Eclesiales de Base*.[57] These communities arose out of theological and pastoral needs and figuring primarily as a restructuring of the Church itself and not as a social or lay movement.[58] From Brazil these communities spread to the neighbouring Chile, Honduras and Panama, and then to other parts of the Latin American subcontinent. Africa and other continents copied from this Latin American way of being Church.[59]

The beginning of the Small Christian Communities in Africa goes back to 1961 when at its 6th Plenary Assembly from 20th November to 2nd December 1961, the Zaire Episcopal Conference (now the Democratic Republic of Congo or DRC) approved a pastoral plan to promote "Living Ecclesial Communities" (also called "Living Christian Communities").[60]

---

[57] Joseph G. Healey & Jeanne Hinton (eds.), *Small Christian Communities Today: Capturing the New Movement*, Nairobi: Paulines Africa, 2006, pp. 7-21.

[58] J. Marins, *Latin America in Small Christian Communities: Vision and Practicalities*, Dublin: Columba, 2002, p. 185.

[59] Gabriel Afagbegee SVD, *Building Small Christian Communities: Foundation and Step-by-Step Approach to Building SCCs*, Germiston: Lumko, pp. 54-56.

[60] Joseph G. Healey, *Building the Church as Family of God: Evaluation of Small Christian Communities in Eastern Africa*, Nairobi: CUEA Press, 2012, p. 3.

The Zaire Bishops opted for these communities to be more important than the well-known mission structures of evangelization like schools, hospitals, church buildings and outstations. They felt that these Living Ecclesial Communities, *Communautés Ecclesiales Vivantes de Base*, were the only way to make the Church more African and closer to the people. So, the very first Small Christian Communities started in the then Zaire in 1961.[61]

In some few countries of the Association of Member Episcopal Conferences in Eastern Africa (AMECEA) region the initiation of the SCCs took place only at the parochial level.[62] For example in Tanzania, the beginning of the SCCs could be traced to Nyarombo Ingri and Masonga Parishes in 1966 in North Mara in Musoma diocese, Northwestern Tanzania with research on the social structure and community values of the Luo ethnic group. The first terms used for these communities were *Chama* (meaning "small group") and "Small Communities of Christians." These were forerunners of the Small Christian Communities.[63] In Kenya the SCCs were started in the parish of Iten in Eldoret Diocese. The SCCs were seen as bearing the people's desire and having the mission of finding good news (gospel) in their own African reality, integrating biblical study with the members' daily life rhythms as well as celebrating life events like birth, marriage, sickness, death and funerals together. They helped the Church to become an indigenous rather than a foreign reality.[64]

---

[61] John Baur, *2000 Years of Christianity in Africa*, Nairobi: Paulines Africa, Second Edition, 2009, pp. 389-392.

[62] In this East African ecclesiastical regional grouping, the member countries are eight: Ethiopia, Sudan, Kenya, Uganda, Tanzania, Malawi, Zambia, and Eritrea. It has a permanent Secretariat in Nairobi-Kenya. Malawi, though geographically in Southern Africa, is ecclesiastically in this East African Association. So too is Zambia, another Southern African country.

[63] Joseph G. Healey, *Building the Church as Family of God*, p. 6.

[64] Jean Marc Ela and R. Luneau, *"Voici temps de heritiers: Églises d'Afrique et Voies Nouvelles"*, pp. 172-176.

In the post-Vatican II era, AMECEA worked hard to promote this communitarian and familial way of being church in Africa. Learning from the situation and ecclesial practice of Latin America and driven by the ecclesiology of Vatican II, in the AMECEA assembly of December 1973, in Nairobi-Kenya, the bishops observed that a means of making the Church in Eastern Africa economically independent and pastorally dynamic was through the building of small Christian communities. Three years later, the AMECEA bishops met in Nairobi for another plenary and at this meeting they unanimously agreed to have the initiation of the SCCs as a pastoral priority. They guided that these SCCs should be considered the 'most local incarnations' of the One, Holy, Catholic and Apostolic Church and that they should be centered on the Eucharist and the Word of God. They further directed that these SCCs were to advocate good and sound leadership among the faithful, promote practical reconciliation among members, stimulate communal spirituality and sharing at grassroots level, effect practical and existential human development, and also become the conscience of society. Many more plenary assemblies of the AMECEA spoke of these SCCs as the most evident way of Christians living together as Family of God.[65]

The new way of being Church as Family of God through the existence and life of the SCCs also spread to West Africa. The SCCs (Small Christian Communities) became a privileged place where the image of Church as Family is translated. The use of the metaphor 'family of God' in reference to the local churches in Africa and the ecclesiastical organization of Small Christian Communities was known to have existed in Burkina Faso and other parts of West Africa. Christians there felt a profound politico-religious experience from the Small or Basic Christian Communities in which they lived. They saw themselves as members of one family of God.[66]

---

[65] Patrick A. Kalilombe, *Doing Theology at the Grassroots: Theological Essays from Malawi*, Blantyre: CLAIM, 1999, pp. 98-104.

[66] Francis Appiah-Kubi, *Church, Family of God: Relevance, and pastoral challenges*, unpublished part of his dissertation.

The origin and development of the ecclesiology and pastoral practice of Church as family of God have been fruits of the participation of both laity and leadership of the church but, of course, with different accents. In Latin America generally, the role of the lay faithful in the initiation of the basic ecclesia communities was stressed even if their initiative received acceptance and support from the bishops. It could be said of these basic communities that they developed from below. In Eastern African Countries emphasis was put on the role of the AMECEA bishops in the initiation and promotion of the Small Christian Communities even if the role and participation of the laity was there and it could be said that there was more accent of the ecclesiological development from above. However, there was participation of both laity and clerics in the practical development of the model of Church as Family of God in Africa.

Popes in these times also assisted in the development of this ecclesiology through there exultations. There were papal pronouncements through various documents which promoted the African model of Church as God's family. Pope Paul VI, for example, stated that the name SCCs belonged to groups which came together within the Church in order to unite themselves to the Church and to cause the Church to grow.[67] He said these communities were the hope of the universal Church and that they needed to be firmly attached to the local Church where they were inserted and to the universal Church.[68] Pope John Paul II stated that the SCCs were a sign of vitality within the Church, an instrument of formation and evangelization, and a solid starting point for a new society based on a 'civilization of love.' These SCCs decentralized and organized the parish community, to which they always remained united. The new basic communities, if they truly lived in unity with the Church, were a true expression of communion and a means for a construction of a more profound communion. This was

---

[67] *Evangelii Nuntiandi* is a papal encyclical that was published by Pope VI in 1975 on the theme of Catholic evangelization in the modern world. It is considered one of the greatest pastoral documents dealing with the mission of the Church which is evangelization.

[68] Paul VI, *Apostolic Exhortation, Evangelii Nuntiandi*, no. 58.

because the Church is a communion. John Paul II reiterated what Paul VI said that the SCCs or Basic Ecclesial Communities were a cause for great hope for the life of the Church.[69]

Development of Small Christian Communities in the Archdiocese of Lilongwe

In Zambia, closer home, the SCCs were started in 1971 in St. Charles Lwanga parish in the Archdiocese of Lusaka.[70] In the diocese of Lilongwe the Small Christian Communities developed in the same veins of Africanizing the Church, bringing it close to the people and going beyond the mission structures of the parish and the outstation. They were begun by a Malawian Bishop, Patrick Kalilombe, who held a Mini-Synod in the Diocese of Lilongwe from 1973 to 1975. He initiated a diocesan pastoral plan of Small Christian Communities at the grass-root level.[71] These Small Christian Communities were called *Miphakati*. He became the first bishop in Eastern Africa and particularly in the AMECEA region to initiate a diocesan plan for the building of the Small Christian Communities. There were examples of how, prior to the innovation of Bishop Patrick Augustine Kalilombe of making a diocesan plan for the initiation of the Small Christian Communities in the diocese of Lilongwe, the initiation of the SCCs in some parts of Eastern Africa was only parochial and not diocesan.[72]

In the first meeting of the Lilongwe Diocesan Mini-Synod from 24th to 28th November 1973 the delegates agreed on the purpose of the Church in the diocese of Lilongwe as being the establishment of the Kingdom of God in this locality. To do this the Church in Lilongwe had to be local and not foreign. The Good News had to incarnate into the culture of the people and be run according to the African cultural

---

[69] John Paul II, *Apostolic Exhortation, Redemptoris Missio*, no. 51.

[70] Int Fr. Jonas Phiri, pastoral coordinator, Archdiocese of Lusaka, Kalundu, Lusaka, 8.5.2016.

[71] For his theology see Patrick Kalilombe, *Doing Theology at the Grassroots: Theological Essays from Malawi*, Zomba: Kachere, 1999.

[72] Joseph G. Healey, *Building the Church as Family of God*, pp. 6-7.

values and by Africans themselves.[73] In initiating a pastoral plan of the diocese for the implementation of its vision of establishing the Kingdom of God in this locality the delegates together with Bishop Kalilombe agreed on inculcating among the faithful the spirit of being in smaller Christian groups in their neighbourhood called *Miphakati ya Chikhristu*. In creating the SCCs in the diocese of Lilongwe, Bishop Patrick Kalilombe, other than having the intentions of making the Church really African and close to the people at the grassroots, allowing them to be and experience being Church as a family, he wanted the Church, through the SCCs, to be self-reliant in financial needs of the Church, self-propagating in the nurturing of the faith, and self-ministering through formation of lay leaders and ministers in these small communities of the Church.[74]

Unfortunately, the elite of the one-party regime of president Hastings Kamuzu Banda wrongly associated the naming of these communities with a political figure, Attati Mpakati, who had been exiled to Zimbabwe. They thought these communities were grass-root machinery of promoting the rebellious intentions of Attati Mpakati.[75] As a result, Bishop Kalilombe went into exile, only to return to Malawi during the multiparty political dispensation that began in 1994. However, in the period of his absence the works of ecclesiological restructuring continued and these communities grew from strength to strength.

The application of the ecclesiology of the Church as the Family of God in the Archdiocese of Lilongwe led to the creation of another ecclesial structure beyond the outstation. These were the Small Christian

---

[73] Patrick A. Kalilombe, *Mabvu Adamvana Kuti Aning'e Pamimba*, Lilongwe: Likuni, 1973, pp. 2-3.

[74] Patrick A. Kalilombe, *Mabvu Adamvana Kuti Aning'e Pamimba*, p. 3.

[75] Attati Mpakati was a Malawian dissident and, following the death of Yatuta Chisiza, leader of the Socialist League of Malawi from 1975 until his death on 24th March 1983. He was killed by a letter bomb while in exile in Zimbabwe. It is widely suspected that the parcel was sent by agents of President Hastings Kamuzu Banda. Mpakati had survived a similar attack in 1979, which President Kamuzu Banda admitted ordering.

Communities and their main purpose was the fostering of stronger human interpersonal relationships, of support and service to one another and in society, among the Christians. The outstations were split into numerous SCCs communities where the Christians were expected to experience being church close to one another and with stronger bonds of human fraternity, fellowship and solidarity. The SCCs developed to become the very basic level at the very grassroots in the structure of the Church. The structure of the outstations would suffice to accord the Christians stronger human bonds of closeness and fraternity as children of the same Father, but the division of the number of the big outstations would be for people to know each other as belonging to the same community of the family of God. Below is a summary of the deaneries, parishes and the Small Christian Communities.

Deanery	Parish	Year Opened	Estimated Catholic Population	Out-stations	No. of SCCs
Mchinji	Kachebere	1902	17,500	10	50
	Guilleme	1935	125,750	46	186
	Ludzi	1942	12,500	22	102
	Kapiri	1966	29,500	26	136
	Mkanda	1984	30,000	30	70
Likuni	Likuni	1902	78,048	29	72
	Mlale	1950	38,463	40	86
	Namitete	1954	68,000	39	134
	Nathenje	1960	27,719	18	54
	Chilinde	2010	25 000	19	42
Madisi	Nambuma	1928	102,640	43	164
	Chiphaso	1930	30,548	30	123
	Mpherere	1939	59,051	57	117
	Madisi	1957	105,273	64	139
	Mtengo wa Nthenga	1959	44,526	34	122
	St.Joseph's – Kasungu	2000	27,000	29	97
	Mponela	2010	-	13	56

Deanery	Parish	Year Opened	Estimated Catholic Population	Out-stations	No. of SCCs
	Kalembe (Chamama-Kasungu)	2010	30 000	29	76
Maula	Maula	1954	-	-	9
	Chigoneka-St. Kizito (Area 47)	1975	8,000	5	14
	St.Patrick's -Chimutu (Area 18)	1976	5,787	2	22
	St. Francis-Kanengo	1976	10,000	4	21
	Lumbadzi	1987	24,970	7	21
	St. Ignatius (Area 30)	1989	350	-	3
	Kaggwa (Area 49)	1992	17,047	8	16
	Chinsapo	2009	3,847	-	9
Mtima-woyera	Mtima-woyera	1955	11,000	1	30
	Chilinde	1974	12,732	-	17
	Msamba, St. John's	1974	25,800	4	36
	Kamuzu Barracks, St. Mary's	1986	1,795	1	-
	Kawale	1991	5,273	1	19
	Don Bosco (Area 23)	1996	11,000	7	42
Salima	Salima	1948	45,400	22	63
	Nkhotakota	1978	18,225	65	163
	Chezi	1992	10,000	33	92
	Nanthomba	1992	14,855	14	54
	Benga	2012	15 000	18	41

Note that Maula parish in the city of Lilongwe, for example, being small in territory, did not have an outstation but had 9 SCCs of which 8 SCCs were for the local Christians whilst one Small Christian Community was for the International Community members who congregated in this parish. They made a community of their own due to the language barrier.[76] St. Ignatius-Police Headquarters at Area 30, being a small parish in the Police Headquarters, it too did not have any outstation. It however had 3 SCCs.

The Mini-Synod, which adopted the diocesan plan for the creation of the SCCs during the time of Bishop Kalilombe, resolved that the Small Christian Community was a vital unit in the Church.[77] The Small Christian Communities gave indications of further growth given the large numbers of catechumens in all the parishes in the diocese and the annual adult baptisms which were done. They also continued to grow in numbers because of the diocesan policy that articulated the size of the SCC. The Lilongwe Archdiocesan Mini-Synod in 2006 resolved that a SCC should not be less than 30 Christian families and not more than 50.[78] The SCC had become a new way of being Church. Whilst it might be possible, due to various reasons, to have a parish without an outstation like those in the city, it was not possible in the Archdiocese of Lilongwe to have a parish without Small Christian Communities. It had become a must-have structure in the Church of Lilongwe and it was neither optional for the parishes to be divided into nor for the faithful to belong to the SCCs. In this vein the 2006 Lilongwe Mini-Synod stated:

---

[76] Int Angella Magalasi and John Magalasi, St. Paul SCC leaders, Maula Parish, Lilongwe, 24-5.2016. The international community that normally congregates in the English service makes up a community of their own in the parish where pastoral services and Sunday school instructions for the children in preparation of the reception of the sacraments and the deepening of faith are done not in vernacular but in English.

[77] Patrick A. Kalilombe, *Mpingo Ndife Tonse*, Lilongwe: Likuni Press, 1975, chapter 2.

[78] Felix Mkhori, *Lilongwe Mini-Synod: Let us March together in Spreading the Good News of our Lord*, Lilongwe: Likuni, 2006, p. 10.

> The Synod General Assembly reiterated that the Small Christian Community is a vital unit in the Church. No Christian should live in isolation. Every Christian belongs to a small local Christian community. It is not enough to go to Church on Sunday without paying due respect to the demands of the Small Christian Community. Leaders of Small Christian Communities must know and fulfill their role with commitment. Different groups and movements in the diocese and in the parishes must respect the fact that the Small Christian Community is paramount.[79]

The development of the Small Christian Communities in the Archdiocese of Lilongwe, as an implementation of the new ecclesiology of the Church as communion and consequently as the Family of God, had a number of advantages in the task of being Church. This development enhanced human relationship among the people of God with a greater sense of fraternity, fellowship, solidarity, and service to one another in the community, the Church and society. Being small in nature, through their participation in the ecclesial life of the SCCs, the Christians were able to know each other, serve (minister to) each other, and could better be attentive to each other's needs.

Through their participation in the life of the SCCs the members supported each other through prayer and social services depending on their spiritual and physical needs. Being small in nature, they knew and encouraged each other. The SCCs thus had become schools of prayer. The SCC members were meant to meet weekly during a day and time most opportune to them depending on their occupational demands and contexts. However, generally during the first week of the month, the members of the community were to focus on sharing the Word of God through Bible reading and open sharing by every member. During the meeting in the second week of the month the members were expected to teach each other some elements from the teaching of the Church through some section of the Catechism of the Catholic Church. In their weekly meeting of the third week the members were meant to do some devotions either in form of the recitation of the Holy Rosary,

---

[79] Felix Mkhori, *Lilongwe Mini-Synod: Let us March together in Spreading the Good News of our Lord*, pp. 9-10.

Novena, or litanies to the saints. In their weekly meeting of the fourth week of the month the members were to look at the different issues affecting their community. This would be something related to spirituality, social life, health, education, politics, and administration. The members in the community assisted each other when some are sick, bereaved or in difficult situations. Thus, together using the strategy of See-Judge-Act they were able to approach their issues in pursuit of arriving at some practical solutions to their problems and challenges. There was also the promotion and growing usage of the Lumko Seven Steps Method of Prayer and Bible Sharing in the Small Christian Communities. These Seven steps were: Invitation of the Lord, Reading the text, Meditation, Silent listening, Sharing, Searching together, Spontaneous Prayers.[80]

The structure of the SCCs had another advantage of providing occasions of participation in the lay ministry of the Church. There were various roles which were to be carried out to sustain the life of the community and these accorded the lay members space to participate in the ministry of the Church. The executive committee of the Small Christian Community in the Archdiocese of Lilongwe comprised of close to thirty members. These were chairpersons and their deputies responsible for particular needs of the organization of the community. Such SCC executive office bearers were the chairperson of the community, secretary, treasurer, chairperson of liturgy and prayer life, choir coordinator, chairperson of the Sunday school teachers for the children, chairperson of the teachers of the catechumens, marriage counsellors, chairperson for development, youth coordinator, and chairperson of the Church groups and associations.[81] These positions of service in the community came through elections in the community

---

[80] www.fabc.org/offices/laity/Seven steps Method of Gospel Sharing/ [14.5.2017].

[81] The pastoral secretariat of the diocese of Lilongwe in its 1978 publication outlined these Church groups, movements and associations, among others as to include family movements, Legionaries of Mary (a Legio), Achigwirizano (prelude of CWO), school committee, development officers in the community and others.

which happened every three years with a maximum possibility of a second term. There were no third terms acceptable in the same position in the service and organization of the SCC. Through such a wide spectrum of leadership there was provision of service of the needs of the community and the individual Christians.[82] The weaker and passive members of the Christian community were easily identified and their needs attended to. There was creation of stronger bonds or links of unity and relationships among the Christians through their coming together in these communities.

Conclusion

Before the Council of Trent, the Church saw itself as a visible entity of an invisible reality and the characteristic model for the Church was that of an Institutional-hierarchical nature and this was carried on to the period of the First Vatican Council. A great watershed in Catholic ecclesiology came in Vatican II when the model of Church as a people of God and as a community became prominent even though the institutional-hierarchical model was still being deciphered. The first formal mention of the Church as God's Family was in the sessions of the Council of Vatican II. In 1994, the model of Church as God's Family was adopted as appropriate for Africa during the First African Synod, and it was reconfirmed by the synods fathers at the Second African Synod in 2009. The model triggered the development of the Small Christian Communities through which the Church was brought closer to the people. The political movement of decolonization in Africa also had some influence on African ecclesiology. Through the development of this model, the people came to appropriate the Church and no longer regarded the church as foreign to them.

The development of the SCCs emanating from the development of the model of Church as God's Family only managed to bring the Christians closer to one another with a deeper sense of fraternity but did not

---

[82] Pastoral Secretariat of the Diocese of Lilongwe, *Maudindo mu Mphakati ndinso Msonkhano wa Bungwe la Mphakati*, Lilongwe: Likuni, 1978, pp. 18-22.

manage to bring people closer to God's creation of which they were part of. It did not manage to bring the people to a sense of fraternity with the environment upon which they depended and which depended on them for the fulfillment of its destiny.

Chapter 3: Biblical and Socio-anthropological Foundations of the African Ecclesiology

The African ecclesiology of Church as God's Family is rich in meaning and has solid biblical and socio-anthropological foundations. The development of this African ecclesiology of Church as God's Family did not only bank on African cultural values, but also on the rich Judeo-Christian Biblical tradition. Though the African model of Church as Family of God was adopted officially by the Roman Catholic Church in Africa during the African Synod, it did not mean that this picture and way of conceptualization of the Church was new. There were some Biblical images which influenced the theological development of the concept of Church as Family.

The viewing of the Church from the perspective of a sociological and anthropological term such as 'family' has some challenges and issues. The insufficiency of the ecclesiology of Church as Family in saving the environment cannot be overemphasized as it leads to the inferiorization of women and the non-human part of God's creation. In appreciating the richness and strength of the metaphor 'family' when applied to the Church, it is equally important to be aware of its biblical foundations before becoming aware of its socio-anthropological foundations and the challenges that come with it. Here below are some of the rich biblical concepts which provide good ground for the understanding of the Church as the Family of God:

The Image of Israel as the People of God

The image of Israel as the People of God is one of these biblical images which influenced the development of the ecclesiology of Church as God's Family. God prepared the Church in a marvelous fashion when he chose the People of Israel as his own special people. The divine election of Israel prefigures the Church as an Assembly of God's people. He made a Covenant with them on Mount Sinai through Moses. With the Covenant, the people of Israel became the Lord's own possession: "Now if you obey me fully and keep my covenant, then out of all nations you will be my treasured possession. Although the whole earth is mine, you will be for me a kingdom of priests, and a holy nation" (Ex 19:5-6). God on his part promised love, care and protection for them in return for obedience saying: "If you listen carefully to what he says and do all that I say, I will be an enemy to your enemies and will oppose those who oppose you" (Ex 23:22). Thus, through the covenant they became the people of God and God became their Father (Lev 26:9-12, Jer 32:38).[133] Through the Covenant established, the Israelites were always conscious of themselves as the elect of God and a people unique for God (Ex 19:6; Ac 10:35; 1 Cor 11:25; 1 Pt 2:9). The Covenant bound the two parties, God and the Israelites, into an obligation of mutual love and faithfulness.

The Church (*ekklesia*) as the new Assembly of the People of God

In the context of the Bible, the Church (*ekklesia*) is understood as the new assembly of the people of God. In the mind of God, Israel had the duty of being light to the Gentiles, that through it the nations may know and serve the one true God. In the events of the Messiah, Jesus Christ (life, death and resurrection), God pulled down all walls of separation and included the Gentiles among his elect. Those who believed in his Son, whom he had sent to redeem the world, became sons and daughters of God.

The believers in Christ Jesus became the new people of God: "But you are a chosen people, a royal priesthood, a holy nation, God's special possession, that you may declare the praises of him who called you out of darkness into his wonderful light" (1 Pet 2:9). Peter compared and contrasted the disobedient and unbelieving Jews and the reconciled community of Christian people (composed of converted Jews and converted Gentiles). He ascribed to Christians a series of phrases quoted from the Old Testament, the various privileges which had belonged to the children of Israel, for example, "a chosen people" (Isa 43:20). The cornerstone was elect, and precious; the living stones

---

[133] Karambai Sebastian, *Structures of Decision–Making in the Local Church*, Bangalore: Theological Publications in India, 1995, pp. 3-7.

built thereupon were elect likewise. The whole Christian Church was addressed as an elect race, one race, because all its members were begotten again of the one Father. In these words, 'a royal priesthood,' Peter followed the Septuagint version of Exodus 19:6. The Hebrew version had the words, 'a kingdom of priests.' The word 'royal' meant the elect would sit with Christ on his throne and reign with him (Rev 3:21). The Israelites were a holy nation separated from the heathen and consecrated to God's service by circumcision. The Christian Church, as comprising the reconciled community of God from all nations, forms one spiritual nation under one King (God), separated in service and dedicated to him in holy baptism.

The African model of Church as Family of God, thus, found itself prepared in the Scriptures in the election of Israel as the people of God. The image of the Christian community as the new people of God was fitting as the promise of the Messiah was accepted by this community as having been fulfilled in the person of Jesus Christ. In him Christians understood themselves as being the new elect of God. Through the salvific works of Jesus Christ, they had been adopted as children of God and brothers and sisters of Jesus Christ. Hence, they formed the Family of God.

The Church as a Community

The African model of Church as God's Family was also founded on another inference from the Biblical presentation of the nature of God as community. The nature of God, as understood by the Catholic Church, was that he is a Trinity. He is one God in three persons of the Father, the Son and the Holy Spirit.[134] He is One but not lonely. So the God of the Christians is not a lonely being, he is a family. He revealed himself to human beings as such and in creating human beings God wanted them to share in his divine life. The communitarian nature of the God of Jesus Christ was evident in and inferred from a number of scriptural passages. For example, when God decided to create human

---

[134] Dennis M. Doyle, *The Church Emerging from the Vatican II: A Popular approach to contemporary Catholicism*, Connecticut: XXIII, 1992, p. 37.

beings he said: "Let us make mankind in our own image, in our likeness" (Gen 1:26). Notice that God said, 'let us' and the subject to perform the action identified himself in the plural form. This showed that even if he is one, he is not alone. The Bible also presented the story of human pride when the peoples, created as they were, sought totalitarian power and independence from God. Human beings scattered over the earth decided to build an impressive tower out of pride not to be under God's rule (Gen 11:1-9). They built what is known as the tower of Babel, which was an imitation of the Babylonian temple towers, known as ziggurats, which were built to 'reach heaven' so that people could be in contact with the gods. In reaction to this the Lord came to the city and the tower that the people had built. He, the Lord, said, "Come, let us go down and there confuse their language so they may not understand each other" (Gen 11:7). In his reaction to the action of the people God presents himself in plural (*us*). He convoked the others divine 'persons' to respond to the pride of human beings. This again showed the nature of the Christian God, that even if he is one, he is not alone. The nature of this one God is plural; he is a community and a family living in close communion and unity in the Godhead.[135] Christian living is hence to imitate the familial life of God himself.

The Plural and Trinitarian Nature of God

The plural and Trinitarian nature of God got further revealed in the biblical narrative of Abraham welcoming three strangers (Gen 18:1-15). Abraham saw three men standing in front of him, as he sat under the oak of Mamre, while the day was growing hot. He welcomed the strangers under the oak tree and showed them great hospitality. As the three men bade farewell, after a good treat, they left a blessing to Abraham that the same time next year, Sarah, his wife, would be with child. The three men were a mystical representation of God. In this narrative God came down to be a guest of human beings; a pre-figuration of the mystery of the incarnation. Abraham discovered who the

---

[135] Fernando Armellini, *Celebrating the Word: A Commentary on the Readings*, Nairobi: Paulines, 1992, pp. 140-145.

guests were only when they repeated the promise of a son, reminding him of the God of the Covenant. It was the triune God himself, in his plurality, whom Abraham entertained without knowing it.

God revealed himself, his true nature and his life to humanity in three stages. In most of the Old Testament, God revealed himself as the 'Father.' Even though in earlier Judaism it was not common to give human attributes to God, the relationship between God and Israel was like that of Father and child. The latter prophetic books began to prophesy the coming of the Messiah, the Son of God, and the full revelation of God's love. The first four books of the New Testament present to humanity the second person in the Godhead, Jesus Christ, Saviour of the world. He is the incarnation of God. In his public life Jesus cemented the teaching of God as Father who is in heaven (Mt 6:9-14). When asked by the disciples to teach them how to pray he said to them that they needed to have a filial relation to their God who is their Father. In his public life Jesus Christ made the revelation of the third person of the Trinity, the Holy Spirit. In the foretelling of his passion Jesus comforted his disciples that he would ask his Father to send them the advocate, the Holy Spirit. The Trinitarian nature of God was further revealed during the baptism of Jesus when the Holy Spirit descended like a dove and rested upon him (Jesus) while the Father's voice sounded saying this was his beloved Son in whom he was well pleased (Mt 3:13-17). The inherent and inseparable communion of these three divine persons was made clear in John 14:1-11 where Jesus said he was one with the Father, and consequently with the Holy Spirit shortly to be sent upon the disciples. The mission of the apostles, as given in the great commission, is to make disciples of all nations, teaching and baptizing them in the name of the triune God (Mt 28:16-20).

Thus, God revealed to humanity his true nature that even though he is one, he is not alone. The God of the Christians is a family, a community, and this family is open to all.[136] There are three persons in

---

[136] Fernando Armellini, *Celebrating the Word: Year. A Commentary on the Readings*, p. 145.

the Godhead (the Father, the Son and the Holy Spirit). God, who is a family, wanted not only that human beings share in his life, but also that they are introduced into his family. Even if God is transcendent, he is not one who lives far away from people. He is also immanent. In this family of God, people of all nations are welcome. The African Catholic Church saw the believers as an assembly of the people belonging to this Family of God.

The Holy Family of Jesus, Joseph and Mary

In African Catholicism the Church was understood as the Family of God and this model also found its remote preparation in the Holy Family of Jesus, Joseph and Mary (Mt 2:14-15). The Holy Family was the prototype and example for all Christian families, the entire Church, a model and spiritual source for every Christian family.[137] The Roman Catholic Church in Africa found itself greatly edified by the unity, love and sharing of life among these three persons in this Holy Family. It also found a lot of examples in the different roles each of the three persons in the Holy Family were each to the other and their responsibilities, and further too what their responsibility was to the wider community.[138]

The life of the Church was to be like that of the Holy Family in terms of the interrelatedness of the believers with one another and with the triune God. The mother Mary carried the Lord in her womb and gave birth to the Son of God, Jesus Christ. She, in a way, presented to the world the Saviour. Joseph gave loving care to both Jesus and Mary and he was a powerful support of the family. The birth of Jesus Christ was good news to the world. The Catholic Church in Africa understood itself as being at the service of the Good News of Jesus Christ in which all members (laity, priests, brothers and sisters) needed to participate. The Catholic Church in Africa saw itself with this Marian role of presenting and showing the face of Jesus to Africa, a continent

---

[137] John Paul II, *The Church in Africa: Post-Synodal Apostolic Exhortation (Ecclesia in Africa)*, no. 81, pp. 63-66.

[138] John Paul II, *The Catechism of the Catholic Church*, nos. 1601-1666.

afflicted by diseases, hunger, poverty, political turmoil, civil and tribal wars. The Church saw itself with the role of presenting the caring and merciful Jesus to the people. It saw itself with the role of being a servant at the service of Justice, peace and reconciliation.[139] The Church needed not only participate in the spiritual and pastoral roles but also work towards the social development of the peoples of Africa.

Community Life of the Early Church

Another biblical image from which the model of Church as the Family of God drew its roots was the community life of the early Church. The Old Testament spoke of the personal and communitarian relationship that existed between God and his people Israel. Among the new people of God, the Christian community, the same communitarian aspect came out. From the Bible the believers in Jesus Christ were known to comprise a special group of people with special relationship to their God but also to one another. There were many images that were used by the Scriptures to describe this community of believers to show there was something that drew them close to one another and that separated them from other communities. This community aspect and element was depicted in a number of ways using different images. The community of believers, the Church, was described as a sheepfold whose gateway is Jesus (Jn 10:1-10). They were compared to a special flock whose shepherd is Jesus Christ (Jn 10:11, 1 Pt 5:4). Those who received the good news and accepted to follow Jesus Christ and were given the kingdom were called the 'little flock,' which emphasized the sharing of life, living together and following the same shepherd (Lk 12:32). These images of flock and sheepfold were prefigured and foreshadowed in the Old Testament in many ways (Isa 40:11, Eze 34:11ff).

The Church which was born after the resurrection of Jesus Christ came out right from the very beginning as a community of living together and sharing faith and life. The early Church, as depicted in Acts 2:42-47, devoted themselves to the teaching of the Apostles, to the

---

[139] Agbonkhianmeghe E. Orobator (ed), *Reconciliation, Justice, and Peace: The Second African Synod*, pp. 1-12.

communal life, to the breaking of the bread and to prayers. All who believed were together and had all things in common. They used to gather together in what were house churches to pray and eat together. The spread of the Church out of Jerusalem, following the persecution of the Church, developed on the same pattern. The apostles and evangelists, wherever they went to preach the good news, founded churches on the same pattern of communities. There were thus founded Petrine, Pauline, Johannine communities among the many. In these communities, while responding to the divine call to holiness, people were at the service of each other through the various ministries that developed.

Since *ekklesia* meant "convocation or assembly," God called and urged all to escape from individualism, and from the tendency to withdraw into themselves and convoked all to be part of his family. This convocation had its origin in creation itself. God created human beings in order that they might live in a relationship of deep friendship with Him, and even when sin had broken this relationship with God, with others and with creation, God did not abandon them. This communitarian nature of the early Church prefigured the African model of Church as Family of God since the element of community was foundational to the family.

Church as a Temple

The image of Church as a temple is in a way connected to this communitarian nature of the Church because connected with this was the understanding that the Church is the household of God in the spirit that gathers in this building. The Church was conceived as a household where the family of God dwells (Eph 2:19-22). In this temple, in this building, Jesus Christ is like the foundation stone that the builders rejected but that later became the cornerstone (Ac 4:11, Mt 21:42, 1 Pt 2:7). It was where God and his people dwelt in communion and solidarity. There were other images that were used to describe this communitarian nature of the Church such as a brotherhood, bride of Christ, the poor of the Lord, and the new creation.[140] The same

---

[140] Geoffrey Preston, *Faces of the Church*, Edinburgh: T & T Clark, 1997, p. 3.

relationship that existed between God and the people of Israel continued between Christians and their God. But furthermore, there was also a familial relationship among the disciples. This is *koinonia*.[141] In the same vein, the Church was to be understood as a community of disciples and every believer was understood to be a brother or a sister in the Lord.[142]

The Socio-anthropological Foundations of the Contemporary African Model of Church

The model of Church as Family of God had foundations not only in the Biblical tradition and in some Church events and consequent documents, particularly those of the Second Vatican Council and the synods of the African Church, but also in the cultural traditions and histories of the people of Africa.[143] There were a lot of values tapped from African culture in general and the concept of family in particular which provided a strong basis for the ecclesiology of Church as God's Family. This, however, was not to say there were no negative elements in this culture and its concepts. But, the proponents of this ecclesiology based it on the values and positive elements that were available in this culture. These values and positive elements in the African traditional culture related to the concept of family strengthened this metaphor of family and it was in these that the contemporary African ecclesiology had its cultural foundations.

---

[141] John Mary Waliggo, "The African Clan as the True Model of the African Church", in J.N.K. Mugambi, and Laurenti Magesa (eds.), *The Church in African Christianity; Innovative Essays in Ecclesiology*, Nairobi: Acton, 1990, pp. 111-116.

[142] Avery Dulles, *Models of Mission*, New York: Doubleday, 1978, pp. 197-204.

[143] When John XXIII (the convener of this ecumenical council) died in June 1963, Paul VI reconvened the council and he described its objectives as: "the self-awareness of the Church, its renewal, the bringing together of the Church with the contemporary world."

The African Understanding of Family

The word "family" has been defined in different ways, but the essence appears to be the same that it is the basic cell of society. It is the basic social unit and the vital cell of society. The family is important for both the persons belonging to it and the society in which they live. The importance and centrality of the family with regard to the person and society is not only repeatedly underlined in the Sacred Scriptures but also in African tradition. The family is the first natural society and it is presented in the creator's plan as the primary place for humanization for the person and society, and the cradle of life and love. It is in the family, the natural community in which human social nature is experienced, that makes a unique and irreplaceable contribution to the good of society.[144] The family could further be defined as a fundamental social group in society typically consisting of two parents and their children. This could be a good starting point towards understanding what the family is but it has the disadvantage of excluding several family structures such as single parents, female headed families, childless couples or all-child families.

In Africa the sense of family goes beyond the parents, children and one's siblings. It is extended and covers others related to the spouses, such as parents, aunts, uncles, cousins and grandparents. It includes the living and the dead. In this wider sense the family is understood as a group of people who share common ancestors. All the descendants of a common ancestor are regarded as a family and in this sense, it is synonymous to ancestry, parentage, pedigree, genealogy, background, family tree, descent, lineage, bloodline, blood extraction, stock and many more. Thus, it could be seen that for African peoples the family has a much wider circle of members than the same word suggested in European or North American cultures. In the African traditional society, the family includes children, parents, grandparents, uncles, aunts, brothers, sisters who may have their own children, and other immediate relatives. In many areas this was what anthropologists

---

[144] John Paul II, *Post-Synodal Apostolic Exhortation: Christifideles Laici*, no. 40: AAS 81 (1989), 469.

called the extended family, by which it was meant two or more brothers (in the patrilineal societies) or sisters (in the matrilineal societies) established families in one physical and mental compound or close to one another.[145] In modern times, even if they might not live in the same close compound geographically, the members are able to know and trace each other, even when others might be living far due to urbanization and employment opportunities. The joint households, through geographical proximity, mental construction and social cohesion, are like one large family.[146]

The family, for African peoples, also includes one's own clan and departed relatives. These departed relatives are called by some religious anthropologists the living-dead. As the name implies, these dead are alive in the memories of the surviving family members and are thought to be still interested in the affairs of the family to which they once belonged in their physical life. Surviving members needed not forget the departed; otherwise misfortunes were feared to strike them or their relatives. There were various religious rituals offered to the ancestors. Some of these offerings were in form of morality whereby good conduct and respect of the rules and taboos were considered as offerings to appease the spirits of the dead. On other occasions there was performance of dances to make the spirits of the ancestors happy. Sometimes the living offered food and drink to the living-dead to appease them or as prayers for special intentions according to the needs of the time. This was because the living-dead were still considered an integral part of the human living family. To this extent the ritual offerings in forms of dance, food and libation offered to them were tokens of fellowship, communion, remembrance, respect and hospitality, being extended to those who were considered the pillars or roots of the family. The living-dead solidified and mystically bound together the whole family. As such they needed always to be appeased. If the living-dead were offended by the bad behaviour of the living-living or their failure to carry out their

---

[145] John S. Mbiti, *African Religions and Philosophy*, Nairobi: Heinemann, pp. 100-106.

[146] John S. Mbiti, *African Religions and Philosophy*, p. 106.

instructions, it was feared they would take revenge and demand a rectification.[147]

The African concept of family also includes the unborn members who are still in the loins of the living. These are considered to be the buds of hope and expectation and each family makes sure that its own existence is not extinguished. The family provides for its continuation and prepares for the coming of those not yet born. For this reason, African parents are anxious to see that their children find husbands and wives, otherwise failure to do so means, in effect, the death of the unborn and the diminishing of the family as a whole.

However, it is important to know that the African traditional family patterns are slowly but progressively being altered as a result of the process of modernization which is exhibited through trends like globalization, urbanization, and secularization.[148] These are challenging the African way of life. Family patterns that were the norm in traditional rural African societies are being altered and substituted by modern values. Sub-Saharan Africa has had the fastest rate of urbanization in the world. The demands and challenges of urban life influence the change of the ways in which they look at the family and some of their values. African families are increasingly faced with the pressure emanating from the prevailing competition between traditional and modern family values. That is why contemporary family patterns are going through adaptations, changes and transformations in the attempt to adapt to the changing times. There has been a steady increase in the pace towards abandonment of traditional practices for modern ones. However, the most popular trend has been the merging of traditional and modern family norms and practices. In other words, there is both traditionalism and modernism in today's family concept in Africa.[149] The African concept of family is very rich

---

[147] John S. Mbiti, *African Religions and Philosophy*, p. 107.
[148] Aylward Shorter and Edwin Onyancha, *Secularism in Africa*, Nairobi: Paulines, 1997, pp. 11-57.
[149] www.su.diva-portal.org/ [2.6.2015].

and indeed the African Church has drawn a lot from the familial concept of life and existence.

The African model of Church as the Family of God drew a lot from the African worldview and way of being. In African existentialism, being is "being in family or community." This concept of family has profound influence on the way of being Church in Africa. The Church, the people of God, is made up of human beings who, on becoming Christians, do not cease to be human, but are expected to be truly Christian and at the same time fully human. Jesus Christ said: "I have come that they might have life and have it to the full" (Jn 10:10). This abundant life that Jesus brings is only possible in interrelatedness to others. Every individual human being needs others to live their full potential. Human beings are created as social beings. This social dimension of the human being was already echoed in the first book and second chapter of the Scriptures when the Lord God said: "It is not good for the man to be alone. I will make him helper suitable for him" (Gen 2:18).

Man and woman have lived in community since time immemorial. The fundamental unit of community and society is the family. There is no society without the family. Sociologically speaking society is like a mental construct and what is concrete is the human family. The dependence of human beings on others in the family is a miniature of their dependence on society and community. They live in the community by nature, but also for their existence and welfare. Living with and interacting with others presupposes some level of relationship between them, thus, it could be said that the human being is by nature a relational being. However, not only are human beings social animals, they are also cultural beings. As a group or community, they have their own particular way of life that distinguishes them from other groups of people. This way of life, their culture, includes all that which makes them who they are: their customs, beliefs, knowledge, moral and laws, art, architecture and much more. It is in this way that Africa has stood out in its sense of family and community. Though the human being is by nature a social being there is still the tendency and propensity towards individualism in the world. In certain societies this individualism has been gaining ascendancy over communitarian living. Within the traditional African context, studies have shown that there is still a strong sense of community in Africa.[150]

At the heart of African cultures and worldview are strong social and family links. There are many proverbs in African culture that describe this deep philosophical thought of the close link between man/woman and their society and how each depends on the other for survival right away from the family.[151] A Setswana proverb says, *Motho kemotho kabatho* (a person is truly human only with others).[152] A similar Chinyanja proverb, teaching the social and family links among Africans, says, *Kali kokha n'kanyama tili tiwiri n'tiwanthu'* (what is by itself is a little animal; those that are two are human beings).'[153] It carries the Aristotelian meaning of 'that who is alone is a beast and those that are two are human,' while at the same time meaning that solidarity promotes social well-being. Traditionally Africans have lived in community with strong sense of belonging i.e. belonging to this or that family, group, tribe or clan. In Africa "the community takes precedence over the individual, although it depends on him or her for its existence, stability and progress."[154] Therefore it is not surprising that there were sayings like, 'we are therefore I am,' 'I am because we are,' or 'I share in the community, therefore I am.'[155] The deep sense of kinship, with all that it implies, has been one of the strongest forces in African traditional life. The individual person owes one's existence to other

---

[150] www.emeka.at/africa_cultural_values/ [16.10.2015].

[151] Ian D. Dicks, *An African Worldview: The Muslim Amacinga Yawo of Southern Malawi*, Zomba: Kachere, 2012, pp. 91-97.

[152] Gabriel Afagbegee SVD, *Building Small Christian Communities: Foundations and Step-by-Step Approach to Building SCCs*, Germiston: Lumko, 2007, 41.

[153] Joseph C. Chakanza, *Wisdom of the People: 2000 Chinyanja Proverbs*, Zomba: Kachere, 2000, p. 99.

[154] Andrew Moemeka, *Communication and Culture: An African Perspective*, Nairobi: African Church Service, 1989, p. 5.

[155] John S. Mbiti, *African Religions and Philosophy*, Nairobi: East African Educational, 1969, pp. 104-105.

people, including those of past generations (ancestors) and one's contemporaries. Persons are simply parts of the whole. The community therefore makes, creates or produces the individual; for the individual depends on the corporate group.[156] For the traditional African, life is lived and realized in community. The traditional African lives with "others" and outside the community the individual is disoriented, somewhat marginalized and easily lost. This strong communitarian life in African Culture laid strong sociological and anthropological foundations for the model of Church in Africa as God's Family.

There was in and among African peoples a great sense of spirituality. They believed in a being and power greater than theirs and to this power and being they owed their creation. John Mbiti stated that in Africa, within traditional life, the individual was immersed in a religious participation which started before birth and continued after his death. The whole of existence was a religious phenomenon; the human being was a deeply religious being living in a religious universe.[157] In light of the above, if Christianity in Africa was to be relevant and a way of life, the challenge that lay on African Christianity was to create a forum (space) and context within itself which would see African spirituality well integrated.

Strong Sense of Kinship

In African traditional life there is a very strong sense of relationship between and among members of the same family and of a common heritage. Family life in African societies goes beyond the nuclear family. There is a strong relationship between persons and their parents, siblings, aunts, uncles, cousins, grandparents both living and those that join the world of the ancestors. African life least aims at living it in such a way that this journey of life is meaningful, happy, safe and satisfactory for both the individual and the community of which one an integral part. This is very different from the Western world where life rotates around self-centeredness, privacy and respect

---

[156] John S. Mbiti, *African Religions and Philosophy*, pp. 104, 108.

[157] John S. Mbiti, *African Religions and Philosophy*, p. 15.

for personal space. A person in the Western world can be described in terms of 'cogito ergo sum' (I think; therefore, I am). In Africa there was a strong connection between the individual and his community and this led to the African adage, "I am because we are, and since we are therefore I am."[158] The Zulu people of Southern Africa would say "*Umuntu Ngamuntu Ngabantu*" which means "a person is a person through other persons." An African affirms one's humanity when the person acknowledges that of others.[159] To give another example, when the *Zulu* people meet and greet one another, they say: "*Siya kubona umfowethu*" (I see you my brother/sister). The person so greeted will respond by saying "*Ngiya kubona umfowethu*" (I see in you my brother/sister). This concept of greeting hold elements of strong kinship, affirming and caring for life in one another.[160]

This strong sense of kinship, in Africa societies, is also expressed in other peoples' greetings. Among the Chewa people greeting someone, how they are, is considered incomplete and impolite if one did not ask how the rest of the members of the family were. The person so greeted would respond by saying not only about oneself but also say how the rest of the family members were feeling. Many times, it would not be a response of simply saying 'fine and you, thanks' (as it is in the Western tradition) but they would even explain details of what the family was going through that made them fine or otherwise. A visitor to Africa is soon struck by the frequent use of the first-person plural 'we' or 'ours' in everyday speech. The sense of community and humane living are highly cherished values of traditional African life. Greeting, among the traditional *Chewa* people, would not take less than thirty seconds as is in the Western world but it would in fact take a good number of minutes. Thus, among the *Chewa*, in greeting, you are not greeting only the individual person but also their family and community because of this close sense of kinship. That is why, when

---

[158] John S. Mbiti, *Introduction to African Religion*, 1975, p. 87.

[159] www.africafiles.org/articles.asp?ID=20359/ [3.10.2015].

[160] Int Michael Ndau, a Malawian priest belonging to the Pallotine Congregation doing missionary work among the Zulu people of South Africa, Pietermaritzburg, Zululand (Kwa-Zulu Natal Province), 20.10.2015.

they meet and greet one another, they would say: "*Muli bwanji*" (it is 'how are you' in the second person plural). Sometimes this would be considered as a plural of politeness but at other times it is not necessarily that. It is a greeting to the community through this person so much so that if the person in response only said about oneself, the individual is considered rude and selfish. When greeted thus, there was expectation that the person being greeted would say something more of the family and community they were coming from. The greeting is almost always in plural, despite the person being one or even if it is a small child. Greeting someone in the second person singular is done not necessarily to show that the person is one, but to show familiarity and acquaintance. Thus, it is viewed that in the individual, people see their family and community.

Life is seen as participation in the celebration of this gift from the great ancestor, God. Communal celebration and joy accompanied them all as an individual passed through the stages of life: birth, initiation, marriage, and death. They are not considered as individual celebrations or rites of passage. They are communal celebrations and involve participation of everyone in the traceable kinship line. A person understood that there was a special bond between them and their community.

In some societies, this bond to the community is made by the shedding of blood. This could be done during birth by the disposal of the umbilical cord of the baby in the land of its ancestors. In some societies this blood is shed through circumcision and other initiation ceremonies. The initiation binds them to the land and to their community both living and dead. Through the initiation ceremony the individual is sealed, as it were, to one's people and the people to the individual. An individual is bound to one's people and the people to the individual. It is a solemn mark of unity and identification. Through the initiation ceremonies it was understood that the spirits of the ancestors were present so much so that the person was not only bound to the present generation but also to the past and future generations.[161]

---

[161] John S. Mbiti, *Introduction to African Traditional Religion*, pp. 96-101.

In African societies and in African life, marriage is at the center of the rhythm of life. Marriage is a sacred duty in which every normal person needs to participate. It is at the very foundation of human life as Africans believe God commanded people to get married and procreate. Bearing of children is an obligation and a sacred duty. It is a uniting link in the rhythm of life. All generations (past, present and future) are bound together in the act of marriage. The past generations may be many but they are all represented in one's parents. The present generations are represented in one's own life, and the future generations are represented in the children to be born in the family. It is through marriage that families are built, and they form the basic cells of society. In African societies, marriage has further meanings of creating relationships between families, bringing people together, and ensuring remembrance of parents after death,[162] regaining a lost immortality,[163] giving a person status in society and giving completeness. Through marriage one's kinship frontiers are said to be expanded.[164]

Emphasis on the Care for Others

In African traditional life there is the belief that the safety, joy and well-being of each member rests on all and each member. For example, when a woman is pregnant, all have to be careful. They have to observe certain regulations and taboos so that the life of the

---

[162] In African societies it is believed that through marriage and childbearing, the parents are remembered by their children when they die. Anyone who dies without leaving a child or a close relative is a very unfortunate person for tose who will remember him. Marriage is intimately linked with the religious beliefs of continuation of life beyond death.

[163] Through marriage, the departed are reborn not in their total being but by having some of their physical features, characteristics and personality traits reborn in the children of the family. If no children were born these traits and features of the departed members of the family would not be seen again.

[164] In African societies marriage makes a person truly a man or woman. Through marriage a person becomes somebody. Without it one is only a human being minus.

mother, the expected child, of family, and community is cared for, protected and safeguarded. Everyone in the community has roles, duties and responsibilities to take care of others. Everyone is expected to be careful for the safety and protection of all. That is why there were regulations and taboos which describe the unwritten moral code of African communities as they accompanied everyone when they were going through the stages of life. The Chewa call this unwritten moral code, *mwambo*. When people kept *mwambo* then they were safe.

In some African societies there were different ways of observing regulations and taboos assuring the safety of all (departed, born, and unborn). A pregnant woman stopped sleeping with her husband altogether until several months after delivery, even until after weaning the child, so that it could go well with her and the baby. In some areas such a woman is not allowed to do certain types of work like cutting firewood, using knives, drawing water and so on. Some people groups perform rituals and make offerings to thank God for the expected child and to pray for the safety of the child and the mother.[165]

In African traditional life there is communication taking place between and among all when people are going through the various stages of life so that appropriate steps are taken which would ensure the safety of each and all in the community. For instance, the *Chewa* people hold that the un-careful conduct of some in the community is thought to bring some catastrophe on others or even the entire community in form of some misfortunes.[166] A woman menstruating or going through her monthly cycle is not supposed to put salt in the relish as this could bring some unknown sickness on the man and the family members, but that when she was in such a condition she is to use a child or anyone in a cool state to do it for her. The chief and the parents of a

---

[165] John Mbiti, *Introduction to African Religion*, pp. 87-90.

[166] The Chewa Nyanja people are Bantu people found mostly in Malawi, Zambia and parts of Mozambique. They are traditionally matrilineal societies who are believed to have originally come from the Katanga region in Zaire (modern Democratic Republic of Congo).

girl who has experienced her the first monthly period were not to engage in conjugal acts so as not to cause unknown sickness or catastrophe on the girl and the entire village community. When a woman is expectant, the husband is not to misbehave so as to avoid bringing misfortune to the woman and the child to be born.[167]

The care for others is also shown in hospitality. Africans have a strong sense of hospitality and this value is one of those that are still alive today. Africans are welcoming to strangers and only in very rare occasions do they show hostility and violence to strangers. Otherwise they welcome them and even let the strangers settle in their land. In an African community everyone is accommodated and there is warmth in human relationships. Good human relationship based on interpersonal communication is always emphasized. Steve Biko observed:

> Ours has always been a human-centered society. Westerners have in so many occasions been surprised at the capacity we have at talking to each other not for the sake of arriving at a particular conclusion but merely to enjoy the communication for its own sake. Intimacy is a term not exclusive for particular friends but applying to a whole group of people who find themselves together whether through work or residential requirements.[168]

Hence in an African traditional community, everyone is accommodated. This entails a great sense of hospitality. The African peoples have many symbolic ways of showing this hospitality. In some West African communities there would be presentations of kola nuts, traditional gin, and coconut and so on. Festus Okafor summarized the African attitude to strangers in this way:

> In traditional African culture, whenever there is food to be taken, everyone present is invited to participate even if the food was prepared for far less number of people without anticipating the arrival of visitors. It would be a highest of incredible bad manners

---

[167] John W. Gwengwe, *Kukula ndi Mwambo*, Blantyre: Dzuka, 1965, p. 115.

[168] Steve Biko, *I Write what I like*, Chicago: UCP, 1978, p. 41.

for one to eat anything however small without sharing it with anyone else present, at least expressing the intention to do so.[169]

For the traditional Chewa people of Malawi, when a visitor came to a household, it was not uncommon to see the hosts not greeting them until after they have given the visitors something to drink or to bite; like water, sweet beer, alcoholic beer, and even the traditional staple food, *nsima*. A chicken would be killed, in some communities, so to show that they are welcome. A son or daughter of the village who had been out for a longer time, upon return to the village for a visit or holidays is greeted and welcomed with plates of *nsima* from almost every family in the village. Even if the food is more than the stomach can take, one is expected at least to eat a portion from every household's *nsima*. The rest is then shared by all in the house.

The Chewa people of Malawi have a proverb that conveys the same meaning of sharing and hospitality: "*Chakudya sichichepa, chichepa ndi chovala*" (food is never little, only a garment can be little). This means people can always share the little food that is there. This proverb emphasizes sharing, hospitality, kindness, and generosity. And in many African societies one does not need to make an appointment for a visit or give notice if one would be available at meal time at somebody's place. A similar proverb says: "*chakudya chawekha sichikoma, koma cholimbilana*" (food taken on your own is not nice but struggling for it with others).[170] This tells the African spirit that in most things companionship is indispensable.

Emphasis on Solidarity

African traditional life is marked by a high sense of solidarity among the family and community members. Solidarity highlights in a particular way the intrinsic social nature of the human person, the equality of all in dignity and rights and the common path of individuals and peoples towards an ever more committed unity. It entails in African societies a widespread awareness of the bond of interdependence

---

[169] Festus Okafor, *Africa at Crossroads*, New York: 1974, p. 21.

[170] Joseph Chakanza, *Wisdom of the People*, pp. 36-37.

between individuals and peoples in their families, communities and societies. There are strong relationships between individuals, peoples and their families and communities.

In African life, solidarity is not only a social principle but also a moral virtue which puts an obligation on an individual to be depended upon in society and in turn to depend on other individuals in that society. Solidarity in African life is understood not just as a feeling of vague compassion at the distress and misfortune of others in the community, but as a firm and persevering determination to commit oneself to the common good. This is to say in solidarity African people commit themselves to the good of all and of each individual, because there is a strong feeling of all being responsible for all.

In effect, solidarity demands that the problems of one became the problems of all. Death, sickness, poverty, misfortune and different forms of catastrophes experienced by the individuals are shouldered by all. It becomes imperative for the community to assist those who are experiencing different kinds of sufferings and problems. There is, hence, some connection between solidarity with the value of care for others in the African traditional family. The care for others rose out of the African feeling and moral duty of interdependence.

Sense of Community Life

In Africa there is a strong sense of community. It is in the community that the African finds safety, security and identity. The individual is expected to actively participate in all aspects of the life of the community. This involves their participation in rites of passage, memorials, communal tribunals, games and sports. In African societies the events of the community are well known to all and it is expected that all participate in them and carry out their different roles.[171] Sometimes it may be thought that the sense of community has disappeared in the cities and towns of Africa due to the factors of urbanization, globalization and modernization. But not all is lost. In

---

[171] Aylward Shorter, *African Christian Theology*, London: Geoffrey Chapman, 1975, pp. 122-123.

modern African cities, primary community loyalties of one's extended family and village, continue to exert their hold over people who live away from the communities of their home villages. People generally return to their villages from their town residences from time to time to join members of their village community to celebrate important rituals and cultural events like initiations, marriages, funerals, death memorials, tombstone unveilings, chieftaincy installations and others.

The community provides a sense of identification to the individual and in actual fact the individual identity is not emphasized at the expense of the community identity. That is why, in Africa, individualism is not encouraged, even if it is not completely absent. In this sense, Steve Biko wrote that:

> We regard our living together not as an unfortunate mishap warranting endless competition among us but as a deliberate act of God to make us a community of brothers and sisters jointly involved in the quest for a composite answer to the varied problems of life. Hence in all we do we place human beings first and hence all our action is usually joint community-oriented action rather than the individualism.[172]

So, living together and the sense of community of brothers and sisters are the basis and expression of the extended family system in Africa. The rationale behind it is the balance of kinship relations, seen as essential to the ideal balance with nature that is itself the material guarantee of survival. Individuals might have rights, but they have them only by virtue of the obligations they are to fulfill in the community. An African adage states: "The prosperity of a single person does not make a town rich. But the prosperity of the town makes persons rich."[173] Put in other words, this means basically that a person can only truly be safe in a safe community. Personal poverty is a foreign concept. Communal poverty can only be brought about by an adverse climate during a particular season. It is never considered repugnant to ask one's neighbours for help if one is struggling. In

---

[172] Steve Biko, *I write what I like*, p. 42.

[173] www.emeka.at/africa_cultural_values/ [4.10.2015].

almost all circumstances there is help between individuals, families, societies and communities. The traditional African community has the attitude to work together which makes it almost impossible to have the poor and beggars.

Sense of the Sacred and of Religion

The traditional Africans as they live their life in families, communities and societies are filled with a great sense of the sacred and all aspects of life are filled with elements of religion. The life of the traditional African is essentially religious. They believe in a being and a power greater than their own from where they own their existence. This feeling is common for all human beings, but in the case of the African this religious sense and sentiment is very strong. The opening words of John Mbiti's classical work, *African Religions and Philosophy*, states that Africans were notoriously religious.[174] A feature that made the Africans' religiosity distinctive was that they put no division between their daily life and religion. The two are literally intertwined and inseparable. That is why, for instance, in African religion there are no special days of worship. All days are days of worship. In traditional African societies there were no atheists. This is because religion, in the indigenous African culture, is not an independent institution. It is an integral and inseparable part of the entire culture. The whole life is understood and lived as religious. This religious participation begins before birth and goes on after their death. The whole of their existence is a religious phenomenon. A human being is conceived as deeply living in a religious universe. Concrete actions and morality are all under the watchful eye of the sacred being, spirits of the ancestors, and the living community. Hence there is always the consciousness of the other.

Religion in the African sense is practical. One's entire action is reflective of one's religious concepts and practices as is seen in the

---

[174] John S. Mbiti, *African Religions and Philosophy*, p. 1. See also Gabriel Afagbegee SVD, *Building Small Christian Communities: Foundations and Step-by-Step Approach to Building SCCs*, Germiston: Lumko Publications, 2007, p. 44.

ordering of society. This is because social morality is dependent on religion. For example, with the Yoruba, morality is certainly the fruit of religion. They did not make any attempt to separate the two; and it is impossible for them to do so without disastrous consequences.[175] This is paradigmatic in all African cultures of sub-Saharan Africa.

Sense of Respect for Authority and the Elders

In African tradition, political, religious and social leaders such as elders, kings, queens, priests, priestesses, medicine-men, rain-makers, mediums, prophets, diviners, authorities and elders hold a special place in the life and concepts of the people. Not among all African peoples are these rulers found. But where they are found, people accord great respect to them and they have a lot of authority. They are not simply religious, social or political heads. They are mystical and divine symbols of the peoples' health and welfare. The individuals holding these different offices or being elderly may not as such have had outstanding talents and abilities, but the office and position is the link between human rule and spiritual government. They are therefore the shadow of reflection of God's rule in the universe. People fear and respect those in socio-political and religious authority as well as the elders because they are considered viceroys of God on earth. People take them as the link with the spiritual and ancestral world. The society expects people to speak well of those in authority, bow or kneel before them, obey them, refrain from having direct contact with them and even render them acts of reverence and obeisance.

African people accord the elders great respect. This is because they think of the elders as joining sooner or later through death the rank of the ancestors. To disrespect the elders is thought to provoke and incur the wrath of the ancestors who see in the elders of the community the closest of kin. Various misfortunes are thought and feared to come upon all children who do not respect the elders. In turn the respect of the elders is thought to bring blessings on the younger generation.[176]

---

[175] Bolaji Idowu, *God in Yoruba Beliefs*, London: Oxford University Press, 1962, p. 146.

[176] John S. Mbiti, *African Religions and Philosophy*, pp. 166-183.

The deceased elders are accorded even more respect. In fact, people fear them. To disregard the wishes of the ancestors and spirits of the dead is thought to be catastrophic on the living. The elders are thought to take interest in the affairs of the living: time and again, and through dreams and visions, they are thought to visit the living. When they visit they can give their assessment of the state of affairs of the family, the community and the society. If they are not impressed with the conduct of the living they demand change of moral behaviour, rectification, and sacrificial appeasement.

Accompanying these values are social and religious virtues of love, care for one another, warmth in human relationships, acceptance, trust, dialogue and respect. These are not exhaustive of the richness of the image and metaphor of family from the African context. They are representative enough, though, of how rich this concept of family is. It is on such values and positive elements in the African institution of family that the African ecclesiology of Church as God's family laid its strong foundation and emphasis. This does not mean that from the African context there are no weaknesses and negative elements related to this cultural institution of family as lived and experienced in Africa. It is very clear today that to actualize these values is becoming a challenge in today's Africa. This is evidenced by the social, economic and political upheavals in this continent. Many African prelates during the first Post-Vatican II Synod of bishops, through their interventions, highlighted present-day threats to the African Family.[177] However, the values of the African concept of 'family' present the richness and strength of this metaphor. When such a metaphor is used in reference to the Church one can imagine how this avails strength of meaning to the Church in Africa in whose spirit the Church in the Archdiocese of Lilongwe emerged.

Conclusion

The concept of Church as the Family of God is solidly grounded in the Scriptures, Christian theology, and in African sociology and anthropol-

---

[177] John Paul II, *Ecclesia in Africa*, no. 84.

ogy. The image of Israel as the people of God, the *ekklesia* as the assembly of the people of God, and the communitarian nature of the Church derived from the plural nature of the triune God were all remote preparations for the understanding of the Church as the Family of God. The African values of community, family, kinship, participation, solidarity, respect for authority and the elders, and sense of the sacred all laid solid ground for the growth of the concept of Church as God's Family. However, there were challenging issues with the concept of family from the African perspectives.

Chapter 4: Challenging Issues with the African Concept of Family

Despite the strengths and values that were associated with the African concept of family, socio-anthropological studies and analyses indicated that this basic unit of society (nuclear family or extended) was undergoing drastic changes due to factors emerging from globalization, modernization, and secularization.[178] How could the Church justify the self-definition using such a metaphor whose reality was going through such changes? The composition and structure of families in the African as well as the Malawian society was changing. The extended family bonds, for example, were much less pronounced than before even in the rural areas. With the economic strains the Africa continent was going through with the development of the market economy, each nuclear family was getting more and more concerned with its own problems and challenges than with the challenges of the whole community. The extended family bonds were much less pronounced in the urban populations and especially among the professional classes. Many of the urban inhabitants were increasingly having little connection with their village backgrounds though they regularly returned to their rural villages for funerals and renewal of family ties. It was in such occasions that they were re-united with their extended family.

The traditional social values were more evident among rural than urban populations but there too, change was taking place due to ever-changing socio-economic circumstances surrounding Africa. Whereas in the past almost all families would be under the headship of a man, a father, there were many households that women headed and principally ran. Numbers of divorce and separation were on the increase making many households to be female headed.[179] The women-men ratio difference was so big that there were ever growing

---

[178] Aylward Shorter and Edwin Onyancha, *Secularism in Africa: A Case Study of Nairobi City*, pp. 11-57, 116-130.

[179] www.everyculture.com/ [21.10.2015].

numbers of women not married. Others remained unmarried by choice and for various reasons but they would certainly be living with some children of their own and/or of relatives. Gender based violence in families too was on the increase and much of it was perpetrated by men leading to the suffering of women. It thus became a big challenge for the Church to use the metaphor of an African family that was going through drastic changes in defining a reality that had a dual constant with evolving identity.

What made it permissible and possible to make use of such a term and metaphor that was going through changes was the fact that not everything good and positive of this socio-cultural institution was washed away by the effects of modernization and globalization. There were still good and positive elements which remained and were relevant. With such values the term family could still be applied to the Church in a metaphorical sense by ideally rising above these negatives. It was nevertheless difficult for people whose illiteracy levels were very high to think of the sense of family outside its sociological confines. It was still pertinent to take into consideration the fact that there were weaknesses with this concept of family that was lived, understood and exhibited, whether directly or indirectly, by the peoples of Africa. The weaknesses of this concept had historically been a source of trouble among different communities, societies and cultures in Africa. When applied to the Church, they had negative repercussions. These weaknesses provided a fundamental flaw in thought and vision about the Church which eventually impaired the real picture of God, creation, and human relations to other human beings and nature.

Patriarchy

Patriarchy is one of cultural traits that are still deep in the African society in actualization of the concept of family. It is a gender power system and a network of social, political, religious and economic relationships through which men dominate women. Through this system the males control female labour, reproduction, economics, household leadership, national leadership, sexuality, as well as define the women's status, privileges and rights in the society. In this social system males held primary power, predominated in roles of leadership, authority, social privilege and control of property. In the African domain of the family, fathers or father-figures hold authority over women and children. Patriarchy manifests itself in the social, political, legal, economic and religious organization of a wide range of not only the African societies but also of many other different cultures. As a social system it is closely comparable to the social models of male privilege, androcracy and kyriarchy.[180]

It is a successful system because those who are privileged with this, the males, are often not aware of it. The males in many African cultures think that this is normal and the way things were ordained to be. They are inadvertent towards the ill-treatment of women. This system has stayed for so long in the African society and has covered a wide area. This enormity and longevity in coverage has become a psychological and mental weapon for its survival in many communities. It is difficult for many ordinary people in African societies to imagine a time when the patriarchal system did not exist or when men were not in charge of their households, families and nations. It is also difficult for many people in African society to imagine a future in their families, communities and nations minus patriarchy which is so entrenched in most African settings that trying to separate it from the African way of being is deemed unfathomable for most. Some people,

---

[180] Androcracy is a form of government in which government rulers are males. Even if African countries attained independence and democratic rule, a critical study indicates many of the African governments are run by males, occasionally with the help of few females. This is thought to begin from the cultural assumption of leadership. Kyriarchy is a term coined by Elizabeth Schüssler Fiorenza in her 1992 publication in which she uses this term to describe her theory of interconnected, interacting, and self-extending systems of domination and submission, in which an individual person might be oppressed in some relationships and privileged in others. It is an intersectional extension of the idea of patriarchy beyond gender and it encompasses sexism, racism, homophobia, classism, economic injustice, colonialism, and ethnocentrism in which subordination of a person is internalized and institutionalized.

like those of the Black Consciousness Movement, thought it was a parasite that the African culture needed to rid itself of if African culture was to survive. It appeared it was proving difficult to completely separate and eradicate from African culture those social systems that oppressed women. African culture has strong patriarchal undertones and many of its people think it is closely connected with what it means to be truly African, which is not the case. African culture has the daunting task of separating the culture from this oppressive patriarchal trait.

The mentality is so deep in African communities so much so that even if there is a lot of political propaganda towards the creation of an equal society between males and females in Africa, it is often utter rhetoric. In the main women are still expected to be submissive in most communities. They are not only expected to be submissive to the males but they are in fact exposed to oppressions and dominations whose occurrences are multifaceted. There still exist stigma against women in society in various roles such as leadership, privilege and property. Many people in Africa still think women need not take active part in leadership and governance and as a result there is still limited participation of women in such roles in society. The reasons for this attitude in the societies are varied but the predominant ones are that it is thought that women are generally the weaker sex and that the women's biological make up so demands. In many African societies they believe that women's biological clock and metabolism implies that their primarily duty is of bearing and raising children, producing the family's food and taking care of the household tasks. In many African societies it is still thought that women are very sensitive and emotional so much that these are considered weak qualities for them to be able to perform to the best of their capability in the stressful circumstances that leadership entails. Thus, women are not given enough space to be able to involve themselves in the society's life and matrix. Even though they form the largest group, demographically, in the world in general and in Africa in particular, their involvement in societal and global affairs is quite limited as compared to the participation of their male counterparts. Patriarchy which appears in many life settings limits them. [181]

The concept of gender equality is still perceived by some people in Africa as merely foreign to Africa and as a Western cultural trait. There are family related traditional practices which perpetuate the objectification, submission and oppression of women and these include the gender division of labour, gender related decision-making processes, bride price and wife inheritance which still continue to take place in many communities in Africa. Education, work and employment opportunities and property rights are often in favour of boys and men as to the disadvantage of girls and women. Some initiatives are being undertaken by some states to improve the well-being and status of women in Africa by promoting girls' education and women rights. But to change the patriarchal attitude has never been easy.

This is not to say there have not been strides made in Africa dealing with the improvement in the status and participation of women in the affairs of the society. A number of women have been and are taking part in leadership roles in Africa in government, civil society, and the private sector. Of late there have been some women in Africa who, against the odds of patriarchy, have shown extraordinary strength, resilience, courage, vision and dedication. In country top leadership roles examples are often given of Hellen Sirleaf Johnson who became president of Liberia (2006), Joyce Banda who became president of Malawi (2012) and Dlamini Zuma who was elected first woman chairperson of the 54-nation African Union Commission (2012).[182] These three female leaders are a success story but nothing really for Africa to rejoice about being fair and just considering that Africa then was a continent with 54 nations. Another women participation in politics example is given of Rwanda where women representation in the elected parliament was 56% of the entire elected lower house. Rwanda gained the distinction of having the largest female majority of

---

[181] www.mtholyoke.edu/abdul20j/classweb/politics_116/AWIP. html/ [20.11.2015].

[182] www.state.gov/s/gwi/rls/rem/2012/201503.html/ [20.11.2015].

elected members of parliament in the world. Other African women have been active at the grassroots, national, regional, continental and global levels in peace building, negotiations and conflict resolutions. However, suffice to say that their involvement and participation is limited compared to that of their male counterparts. This is due to the patriarchal undertones that African culture, from the family, community to the entire society, still has. This cultural trait has had consequences on the religious life of the people since religion in some sense is a product of culture.

Ethnocentrism

One of the negative elements and dangers of the African cultural concept of family, when protracted, has been and was ethnocentrism. The excessive sense of 'my family' breeds ethnocentrism, tribalism and nepotism. Every ethnic people, tribe, clan and even communities have their particular culture. Ethnocentrism is judging another culture solely by the values and standards of one's own culture. As such ethnocentric individuals and communities tend to judge other groups relative to their own ethnic group or culture, especially with concern to language, area of origin, behaviour, appearance, customs, and religion.[183]

Ethnocentrism emerged from being too passionate and too obsessed with one's own family's, community's and society's values and cultural articulations. The individuals and communities tend to think the others are lesser than them and they endeavor to force the others to follow their cultural traditions which are thought to be the best and the ideal. Ethnocentrism is bad when people make false assumptions about cultural differences. It is bad when they use their cultural norms to make generalizations about other peoples' cultures and customs. Such generalizations—often made without a conscious awareness that they have used their culture as a universal yardstick—can be ways off base and cause them to misjudge other peoples. Ethnocentrism leads to cultural misinterpretation and it often distorts communication between human beings. It leads to fighting with the aim of getting rid of the other ethnic grouping. When the sense of family is too much in

---

[183] www.wikipedia/wiki/ethnocentrism/ [21.7.2015].

the Church it can create some kind of ethnic churches in which one's blood would be the first to be considered and the baptismal waters later. It is said that blood is thicker than water.

This, in the history of the African continent, has had disastrous consequences. Ethnocentrism has been one of the greatest obstacles to peace on the African continent. Taking the Church as Family of God as a model of evangelization in the 21st century and using this inculturated ecclesiology, accorded the African Christians an occasion to use Christianity in critiquing their cultures and use Christianity as a transformation agent.[184] However, seriously looking at the other side of the coin shows how it was possible in the Church to have this extreme understanding of family and how it could create ethnocentric connotations in the Church. Despite its ideals of solidarity, hospitality and compassion, religion is said to have been one of the origins of ethnocentrism in many parts of the world. Religion is an important factor among the many that affect this complex relationship. Images of God, Jesus, Spirit, Salvation, and Church, have contributed to ethnocentrism.[185] In Africa two such historical structural sins of ethnocentric nature can give a clear glimpse of how religion can breed ethnocentrism and these were apartheid in South African and the Rwandan Genocide. This tendency becomes a major reason for divisions and fights among members of different ethnicities.[186] Though in the Archdiocese of Lilongwe, it has not reached those levels of physical fighting between Christians of different tribal origins; nevertheless, it has not been so peaceful. There were claims at times that ecclesiastical nepotism existed in the leadership of the Church and the selective provision of privileges to clergy and religious. From this it can be deduced that the sense of family in the church, by extension, can

---

[184] Gerald K. Tanye, *The Church-as-Family and Ethnocentrism in Sub-Saharan Africa: Tubingen Prospects on Pastoral Theology and Religious Pedagogics*, Berlin: LIT Verlag, 2010, pp. 1-42.

[185] Dave D. Capucao, *Religion and Ethnocentrism: An Empirical-theological study*, Leiden: Brill Publications, 2010, pp. 179-219. Also see www.brill.com/religion-and-ethnocentrism/ [20.7.2015].

[186] www.unitedhumanrights.org/genocide/rwanda/ [3.6.2016].

breed tribalistic and nepotistic favouritism. This sense of family can emerge exaltation of one's own ethnicity and hatred and segregation of those other people from another district, region, tribe and clan.

Excessive Particularism

The strong sense of family has the potential to breed excessive particularism. It is true that each culture is particular in that there are elements which differentiate it from the others. It is also true that there are elements common to all cultures be it in Africa or the whole world. Some cultural elements transcend race and tribe and they are simply human cultural elements e.g. love, mercy, goodness, kindness etc. There is a close similarity between ethnocentrism and particularism. However, the latter puts emphasis on 'my family, community, tribe and clan' as being very particular and that those who belong to this family only are to have privileges over the others. Each tribe and clan is particular but excessive particularism comes with the sense of 'my group is the first and number one.' All the other groupings of people come second. When this comes to the Church, it can also breed an attitude of contempt towards people who belong to other denominations and faiths, since one group has a feeling of being particular and close to God in the sense of a family to the Father. This breeds contemptuous feelings for other churches. This has been evident in the Archdiocese of Lilongwe as some of the local Christians, who may have had difficulties to conceptualize the sense of mystical family, thought that this family of God was the Catholic Church which they considered to be the first Church. Thus, the concept of Church as a family can be misleading.

Diminished Idea of the Individual

Africans have a strong sense of community. The communal life common to the Africans is different from communism and it is what some of the early African leaders, after decolonization, ideologically defined as communalism and which they sought to promote in Africa. Practically all African leaders who came after decolonization said for the human being, human life is the all-important and central reality.[187] Though conceived and coined differently, the essential element common to all of them is the promotion of an existential philosophy called *Ubuntu Philosophy* expressed in communal consciousness and life. *Ubuntu* is a Bantu-Nguni term roughly translating to human kindness or the quality of being human. This means being human in the sense of being sensitive to the feelings, needs, and requests of others. The expectations, feelings and needs of the community come first and through their fulfillment are personal feelings, needs and expectations fulfilled. This African way of existentialism is one of the several African approaches to a comprehensive understanding of the process of cultivating cohesion and positive human interaction with one another and with creation in daily life.[188] It is the direct opposite of what in Western philosophy is called individualism.

Another criticism of this African sense of family and communalism coupled with the pursuance of *Ubuntu philosophy* is that it leads to a diminished idea of individual identity and freedom. In African traditional life the sense of community and humane living can be too highly cherished to accord the individual's true sense of the self. The individual person becomes too conscious of one's community responsibility to respond to the inner call to selfhood. The individual is understood to exist to communicate and enhance the value of harmonious community living. The person has the consciousness of the existence of other beings and factors whose wills he needs to satisfy first. Examples of such beings and factors would be the community elders, the ancestors, the living-dead, taboos, norms and prohibitions. The distinct ethical un-written code with which enshrined norms of acceptable behaviour, taboos and prohibitions are policing factors in the life of the individual as the people are not totally free to do what they would wish to do on their own. They are dictated by the expectations of the family and community. Thus, one's sense of the

---

[187] Joseph G. Donders, *Non-Bourgeois Theology: An African Experience of Jesus*, p. 4.

[188] www.msue.anr.msu.edu/news/ubuntu_a_south_african_philo sophy/ [20.9.2015.

self, personal fulfillment and satisfaction, and independence is impaired.[189] However, the proponents of the worth of community life in Africa would sometimes dispute this and say that in addressing the needs of the community the person's personal and individual needs are addressed.

Thus, the strong sense of community, while being good, has been criticized as having the potential of diminishing the identity of the individual. This African concept of community life can indeed sometimes crowd and overshadow the individual and one's personal space. The individual 'person' can become melted in the communal 'person.' The sense of family could become a weapon of repression of the individual. The personal expression and fulfillment of one's expectations, feelings, needs and requests are overshadowed by the community and family. The individual can be forgotten in the course of considering the community. This strong sense of family and community can also become a scapegoat for personal abandoning moral responsibility. People can at times refuse to take moral responsibility for what their actions brought about and say it was what the community or family expected them to do. Hence, one can imagine how such ways of thought can be erroneous when applied to the Church

Conclusion

The concept of Church as God's Family is not new but has been arrived at with influence from some biblical images as well as from values found in African sociology and anthropology. There is also a multitude of values that contributed to the current African ecclesiology of Church as God's Family and these include; the African understanding of family, strong sense of kinship, emphasis on the care for others, emphasis on solidarity, sense of community life, sense of the sacred and religion, and the sense of respect for authority and the elders.

A genuine analysis of the African concept of family gives rise to a solid critique of the challenges that come along the conceptualization of the

---

[189] www.afrikaworld.net/afrel/community.htm/ [21.9.2015].

family in African culture. Some of the challenging issues with the African concept of family are: patriarchy, ethnocentrism, excessive particularism and the diminished idea of the individual. Such challenges leave some questions regarding the justification of the application of such an imperfect concept of 'family' upon a perfect reality like the Church, and the justification of such an imperfect term which was sociologically and anthropologically exclusive on a reality such as the Church which was commissioned to be an instrument of a salvation encompassing all of creation.

Chapter 5: Applications of the Model of Church as Family of God in the Archdiocese of Lilongwe

The application of the model of Church as God's Family in the Archdiocese of Lilongwe led to carving of a character of the Church which was not there before in this local Church. The Church was a developing reality that was changing goal posts depending on the circumstances. The language too that was used in defining the Church was finite and did not encompass the total reality of the Church. There are limitations which come along the conceptualization of the Church as family, as such, there was need discover its complementarity with other Biblical images to come close to the real meaning of the Church in terms of its nature and mission.

There were new demands and challenges in Africa, one of these has been natural environmental degradation or the environmental crisis. In the present crises of the destruction and degradation of nature and the environment the Church needed to think on the new avenues it could model itself in response also being mindful of the mission of deeper evangelization in the third Millennium of Christianity in Africa. This is because the experience of the people of Africa had to become one of the fundamental sources of their theology, ecclesiology and pastoral practice.

The understanding of the Church in the Archdiocese of Lilongwe led to the development of definite ecclesial behaviours, attitudes and structural organizations through which the concept of Church as God's Family was being exhibited. Like in an unending cycle these in turn became factors which influenced the self-understanding of the Church as God's family. The model of the church as the Family of God was developed and consequently applied in very different ways.

The Sense of Local Church

When the Church was planted by the missionaries, the picture that most of the Christians had was that it was a foreign church. Most of the people thought it was the Church of Rome whose leader was the pope. The model that was emphasized by the missionaries was that of a hierarchical institution. The people who accepted Catholicism were like subjects in this Church of Rome.[190] But the historical event of decolonization and the ecclesial event of Vatican II in the second half of the 20th Century marked the shift of self-conceptualization of the Church in Africa too.

The publication of one of the Council's documents on the missionary nature of the Church, *Ad Gentes,* contributed to this change of understanding and attitude. The council's ecclesiology of communion and the theology of the local church which were more and more explained in later post-conciliar documents, most importantly *Evangelii Nuntiandi* and *Redemptoris Missio,* brought about change in the way of understanding and being Church. Such publications brought about change in the Catholic Church's attitude toward mission.[191] The concept of the Universality of the Church had been over emphasized and was being balanced with the concept of the local church. With the theology of the local church, the Church that was previously understood as foreign was brought close to the people and it was understood as composed of them. The ecclesiology of communion and of the local church brought about the mentality of living together as Church in a family spirit. They brought the feeling among the Christians that they are the Church as such have to participate in its life, organization and ministry. To be able to live this Africanized and localized Church life they had to be close to one another in a spirit of family and community in which they were called to understand the Gospel in their particular cultural context.

---

[190] Personal interviews which I had with some older generations of the Catholics in the rural parishes of the Archdiocese of Lilongwe were quite revealing of this understanding of the Church in the early days before the initiation of SCCs. Asked to what Church they belonged, they answered, *Mpingo wa Roma* (we belong to the Church of Rome). Some of the older generation still did not understand that they were the Church, a concept shared by the younger generation born in the times of the concept and model of Church as the Family of God.

[191] ttp://www.catholicworldreport.com/ievangelii_nuntiandi/the_greatest_pastoral_document_that_has_ever_been_written.aspx/ [11.11.2015].

In the Archdiocese of Lilongwe, there was a progressive development in the understanding of the Church in ways that were different from the original understanding and response of the people to the missionary effort of planting the Church. This understanding of themselves being church in their locality and the deepening in the sense of local church functioned as a cohesive factor of the Christians to come very close to one another and develop a sense of family. From the 1970s the Christians in the Archdiocese of Lilongwe, as is in many parts of Africa, began to understand themselves as the actualization of the Church in their own culture marked by a shift from missionary dependence to African selfhood.[192]

Evangelii Nuntiandi was one of the most important documents which promoted the localization of the Church in the Archdiocese of Lilongwe and led to the living of ecclesial life in a familial spirit. It emphasized the dignity of the local church. The document dealt with the theme of evangelization but also, with reference to the local church, discussed the agents of evangelization. In the document the local churches are seen as the actualizations of the Church of Christ, in the *hic et nunc* (here and now) situations. Evangelization, as the preaching of the Gospel, is always an ecclesial action. This ecclesial action (evangelization) by the universal Church is always present in the activities of the local Christian community because the Gospel proclaimed is lived by men and women who are linked to a culture. The document reminds the local Christians that their culture is to have an influence on their way of living the Gospel.[193] Therefore in any specific action the local church and the universal church are linked in a central way. This understanding changed in Lilongwe the concept that they were the passive recipients of the action of the Universal church and that they were to be active members participating in the ecclesial action of evangelization (announcing of the good news of Jesus Christ). The actualization of the idea of the local church in Lilongwe meant

---

[192] John Baur, *2000 Years of Christianity in Africa: An African Church History*, Nairobi: Paulines, 1994, pp. 447-451.

[193] Paul IV, *Evangelii Nuntiandi: An Apostolic Exhortation on the proclamation of the Gospel*, 1975, no. 20.

their understanding that they shared in the ministry of the Church. While in the past, the Christians would see themselves as receivers of the ministry of the Church; in the local church they saw themselves as having responsibility. The Vatican II principle of collegiality was implemented at the lower level of the Church structure and it led to the creation of parish councils with representation from the grassroots. This structure facilitated the involvement of the lay faithful in the Church of which they had a sense of ownership.[194]

In these times the church in the Archdiocese of Lilongwe shared the understanding of Paul VI that the local church form was not necessarily a diocese or parish. The local church was a church of a particular area and cultural background. Thus, people in their own communities and in different and varying cultural, social and economic situations began to understand themselves as the Church. The Church was even lower beyond the diocese and the parish. The church was now moved, in understanding and actuality, to the neighbourhood. The baptized were to be united then so as to live this ecclesial life together and hence they lived as Christian families at the grassroots. In living their life as local churches in the Archdiocese of Lilongwe the Christians drew from the community or familial life of the early church. When they gathered for prayer and ecclesial action they were aware of the fact that they were the Church for they gathered and acted in the presence of the Lord: "For where two or three gather in my name, there I am with them" (Mt 18:20). They had regular calls for meetings for prayer, scriptural discussion, socio-political discussion and sharing of life in the spirit of the early church: "They devoted themselves to the apostles' teaching, and to fellowship, to the breaking of bread and to prayer" (Ac 2:42). Membership was first through profession of faith and baptism, geographical proximity and fellowship. In the local Church there was devotion to the Lord but also to one another which comprised a level of commitment to one another and the group which raised the assembly above an informal getting together: "Be devoted to one another in brotherly love. Honour one another above yourselves" (Rom 12:10), and "You know that the household of

---

[194] John Baur, *2000 Years of Christianity in Africa*, p. 456.

Stephanas were the first converts in Achaia, and they have devoted themselves to the service of the saints. I urge you brothers, to submit to such as these and to everyone who joins in the work, and labours at it" (1 Cor 16:15-16).

In these local churches the Christians saw themselves as united still with the universal church through their communion with the parish and the diocese. The understanding of the local church in Lilongwe Archdiocese was not of the Church as an irregular federation of local churches which were essentially different from each other because of their differing or varying social, cultural and economic context. They were not independent of the universal Church. The local churches made up the same universal Church that is universal in vocation and mission and one which acquired varying outward appearances through these local churches. The Christians in the Archdiocese of Lilongwe, in their local churches, lower than the diocese and parish, saw themselves as an important integral part of the universal Church.[195] Just as there was, sociologically, nothing in the world but local cultures, there was no universal Church without the local churches. The making and strengthening of the local churches was seen as a must for the making and survival of the universal Church. The key feature in the actualization of the local church was not, however a juridical connection, to a place far away that governed what it meant to be church, it was a community of faith that was bound to a definite geographical location, within a linguistic and cultural setting, with the responsibility of living and translating the faith into the local culture because it was this particular community that had the potential or competence to know the culture by virtue of the fact that its members were also members of the culture.[196] Principles of the local church, participation of the lay faithful in ministry and decision making processes, the priesthood of the lay faithful, and the principle of subsidiarity helped the Christians at the grassroots in the Archdiocese of Lilongwe to come together to brace up for their ministry. This

---

[195] John Baur, *2000 Years of Christianity in Africa*, pp. 462-467.

[196] www.ejournals.bc.edu/ojs/index.php/ctsa/article/viewFile/3020/2639/ [20.11.2015].

coming together facilitated the living together of the local church as a family of God.

The concept of local church facilitated and functioned to help the Christians in this locality that they were called to receive the gospel, celebrate it, and transmit it in their cultural categories. The local church felt called to understanding the gospel of Jesus Christ in its own setting and thus the element of inculturation became integral in the life of the Church. The Christians desired to live the gospel using the values present in their cultural context and understood that the good news and culture enriched each other. Not only did they find closeness in the Christian spirit of communion with the concept of family that they as Africans do have, the whole web of life in the local church was filled with the desire to understand and connect the good news with their reality.[197] The concepts of life, liturgy, organization, leadership, and celebration were performed and lived in ways that were already familiar to them from their culture. Inculturation was an integral part of life in the local church since the people desired to live the church in their African way as composing the church itself and not thinking of belonging to a foreign church.[198]

The Realization of the Insufficiency of the Missionary Church

The making of the local Church was felt as a must because there was a realization of the insufficiency of the Church structures brought by the missionaries. With the missionary structures it was difficult for the Christians to appropriate the Church as their own. The localization of the Church led to the development of the Small Christian Communities.[199] The SCCs were and remain the outstanding forum where the

---

[197] Paul IV, *Evangelii Nuntiandi*, no. 20 See John Paul II, *Ecclesia in Africa*, nos. 55-62.

[198] In this connection the purpose of evangelization must be understood that it is to transform humanity and the world from within and making it new. Without inculturation the Gospel and the Church still appear foreign to the people.

[199] John Baur, *2000 Year of Christianity in Africa*, p. 456.

model of Church as the family of God finds its expression and manifestation. They became the dominant model of the Church in Africa on the upswing and enjoying both robust hierarchical support and impressive grassroots energy.

Through these communities Christians were to live together their Christian life and calling in a spirit of family. Church life was to be based on these communities where everyday life and work took place. In these communities the people were to pray together, discuss the scriptures, relate the scriptures to their situation and plan consequent concrete actions.[200] These communities were understood as manageable and basic social groups of Christians in the same geographical proximity where they would experience real inter-personal relationships and feel a sense of belonging both in social and Christian living. In these communities the members looked at each other as related, through faith and baptism, and were meant to be supportive to each other not only in their spiritual life but also in their social and physical life. Encouraged by the subsequent plenary meetings of the AMECEA bishops, these communities graduated from being a movement in the Church in Africa to being a whole new way of being Church. The SCCs were lay led ecclesial communities. However, the plenary meetings that came later also encouraged bishops and priests to see themselves as regular members of these ecclesial communities, participate in their life and not to see themselves as leaders or occasional visitors.[201]

---

[200] The initiation and formation of the Small Christian Communities in Lilongwe by Bishop Kalilombe in the 1970s did not go down well with the Malawi government. In 1976 a conflict arose between the Church and the Malawi government under the presidency of Hastings Kamuzu Banda. According to Kalilombe, the Church was accused of forming clandestine subversive communities or groups which were working against the party and the state, and that these communities did not show respect and obedience to the life president. Kalilombe was forced to leave the country.

[201] Joseph G. Healey, *Building the Church as Family of God: Evaluation of Small Christian Communities in Eastern Africa*, Nairobi: CUEAP, 2012, p. 5.

The development of the SCCs in the Archdiocese of Lilongwe made the Christians to see themselves as part and parcel of the people and family of God. The Christians saw the SCCs as the basic unit in the life of the Church just as the family was the basic unit of society. It led to the institutional and ecclesial restructuring of the particular Church or the diocese. In the past the Church structure ended at the parish or mission, but that changed; the people of God in the SCCs saw themselves as the most fundamental level of the structure of the Church. From the most important below to the top the structure of the diocesan local church went in form of clusters of groups according to geographical proximity like this: Small Christian Communities, whose clusters make an outstation, zone (center), parish, deanery, and then the diocese. The SCCs provided to the Christians a structure with which they could identify. The requirement was that they were to remain small to allow people to know one another. In the Archdiocese of Lilongwe, the SCCs' composition was supposed to range between 30-50 families. The essential idea was identification of one another as a brother and a sister in the Lord. The SCCs provided a structure of service and participation in the life of the Church. Nobody was expected to be a spectator in this family church but an active member involved in all the Church's spiritual and social activities.

The essence of ecclesial life of the SCCs in the Archdiocese of Lilongwe was the creation and living of life in a church that was self-propagating, self-ministering and self-supporting.[202] During the time surrounding Vatican II the countries of Africa were becoming independent and self-governing nations. The political and economic optimism was also felt in the Church. The Church in Africa was optimistic and hopeful that the Church too would become self-dependent by becoming self-ministering, self-supporting and self-propagating. In regard to self-ministering, there were encouraging signs as the local churches in Africa witnessed the handover of responsibility from missionaries to local leadership. The development

---

[202] Patrick A. Kalilombe, *Doing Theology at the Grassroots: Theological Essays from Malawi*, Zomba: Kachere, 1999, pp. 1-173.

of a self-propagating church was a success as in these SCCs the laity played different roles and participated in various ministries.

Self-propagating Church

Self-propagating means that the Christians see themselves as bearing the duty of teaching and propagating the faith. Whilst in the past they waited for somebody to come from the parish to teach them the faith, prayer and the Word of God, Christians realized that it was *their* duty as they had been baptized into the prophetic life of Jesus Christ. The participation of the laity, to some degree, meant linking with the concept of self-ministering as it implied the people's belief that in these communities they were to minister to one another. There were different office bearers in the community, but together with every member of the community they were to participate in the service of the group and one another in the spirit of family. The leadership of the SCCs was not by the priests but by the lay faithful, even if priests and consecrated religious were members of these communities. Lay facilitators gave patronage to the communities. The corporate group facilitators called *Bungwe la mphakati*, while having distinct roles to play in the running of these communities, worked with a sense of interconnectedness and they met regularly to plan, discuss, evaluate and re-plan the organization and sustenance of these communities. The priests played their own role in these communities but most importantly they were a link point with the universal Church. The SCCs animators had these roles: *a pampando* (chairperson), *alembi* (secretaries), *asungi chuma* (treasurers), *a pampando a bungwe la amayi* (chairlady of the Catholic women), *amabungwe* (representative of all the ecclesial associations), *alangizi* (marriage counsellors), *amtsogolo a chinyamata* (youth group leaders), *aphunzitsi a kalasi* (catechumen instructors), *and aphunzitsi a tilitonse* (Sunday school and catechesis instructors). Nevertheless, not all these animators of the communities were present for the Parish council meetings. It was only the chairpersons of the SCCs, parochial leaders of the major church groups (women, youths, and men), parochial representatives of the spiritual associations and movements, who were called and attended the parish council meetings in most of the parishes.[203]

Self-supporting Church

The self-supporting Church was another concept strong in these communities of the local church. When the Church in Africa in general and in the Archdiocese of Lilongwe in particular was being localized there was optimism too that the Church would be self-reliant and no longer depend on donor support from the west if they were to claim to be a local church. In the self-dependence of the Church in Africa, the concept of self-reliance was being pursued together with the concepts of self-ministering and self-propagating. It was understood that a Church that depended for its existence and essential services upon the continuous charity of other churches was not a healthy, properly established Church. Basic economic self-reliance was as much a part of the establishment of the Church, which was the specific purpose of missionary work, as was the indigenization of its hierarchy.[204]

Self-reliant Church

The process of the establishment of the local Church entailed the necessity of making the Church self-reliant. The realization of this necessity in the Archdiocese of Lilongwe to make the church self-reliant had been there with which the Church could claim to be truly a local Church. Christians saw that, since they were the Church, it was their responsibility to take care of the economic, material and social needs of the Church. There were familial initiatives of fund raising to take care of the needs of the Church through collections, payment of annual tithes, or *masika* (first fruits offerings). But considering the many needs of the local churches their contributions often fell short by far. While the Church in Malawi could proudly claim to have reached the levels of being self-ministering and self-propagating, still there was

---

[203] Matthias Chimole, *Maudindo mu Mphakati*, Likuni, 1989, pp. 1-31.

[204] Adrian Hastings, *Mission and Ministry*, London: Sheed and Ward, 1971, p. 14.

little progress with the element of self-reliance of the local church. Most of the parishes, with the exception of the urban parishes, were economically struggling. The rural parishes had difficulties to pay their workers, catechists, pastoral workers, support staff, contributions to the diocese and to sustain the parishes in terms of water and power bills. They also had difficulties to pay for the training of the future pastors through their contributions to the seminaries.[205] On the whole it could not be said the local Church in Lilongwe was self-reliant. Neither were the SCCS self-reliant. They had poor prayer structures and always had difficulties to economically contribute to the self-reliance of the out station, center (zone), parish, deanery, and eventually to the entire Archdiocese of Lilongwe.

Thus, not much progress had been made in terms of self-reliance. The reasons for this scenario were numerous. But the bottom reasons were that the people to some level still thought it was the duty of the universal headquarters of the Church in Rome and its hierarchical representatives (bishops, priests and religious) to foot the economic expenses of the Church, and that the country had remained desperately poor and not economically independent with factors ranging from poor political leadership, financial incompetence, confusion, corruption, political selfishness, nepotism, abuse and embezzlement of public funds, disregard of human rights, and abuse of the natural environment. The local political and economic initiatives to get out of poverty had been weakened by the international global economy that favoured the strong and weakened the weak. Prosperity had been achieved for relatively few people and mostly those who were in political leadership positions and those who were well connected to the elite. The majority of the people still lived in abject poverty.

Spiritual Movements and Apostolic Associations

The development in the local Church of the Archdiocese of Lilongwe of spiritual movements and associations other than the SCCs also functioned to further the self-understanding of the Church as family of God and the fostering of fraternal harmony among the people of God.

---

[205] Patrick A. Kalilombe, *Doing Theology at the Grassroots*, pp. 30-80.

A distinctive feature of the Christians of the Archdiocese of Lilongwe was that other than being Christians and belonging with a sense of 'must' to the Small Christian Community, they also belonged to one or more ecclesial associations and movements. The African Synod Fathers in 1994 were able to acknowledge this and exhort their promotion when they said:

> It is a source of joy and comfort to note that the laity are more and more engaged in the mission of the Church in Africa and Madagascar, thanks especially to the dynamism of Catholic Action movements, apostolic associations and new spiritual movements. The Synod Fathers requested that this thrust be pursued and developed among all the laity: adults, youth and children.[206]

In these movements and associations, they met regularly, prayed together, planned and executed socio-spiritual actions together. As they lived their life in these associations they still maintained their bond to the local church and the diocese. Some of these movements attained the status of organizations; examples were the lay Catholic Women Organization (CWO) and the Catholic Men Organization (CMO).[207] Some of these associations and movements were of clerics and consecrated men and women like the Association of Diocesan Catholic Clergy of Lilongwe (ADCCOL), Association of Men Religious in Malawi (AMRIM), and the Association of Women Religious in Malawi (AWRIM). They developed out of the need to better serve the contemporary church and society according to their needs and gain the graces of their spiritual pursuance. Others also developed out of

---

[206] John Paul II, *The Church in Africa: Post-Synodal Apostolic Exhortation Ecclesia in Africa*, no. 99, p. 75.

[207] Int Fr. Francis Lekaleka, the Lilongwe Archdiocesan Chaplain of the Catholic Women Organization, on 11.11.15. In the interview he emphasized the fact that all women and men in this local church belong to either the CWO or CMO because of their being women or men respectively. Their belonging is different from the other groups where they are free because they are associations of some apostolic work and would welcome Catholic Christians from either gender.

the attraction of the Christians to live a spirituality of some saintly figures in the tradition of the universal Church. Examples of these movements and associations in the Archdiocese of Lilongwe which together with the lay organization of CWO and CMO and the religious associations of ADCCOL, AMRIM, and AWRIM served to further the understanding of Church as God's family could be given. They included *Legio ya Maria* (Legionaries of Mary), *Atumiki a Chifundo* (Servants of Charity), Third Order Franciscans, Choir Members Association, Association of Readers, Mass Servers Association, Catholic Teachers Association, Justice and Peace groups, Home Based Care groups, Catholic Development groups, *Ana a Tereza* (Liturgical dancing girls), *Akisiyo Katolika* (Catholic Action group), Catholic Charismatic Renewal Movement, Marriage Encounter (ME), Christian Family Movement (CFM), and *A Mtima Woyera* (Sacred Heart of Jesus Groups). This list is not exhaustive of the different groups, organizations, movements and associations which were there in the local church of Lilongwe Archdiocese. These movements and associations, where the sense of ecclesial family was fostered, were well organized and they permeated the whole structure of the local church starting from the level of the Small Christian Community up to the diocesan level. These movements and associations had leadership structures at all these levels. While living in these groups in fraternal harmony they were to remain in communion with others through the parish where all together aimed to pursue and to express their being Church as Family by devoting themselves to the teaching of the Church, fellowship, prayer and the breaking of bread (Ac 2:42).[208]

The relationship of ecclesial cum spiritual movements and apostolic associations to the Small Christian Communities was expected to be easy to understand. But in actuality it has not been so. The relationships among these movements and associations, which were meant to promote the sense of family of the Church, had not always been as expected. Some of the faithful of Christ occasionally would attach more allegiance to a movement or association than to the SCC to which they belonged. The pastoral instruction of the Archdiocese of

---

[208] John Paul II, *Ecclesia in Africa*, no. 100, p. 75.

Lilongwe on this, however, was that all these apostolic associations and spiritual movements were under the umbrella of the mother community which was the SCC to which every Catholic Christian in the neighbourhood belonged. For Catholics in the Archdiocese of Lilongwe it was not a must to belong to this or that movement or association, but it was a must for the faithful of Christ to belong to the Small Christian Community.

Prominent Characteristics of the New Ecclesiology

These family related values in African culture which had been articulated influenced the contemporary understanding of the Church, as God's family, in the Archdiocese of Lilongwe. The adoption of the metaphor of 'family' for the Roman Catholic Church in Africa formalized the use of the model of Church as the Family of God which emerged from the ecclesiology of communion that stood out in the Second Vatican Council. The use of this metaphor of family for the Church in Africa brought a lot of opportunities and did bear good fruits in the Church in many parts of Africa including Malawi. It changed the way of being Church. Several prominent characteristics of the Church were born from this new ecclesiology which used the African concept of family for a model.

A Church of Communities

In the Archdiocese of Lilongwe, Malawi, the Church witnessed a paradigm shift from an institutional-hierarchical Church to a Church which was a cluster of communities (SCCs, spiritual movements and apostolic associations). When the Missionaries of Africa arrived in the Archdiocese of Lilongwe, they planted a Church whose ecclesiological model was that of a hierarchy. In the early days the Catholic Church was thought to be the Church of Rome, of the Pope, of whom the priests were his immediate collaborators. The religious brothers and sisters who worked alongside the priests were also thought to belong to the group of the foreign proprietors of the Church.[209]

The pastoral behaviour and practice of some priests in the early days of the Catholic Church in the Archdiocese of Lilongwe, before the Second Vatican Council, also perpetuated this concept of the Church of Rome and church of the pope that it was their Church and the lay Christians were like their people and subjects.[210] From 2010 – 2012 when I served as the pastoral coordinator of the Archdiocese of Lilongwe, oftentimes in deanery meetings and *presbyterium* meetings it was not uncommon to hear priests say "our Christians" in reference to the faithful of Christ.[211] I personally took a lot of effort to inculcate among my fellow priests that the laity were not 'our Christians' but that they belonged to God and were the people of God. This is told to give an idea that pre-Vatican II ways of conceiving the Church were evident in the pastoral language used in reference to the laity. There was little participation of the people in the life of the Church. For example, in the liturgical celebration the priest did almost everything alone; leading the prayers, reading the texts from the Bible and expounding the Word, leading the songs, teaching the faith (catechesis) and many more. The people (laity) were just on the receiving end of the services of this 'church of the pope and his priests.' The Chichewa version of the Church's creed which was done by the

---

[209] Int Mr. Dambuleni, Mzira and Mr. Chidzaye, Mndinga, 1.8.2015. These are some of the retired catechists (formal instructors of the faith) who served for a long time in the past in the parish of Madisi. They worked with some of the White Father missionaries who came to evangelize this area of Madisi, Nambuma, Chiphaso, and Mpherere parish areas before the Africanization of the clergy in the late 1970s.

[210] John Baur, *2000 Years of Christianity in Africa*, pp. 455-456. In this section Baur states that missionaries parachuted, as it were, church structures which were a carbon copy of those in Europe.

[211] A presbyterium is an assembly of all the priests in the diocese together with their bishop. The convocation of such an assembly is always done by the bishop of the diocese, or when the bishop is not there, the apostolic administrator.

missionaries translated the article of the descent of the Church from the apostles as being the church of Peter (in reference to the pope).[212] From the developmental perspective, when the Church was being planted in the Archdiocese of Lilongwe, the priests did almost everything. They were in charge of the constructions of the church buildings, the schools and the dispensaries. It was seen as their responsibility to source funds for the development of their missions. The Church of the Pope and the Church in Rome was represented by the Church at the mission run by the priests, religious brothers and sisters. Baptized Catholics and catechumens, in their villages, looked at this mission center Church as their Church.

But the ecclesiology emerging from the Second Vatican Council and the African Synod provided a paradigm shift. In the Archdiocese of Lilongwe, the sense of Church as the Family of God led to the creation and nurturing of *Miphakati*. The Catholic Christians living in the same neighbourhood came together and lived their life as Church. The Church had been localized. Since Central Malawi was still largely traditional, with the exceptions of the city, towns and trading centers, the people coming together in the SCCs were closely related and living in the same or neighbouring villages. The Small Christian Communities were considered the Church in the neighbourhood. They were the Church at the grassroots. In these local places the people of God, the faithful of Christ, in their Small Christian Communities were meant to be self-ministering, self-propagating and self-supporting. The Small Christian Communities were considered Churches and living in communion with the Parish Church where the priests were resident. The development of these communities brought about a restructuring of the Church. The Church was now understood as a Church of Communities. It was a communion of Communities. A cluster of SCCs formed an outstation. A cluster of outstations formed a center (sometimes called zone). A number of zones made up the parish. A number of parishes in the same geographical proximity made up a deanery and consequently a number of deaneries (clusters of parishes)

---

[212] Archdiocese of Lilongwe, *Buku la Nyimbo ndi Mapemphero*, Lilongwe: Likuni, 1989, no. 49, p. 53.

made up the Archdiocese of Lilongwe. It is important to note that the Church is the people of God found at the grassroots in communion with their pastors and servants (the pope, priests and religious men and women).[213] Thus, in the Archdiocese of Lilongwe the application of this model of Church as God's Family triggered the restructuring of the Church through the initiation of Small Christian Communities with which the Church became a Church of Communities. These Communities, as long as they remained united to the parish, the bishop and the pope in faith and practice, were considered churches in the communion of the Catholic Church. The ecclesiology of the Church as the Family of God restructured the Church and brought about this new characteristic of Church in Lilongwe Archdiocese as a communion of communities.

A Church of Solidarity

The application of the new ecclesiology in the Archdiocese of Lilongwe created communities where people felt a lot of interconnectedness as they lived in different facets of life. Solidarity become not only a lived social-moral principle but also an ecclesial one. There was the real desire to build up unity of the human family, striving for integral development for all men and women, who were then interconnected by relationships of mutual concern and support. In these communities of the Church in the Archdiocese of Lilongwe solidarity was first and foremost a sense of responsibility on the part of everyone with regard to everyone.[214] The heart of solidarity is the life of Jesus. Through the incarnation, God becoming a human being (the Word becoming flesh), God is in solidarity with humanity and humanity was called to solidarity with one another and with God. Solidarity is much more than

---

[213] This information on the structures of the Catholic Church in the Archdiocese is gotten from the unpublished research work I conducted in pursuit of and submitted for the Master of Theology degree in the Catholic University of Eastern Africa (Nairobi-Kenya) in 2010, titled "A Pastoral Approach to the Chewa Youth Rites of Passage in Madisi Deanery of the Diocese of Lilongwe, Malawi," pp. 40-50.

[214] Benedict XVI, *Caritas in Veritate (Charity in Truth)*, 2009, paragraph 38.

an idealistic principle for organizing society or social institutions. It was not meant only to exist between individuals, but also within and between social institutions. It needed to be practiced through acts of love, service to the neighbour, support of the weak and humble, mutual respect, and social action.

The Church of communities (most evident in the SCCs) in the Archdiocese of Lilongwe consequently led to the creation of strong bonds of solidarity in these ecclesial communities. The situations of inequality, poverty, and injustice were signs of lack of fraternity and an absence of the culture of solidarity. Ideologies of individualism, egocentrism and materialistic consumerism which weakened social bonds were viewed as anti-ecclesial in these communities. The application of the concept of Church as the Family of God and the creation of the Small Christian Communities, *Miphakati*, brought about the emergence of a Church characterized by a strong sense of solidarity. There was a strong sense of cohesion among the Christian members belonging to the same community. In these communities they valued each other as human beings, respecting who they were as people and as individuals. In these communities they built a sense of family that empowered everyone to attain their full potential through each one of them. They respected each other's dignity, rights and obligations.

In solidarity the people remained sensitive to others, particularly to the humblest and weakest among them in the ecclesial communities. Solidarity in the ecclesial communities was not a feeling of vague compassion, or shallow distress at the misfortune of so many people in the community, near and far. On the contrary, it was a firm and persevering determination to commit oneself to the common good: this was to say the good of all and of each individual belonged to each and to all because they were all really responsible for all.[215] Solidarity became a bond that linked together all in these ecclesial communities and that all were responsible for each other. This sense of solidarity in the ecclesial communities of Lilongwe was like glue that bound the

---

[215] Cf. John Paul II, *Sollicitudo Rei Socialis (The Social Concern of the Church)*, 1987, paragraph 38.

members together for their common good. In some sense it included all the other principles and values that were necessary to create a truly good society.[216] Opposites of solidarity were things like exploitation, inequality, oppression, greed and selfishness. Solidarity is at the heart of what it meant to be human in these communities. It was a summary of the feelings and actualities that there was a deep bond between them all. The members of these communities looked at each other, using the Pauline concept, as members of one another: "Therefore each of you must put off falsehood and speak truthfully to his neighbor, for we are all members of one body (Eph 4:25)." Solidarity in these communities made sure and demanded that all people had a right to freedom, independence, self-determination, family life, security, and other basic necessities.

In these Small Christian Communities where the faithful of Christ built a strong sense of solidarity they recognized that they could not live their ecclesial life independently of God and of others. As Christians living an ecclesial life they realized that they were interdependent beings. Other than the usual Sunday gatherings for prayers, they met together often to strengthen these socio-ecclesial bonds. Though they were meant to meet once every week at their opportune time, the rural communities already living together and interacting almost daily in their villages did not meet together as often as the ecclesial communities in the city and towns. The weekly meetings strengthened these fraternity bonds and the sense of solidarity. The Christians in the Archdiocese of Lilongwe, in the SCCs, looked at this interdependence as a thing to be cherished. Through solidarity the faithful of Christ in the Archdiocese of Lilongwe depended on each other in all moments of life: in life and in death, in good or poor health, in good moments and in bad moments. One always felt supported by the Christian community around them. The image Paul gave of the Church as the Body of Christ (that all are individual parts that together make up the Body of Christ) gives us a visual way to think of this.

---

[216] Cf. John Paul II, *Compendium of the Social Doctrine of the Church*, no. 193.

The society continued to become ever more globalized. This globalization made people neighbours but it did not make them brothers and sisters. Solidarity was simply a demand for fraternity, that people should be able to treat each other as brothers and sisters. The Church as the Family of God, with its privileged locus in the ecclesial life of the SCCs, removed the gap between and among people so that they indeed treated each other as brothers and sisters. The SCCs eventually became tools of transformation for the society. They became centres of transformation where people lived in communities with strong bonds of unity through Christ and discussed their socio-political and economic situations.

A Servant Church

The presentation of the Church as servant was one of the major themes in the Second Vatican Council. The council asserted that the Church is to be a servant Church imitating Jesus Christ who came to serve and not to be served.[217] In this ecclesiological principle the Vatican II Council taught that the mission of the Church included service to human needs in the social, economic, and political orders, as well as preaching of the word and celebration of the sacraments.

Following the Second Vatican Council and the African Synod the Church in Lilongwe saw itself not only to be a servant of themselves as Church but also as a servant of society. Evangelization included the pursuit of justice and the transformation of the world. It involved a message especially energetic about liberation.[218] The Church could not stand idly in the face of injustice and oppression. It was a servant like Jesus Christ himself who came not to be served but to serve, and who gave his life as a ransom for many (Mk 10:45). The Second African Synod, convoked by Benedict XVI, and regarding the history of war, injustice, oppression and conflict in Africa, was aimed at reminding the

---

[217] Austin Flannery (ed.), The Vatican II Constitutions, Decrees, *Gaudium et Spes: Pastoral Constitution on the Church in the Modern World*, no. 3, pp. 164.

[218] Cf. Paul VI, *Evangelii Nuntiandi (On Evangelization in the Modern World)*, (1975), no. 29.

Church that it was to be in the service of reconciliation, justice and peace. The Church was to be salt of the earth and light of the world (Mt 5:13-14).

The Church of Lilongwe, as servant, was involved in the process of transforming the Malawian society at different levels. In the struggle to deal with the evils of the one-party state and the initiation and promotion of the rule of democracy, the bishop of Lilongwe, then Mathias Chimole, was one of the authors of the pastoral letter 'Living Our Faith' which gave a lot of impetus to the struggle for democracy.[219] The development and setting of a diocesan Commission for Justice and Peace (CCJP) in 1992 was another achievement through which the Church sought to be at the service of society.[220] There was also the formation of CADECOM, the Catholic Development Commission. These commissions raised awareness in Church and society of the injustices and misery that were there and how the people from the grassroots needed to participate in self-emancipation.

The Church, through the application of the metaphor of family, developed in its *ad intra* (within) and *ad extra* (outside) mission the characteristic of servant-hood.[221] In the grassroots ecclesial communities going up through the ecclesiastical structure to the level of the Archdiocese, the members visualized themselves as being servants, at the service of God, of others in the community and also being at the service of the society. The members of the Church in Lilongwe developed more and more awareness that they were called to the mission of the Church through their baptismal promises. Christian discipleship in the Church and society entailed service. The faithful of Christ felt that, by the virtue of their baptism, they were called to ministry. These vital Small Christian Communities developed themselves as schools of

---

[219] www.jstor.org/stable/1387707/ [2.9.2015].

[220] www.ppja.org/english/countires/malawi/catholic-commission-for-justice-and-peace/ [2.9.2015].

[221] *Ad intra* and *ad extra* are missiological terms literally translated as 'to the inside,' and 'to the outside' respectively, and they refer to the mission of the Church within itself and outside itself.

faith, prayer and service. From these active communities came active lay faithful, catechists, families, young people, consecrated men and women, deacons, priests and bishops who saw themselves as agents of the mission of the Church which is evangelization. The lay faithful had come to see themselves more and more as agents of evangelization as they came to learn and believe that through baptism they shared in the priesthood in Christ. The priesthood in the Catholic theology had been developed as being duo-faceted: the common priesthood of all the faithful and the ordained (ministerial) priesthood, both emanating from the one priesthood of Jesus Christ.[222]

A Church in Pursuance of Inculturation

The self-understanding of the African Church as a local Church had been done closely with the need for the local Church to understand and live the Gospel in its own cultural reality and this had led to the inseparability of the principle of the local Church with the pursuit of inculturation even in the Archdiocese of Lilongwe. Inculturation is understood as the intimate transformation of authentic cultural values through their integration in Christianity and the insertion of Christianity into the various human cultures.[223] The Christians' realization that it was possible to define and live the Church using African categories led them to take full and lively ownership of the Church. Though remaining in union with the Church of Rome, they understood themselves as the church itself. The church present in Rome was the same church present in their midst. This sense of family and of local church led the Christians in the Archdiocese of Lilongwe to be very

---

[222] The Catholic Church understands the priesthood in two ways: priesthood of all the faithful through baptism and the ordained priesthood. The two faces of the priesthood both come from the priesthood of Jesus Christ, but are different in function and in essence, cf., www.en.wikipedia.org/wiki/Priesthood_(Catholic_Church/ [2.11.2015].

[223] Sebastian Karotemprel (ed), *Following Christ in Mission: A Fundamental Course in Missiology*, Nairobi: Paulines Publications Africa, pp. 110-119. Also cf. John Paul II, *Redemptoris Missio*, no. 52, and Vatican II, *Gaudium et Spes*, no. 58.

active in living their ecclesial life. Individuals and church groups were involved in their different ways in being church. As an incarnated church, it had become an inculturated church in leadership, liturgy, and self-understanding. The leadership roles in this familial church were held in such a manner that roles of service were carried out in the socio-anthropological families in Africa. In African societies there was an active participation of all age groups, including the young people. This latter element was very evident in the Church in the Archdiocese of Lilongwe. The young people were active participators in the Church not only through their youth groups but also in the various structures of the local church beginning from the SCCs, Outstations, Zones, Parishes, Deaneries and the Archdiocesan level. Getting into any church assembly, on a Sunday gathering in the Archdiocese of Lilongwe, would straight away give one the picture of the youth being in the majority in the liturgical assembly and active in the liturgy (reading the scriptures, praying, dancing and singing). They were also active in apostolate and administration of the local church. It was a church full of life. This was in great contrast to the Western countries where faith and the church have since become seemingly attractive only for the elderly.

They were Church communities full of life. This life executed in the way of being church in Lilongwe was typical of African culture. Several generations of anthropologists, ethnologists, philosophers and theologians have argued with consistent veracity and uniformity that the fundamental category of existence in Africa was life. "The primary African philosophical interest is life, the gift that God gave and continues to give to this world and in the peoples' communities."[224] To qualify it as 'philosophical' did not mean that it could be reduced to a purely abstract category. For African religion equally, all principles of morality and ethics were to be sought within the context of preserving human life. Thus, the African world-view defined the ethically good as those actions or orientations which give life and affirm life. The ethically bad, on the contrary, denotes those actions or orientations

---

[224] Joseph Donders, *Non-Bourgeois Theology: An African Experience of Jesus*, New York: Orbis, 1985, p. 4.

which undermined life. The responsibility devolved on the community to struggle constantly to overcome the menace of evil to its corporate life.[225] For Africans, life signified, first and foremost, a concrete experience. Africans experienced life as belonging, communion, sharing, hospitality, celebration and participation. In addition, they experienced life as abundance and well-being, material, spiritual, psychological, and social. One particular element of the expression of life and wellness was through celebration and dance. The liturgical celebrations in the ecclesial communities in Lilongwe Archdiocese were marked by a lot of dancing, expressing their gratitude to God (the giver of life), and expressing their horizontal desire to foster those values in the communities that promoted life for all. Thus, the attainment and preservation of the fullness of life came into play as the constitutive elements of human existence in Africa, even in the religious communities.[226]

Conclusion

The application of the model of Church as God's Family in the Archdiocese of Lilongwe led to the development of the local Church. The Christians at the grassroots began to see themselves more clearly and evidently as the Church. This was in direct contract to the previous model of the Church as an institutional-hierarchical entity that emphasized the universality of the Church which was represented by the hierarchy. Through the development of the SCCs, the Christians at this level came to see themselves as the Church in the neighbourhood. The application of the new ecclesiology in the Archdiocese of Lilongwe led to the development of the realization among the local Christians about the insufficiency of the Church planted and preached about by the missionaries. The missionary Church emphasized the institutional-hierarchical model and through this the Catholic Church, in the minds of many Catholics, was a Church of Rome and the Pope, and the

---

[225] Laurenti Magesa, *African Religion. The Moral Traditions of Abundant Life*, New York: Orbis, 1997, pp. 31-32.

[226] Agbonkhianmeghe E. Orobator, *The Church as Family: African Ecclesiology in its Social Context*, Nairobi: Paulines, 2000, pp. 149-150.

priests and religious sisters and brothers were its representatives. The priests and religious brothers and sisters were the immediate collaborators of the Church in Rome. The lay Christians were passive spectators and recipients of the Church's ministry. But with the new ecclesiology, the Christians at the grassroots were able to see themselves as the Church.

Furthermore, the self-understanding of the Church, in the Archdiocese of Lilongwe, in the new ecclesiology of the Family of God, led to the development of many spiritual movements and apostolic associations. In these movements and associations, the members saw themselves even more as belonging to one family, the Family of God. The development of the sense of local Church, realization of the insufficiency of the missionary Church, and the spiritual movements and apostolic associations led to a Church in the Archdiocese of Lilongwe that had some prominent characteristics and these included: Church of communities, Church of solidarity, servant Church, and an inculturated Church (in leadership, liturgy and in catechesis).

Chapter 6: Challenging Issues with the Metaphor of Family for the Church

Tapping on the richness of the concept of family from the African perspective and using the metaphor of 'family' for the Church in Africa, produced positive fruits in the Archdiocese of Lilongwe through the creation of an ecclesiology that was theologically and anthropologically based. I should not be naïve to think this was easy to understand and interpret especially in modern times when the family, even in Africa, had become one of those social institutions that were going through crisis. There were a number of defects which were associated with the institution of family not only in the world at large, but also in Africa and Malawi in particular. The understanding of the Church as family ran the same risk of inheriting these defects of family and thus hampering the proper understanding of the church. Some people might have difficulties in understanding such a divine reality, the church, from the perspective of an imperfect or defective institution. It became difficult to understand the church in terms of family when one considered how in human families in Africa today there is a lot of infidelity, injustice, and abuse of spouse and children. It became difficult to consider this divine reality, the church, in terms of family when many people were not living in families. The social reality of single parents too became an obstacle to this model. Men, women, and children living as singles by choice, and children living with single parents would not find it ideal to describe the church as family as it would linguistically seem to exclude them from the church. Single parenthood was increasing due to divorces, unemployment, consumerism, modernism, and the so called sexual freedom. Christians living in such groups would find it not easy and comfortable to feel accommodated in a church that defined itself in terms of the African family with these defects.

There were some more negative elements that come up through social analysis when such a metaphor is used for the Church. However, it is important to remember that no metaphor or model is perfect. Each metaphor contributes something towards the explanation of the reality in question. The task which is daunting is to come up with a metaphor which is closer to reality and closer to wholistic understanding of the reality being discussed. The metaphorical definition of the Church in Africa as Family of God added something to the self-understanding but also betrayed something of the whole reality of the Church as a communion in pursuit of salvation; a pursuit that included the totality of God's creation.

A Challenge to Interreligious Dialogue and Ecumenism

The self-definition of Church as Family of God, while bearing some positive elements, could lead to a restrictive understanding of the Church especially among communities like in Lilongwe where illiteracy levels are high and with which it might be difficult to conceptualize the Church in terms of a mystical communion or mystical family. Among such communities what came to the people's minds by the term 'family' were the physical human beings they seemed to be bound to. The concept of family for the Church could, hence, lead to pride in the institution that leads to looking down at others who do not belong to this particular group bound by a common faith and creed. The sense of family if wrongly understood could lead to a negative and contemptuous attitude towards those who do not belong to this family. It had the potential of creating a diminished idea about the universality of the Church and thus making ecumenism and dialogue with the non-Christian religions efforts difficult as there was no level ground. The metaphor of family was naturally exclusive of some who were from without. It created a mental superior and inferior polarization framework which would be difficult for a genuine inter-faith dialogue.

The advantages of applying the metaphor of 'family' to the Church could not be overemphasized when considering the richness of this concept from the African perspective. However, thinking of the reality of the Church from this angle of the term, that was essentially sociological and anthropological, presented the Church with the danger of diminishing its universality. One of the controversial questions, in history, which bogged systematic theology down from the Roman Catholic perspective, was whether salvation is possible for those outside the communion of the Church. It is now a settled question because it was believed the Church goes beyond the institution and transcends peoples.

When the model of church as God's family was understood and interpreted from an exclusivist Catholic understanding, such application of metaphor of the 'family' had serious negative ecumenical consequences. It might lead to the thinking that there are others who are excluded from this family and naturally what comes to the mind would be those who believe and practice differently from what one's church is used to. A Catholic oriented interpretation and understanding of the ecclesiology of church as God's family would run the risk of segregating the others as not belonging to the church and this would deter the pursuit of unity that the ecumenical movement is striving for. Such an understanding is ecumenically insensitive and if understood in an ordinary and narrow sense, as was often the case, it worked against the unity of all believers, and unity with the communion of all the saved of God.

The non-Christian religions had even a salvific value and God in his infinite love and mercy was able to draw and would draw people to himself irrespective of their religious affiliations as long as they did his will. The Church is one and universal and this transcends any religious institution here on earth. There is no particular and temporal ecclesial institution that represents this communion of salvation, understood as a communion of all in the communion of God. Furthermore, humans are not the sole beneficiaries of the effects of the sacrifice of Jesus Christ on the cross. The universality of the Church flows from the universality of God's unique plan of salvation for the world. Benedict XVI had this to say on the celebration of the gift of the Holy Spirit:

> The universality of the Church flows from the universality of God's plan of salvation for the whole world. The universal character emerges clearly on the day of Pentecost, when the Holy Spirit, fills the Christian community with his presence so that the Gospel may spread to all nations, causing the one people of God to grow in all nations. From the origins, then, the Church is oriented '*katholon*,' it embraces the whole universe. So, the universality of the Church does not arise from below, but descends from above, from the Holy Spirit who wishes to make all things new. The Holy Spirit

breaks all boundaries of race, class, nation, and unites all in God. The Church embraces all.[227]

Thus, what made the Church universal was the fact that Christ in his saving mission embraced all humanity whose life and existence is mutually intertwined with the rest of nature. The mission and vocation of Jesus Christ was essentially to call all into the communion and friendship with God, a communion which was lost through sin. The prophet Isaiah had this to say, "Surely the arm of the Lord is not too short to save, nor his ear too dull to hear. But your iniquities have separated you from your God; your sins have hidden his face from you, so that he will not hear" (Isa 59:1-2). At creation there was communion of God with his nature and humanity. But with sin there followed four-fold alienations (separations): (1) humanity was alienated from God; (2) humans were alienated from their humanity; (3) man and woman were alienated from one another; and (4) humans were alienated from their world. Oftentimes sin was considered as three-fold, as alienation from God, alienation from the self and alienation from others. The fourth is also important: alienation from nature (creation).

There was a divorce, using a metaphorical language, in the relationships between God, humanity and earth (creation). Creation needed healing because it was badly diseased through sin. Salvation in Jesus Christ meant creation was now healed. It was about overcoming this divorce so that there was re-marriage of heaven and earth in the new creation (Rev 19:9). This was the healing that was required, an event but also a process and in this process, humans were meant to be at the service of nature just as nature was at the service of humanity in that people fully depend on nature for their life support and survival.

The universality of the Church goes beyond humanity to include the rest of nature. The major problem humans had was to think of themselves as the sole beneficiaries of the redemptive work of Christ. The application of the term 'family' for the Church could breed a form of restrictivism which, by extension, might deny redemption to the

---

[227] www.zenit.org/articles/pope-the-universality-of-the-church/ [30.9.2015].

non-human creatures.[228] It restricts redemption to humanity only and there is no consideration of nature as a co-beneficiary of salvation through Christ. The term Church as the Family of God further could develop in humans an attitude of religious triumphalism. Though triumphalism, in Christianity, could provide impetus for proselytization, conquest of unbelieving communities, and general expansion of the group and its doctrine, it could become negative because, before the harm it did to nature, such conception could also be detrimental to the survival of the social system of which the Church is a part. Such dangers included: impaired ability to judge the value or morality of the group's actions, cessation of creativity and innovation within the group, blindness to other group's strengths and innovations, tendency to over-react against the group's competitors (based on an inflated sense of the likelihood of triumph in conflict) and breeding a form of restrictivism.

With such a term, consciously or unconsciously, humans nurtured in themselves a collective pride in which they would assume they were the first, privileged beings, created in the image of God. They would with pride say they were the children of God and members of his family. This religious triumphalistic attitude of *'we are the family of God'* promoted a sense of pride, security, sense of superiority and self-righteous expectation of ultimate triumph, and had the danger of relegating the non-human part of creation which also bears the spark of God the creator.

An Ecclesial Tendency towards Anthropocentrism

When there is a thoughtless use of the term family for the church there would be a danger of impairing the true image of the church, of salvation and liberation. There developed an ecclesial tendency towards anthropocentrism which is one of the derivatives of

---

[228] Restrictivism, in Christianity, is a theology that views that Christian salvation is possible for those who have heard the gospel of Jesus and put their faith in Jesus prior to their death. It holds that all the un-evangelized are damned. Unless people hear the message of Jesus Christ and respond, they have no hope.

anthropomorphism, the attribution of human form, characteristics, and qualities to entities or beings other than human. It bears the meaning of a negative attitude centered on the human person and the interpretation of what is not human in terms of human or personal characteristics. It is the humanization of something. It could further be described as a literary device and technique of ascribing human traits, emotions, ambitions to things (beings or institutions) that are not wholly human e.g. God, Church, salvation. It is an attribution of human qualities to non-human beings, objects, natural or supernatural phenomena. The word etymologically comes from two Greek words, *anthropos* which means human and *morphe* which means shape or form. The verb form of this word is 'anthropomorphizing' and this means taking something as if it were human. Whilst the possibility was there to use metaphorically the word 'family' for the Church, there was a natural tendency to understand the Church and salvation in very sociological and anthropological terms.

Anthropomorphism has significantly shaped religious thought. The history of both polytheistic and monotheistic religions reveals that these faiths had apprehended the nature of divine being(s) in terms of human characteristics and this brought along with it both advantages and disadvantages. In ecclesiology, specifically, people were trying to define and understand the reality of the Church, which is a mystery. The Church, being a mystery, is a reality whose whole is very difficult to capture. The human device has often been to use categories which aimed at helping human beings understand what they do not know in terms of what they know. However, humans needed to be careful in the way they use these categories so that they did not impair the complete picture of this reality, the Church. No category, because of the richness of this reality, was able to capture in one word or phrase the complete reality of the Church. However, humans needed to use those categories which were closer to the reality in question.

In science and education, we are dealing with the element of sharing knowledge with human minds which are limited and with propensity of misconception even if they have a high degree of conceptualization. The term 'family' was very naturally a sociological and anthropological term and the application of such a term to an entity that was also 'divine' and transcendental like the Church had the chance of misleading. The application of the anthropological term 'family' to a mysterious reality like the Church, which was both human and divine, impaired the proper understanding of such a reality. This made it even worse when people considered the essential pursuit of salvation that the Church began to experience but was to reach finality in eternity. The model of Church as God's family was homocentric and made salvation homocentric. God, of course, existed before humans, and therefore humans were created in the form of God. This resemblance implied some kind of kinship between humans and God. But God was not only present in humans; he was also present in the rest of creation. There is excessive anthropomorphism, fundamentally flawed when applied to realities which are also divine like the Church.

Anthropomorphism tends to project human emotions onto a reality (the Church) that is fundamentally not only human. It has the danger of portraying the Church as if it were only human. The Church is human, but not only human. This danger worsens, with this picturing of Church as family, as the anthropomorphism would in turn limit redemption, which is the pursuit of the Church, as if it were only for humans. It presents ecclesiology with the danger of portraying the Church as if it is the sole beneficiary of redemption. In as far as the Church is a communion of salvation, communion with the triune God and with the rest of nature, the contemporary African ecclesiology of Church as the Family of God has the propensity of describing the Church and redemption as if they are sole human privileges.

Transposition of Androcentric Elements into the Church

Androcentrism means centered on men or male centeredness. It is the practice, conscious or otherwise, of placing male human beings or the male point of view at the center of one's world view and its culture and history. Etymologically, the word comes from the Greek word, *andros*, which means man or male. The related adjective 'androcentric' means dominated by or emphasizing masculine interests or points of view, often to the neglect or exclusion of women. The opposite of androcentrism would be gynocentrism, which is the practice of placing the feminine point of view at the center. In the scientific debate the term androcentrism was coined as an analytic concept by Charlotte Perkins Gilman.[229] The term was coined in her book titled, *The Man-made World: Our Androcentric Culture* published in 1911. Gilman stated that androcentric patterns, mindsets and life styles were evident in many fields and facets of life. They could be seen in education, literature, art, language, and even in religion. She noted that, for example, in language what was called 'generic language' as to refer to both men and women was androcentric. Men were thought of as the norm and women as deviance. Historically much of the development of Christianity has been driven by men and so has seen a lot of the masculine perspective. Even the Bible was largely written from a male perspective and the female experience was interpreted by men in the Bible. All of the known authors of the bible books were male. Even in Biblical translation there was seen the marginalization of the works of women. Of the New Revised Standard Version translators 86% were male, and for the New International Version, 93% were male. The African Bible, based on the text of the New American Bible and published by the Roman Catholic Church in Africa in 1999, had 41 contributors and editors. Of these there were only 2 women.

Androcentrism breeds patriarchy in which fathers or father-figures hold authority over women and children in the family. Patriarchy means the rule of the father. It is etymologically from two Greek words, '*patriarches*,' meaning father or chief of a race, and '*arkho*' meaning '*I rule*.' Though historically patriarchy used to refer to autocratic rule by a male head of the family, in modern times it more generally means a social system in which power is held by adult men.

So, humanity lived in a world dominated by androcentric culture. The ascription of Church as a family could, consciously or unconsciously, function to maintain patriarchy in a Church that was already male dominated. African families, societies and communities usually are male dominated and when the Church is thought of as a family there is the danger of conceiving it in terms of how these African institutions of family, society and community are structured. Even the so called

---

[229] www.wikipedia.org/wiki/Androcentrism/ [30.9.2015].

matrilineal societies are patriarchal. There is a societal fixation on masculinity which in such androcentric institutions is thought to be normative. Masculine patterns of life and mindset claim universality. In such institutions seeking an equivalent female pattern of life and mindset is considered as deviance and weakness. Men are thought of as the leaders and heads of the families, communities and societies. So, when the Church is defined as family there is the danger of making the Church male centered too. This was actually the real trap into which the Church in Africa with the current ecclesiology has fallen. An assessment on the attendance and participation in the Small Christian Communities in the Archdiocese of Lilongwe revealed that they were better attended by women than men. Men in general would be considered as Sunday Christians and for various reasons they attended the prayer meetings of the Small Christian communities comparatively less frequent than women. However, one gets a shock to note that the majority of the leadership of these communities is composed of men. So, it was males, who formed a minority in the Church communities, leading females who formed the majority of the Church.

From the feminist as well as realistic point of view, androcentrism and patriarchy are unjust social systems because eventually they enforce gender roles and are oppressive to both women and men. They include social mechanisms which evoke male dominance over women, and the objectification of women and of the non-human nature. These are social constructs and people can get rid of them. The Church needs to play its role of overcoming these unjust mechanisms in societal institutions by revealing and critically analyzing their manifestations.

Inferiorization of Women and the Non-human Creation

The inferiorization of women was evident in many ways. In the structural organization of the Church there were few women holding leadership positions despite the church opening to have these positions filled by elections every three years. In 2011, in all the 35 parishes of the Archdiocese of Lilongwe, there was only one female parish council chairperson and this was Mrs. Evarista Chafulumira of St. Patrick's Parish in Area 18, Lilongwe. Even then, the male centeredness came out as three years later she was not given a second term of service despite having performed very well. This was not too surprising in an ecclesial electorate where they had many males. The only fora where women leaders were in abundance were in women-oriented sodalities (church groups) such as the Catholic Women Organization and the association of charity works (*Atumiki a Chifundo*). This example was an indicator on how women are held in the Church.[230]

There exists a relationship between religious-theological worldviews and the degradation of women and nature, a relationship between theology and the domination of women and the environmental crisis. These worldviews were some of the sources of human action and ethics, whether consciously or unconsciously. The way Christian Theology defined things had profound impact and implications on the peoples' conduct towards one another and towards the rest of nature. Theology could bring about a proper or an improper understanding of the place of nature in religion. Some scholars in the past blamed Christianity and its teachings to have contributed to the degradation of nature. The models of human dominion over nature, God's transcendence (and by extension humanity's transcendence) over nature, the treatment of nature as a tool for human survival and prosperity were some of these elements blamed for the degradation of nature.

The application of the metaphor of family to the Church and the consequent understanding of Church as God's Family bred anthropomorphic and androcentric accents in the Church and these contributed to the relegation of non-human creation and women both in the Church and in society. It centered the nature and mission of the Church on human beings. The non-human creation was consigned to an inferior and obscure rank of God's creation. The relegation of nature was not right in both its reality and methodology. Methodologi-

---

[230] This information is obtained from the 26 September 2011 parish council minutes in St. Patrick's Parish during which the election of the first female parish chairperson in the Archdiocese of Lilongwe took place, and Int Fr. Francis Lekaleka, then the Acting Parish Priest, St. Patrick's Parish, 10.12.2015.

cally it was not good and right to put God's creation on a hierarchical scale and ladder because this was bound to reduce the importance of some of God's creatures the lower one went. It would again give an impression that one type or species of creation would exist or live independent of others. The reality of the matter was that there was interdependence and mutuality of all of God's creatures and none would exist or live independent or without careful participation of the other. Existence and life needed to be understood as one web. This interdependence and mutuality would best be understood in a cyclical or circular model and not in a pyramidal mode. The human tendency to rank God's creation had favoured males and led to the relegation and domination of women and non-human nature.

There were connections between the domination over women and the domination over nature. The connections were not only in the goals of the two movements (women's movement and environmental/ ecological movement), but also in the causes of the domination of nature and women. There were historical and typical causal connections between women and nature. The domination of nature and women was historical and it was a result of the development of patriarchal culture in the world. There was a time when life was matrifocal (focused on women) and matrilineal and this was during the agrarian era uninfluenced by the industrial revolution and technological advancement as it became.[231] The agrarian era centered life on small scale production of food and maintenance of crops and farmland and during this time women were the focal point and powerful. This agrarian era was preceded by the hunter-gatherer societies and was succeeded by the industrial societies. In the agrarian era women even in Africa played major roles in the socio-economic, political, cultural and religious development of society. They provided food for subsistence, were primary socializing agents, giving values, aspirations and moral foundations for their children and therefore being the

---

[231] Ariel Salleh Kay, *Epistemology and Metaphor of Production: An Ecofeminist Reading of Critical Theory*, in *Studies in Humanities*. Special issue on "Feminism, Ecology, and the Future of the Humanities", Patrick Murphy (ed), vol. 15 (2), pp. 130-139.

pillars for the construction of balanced societies. They were also able to produce surplus food for barter trade and maintained the families when the men were out either hunting, gathering, trading or raiding neighbouring ethnic communities for animals and other related items of survival and prestige.[232]

This agrarian and matrifocal period changed in history and there was the transition to industrial societies which ushered in patriarchy in human culture. The roles and status of women changed with the introduction of industrial culture which brought about patriarchy. Women were inferiorized or pushed socially to a lower rank. Nature began to experience exploitation in order for the male centered society to maximize production and achievement in the new economy. History shows some connection between the domination of nature and women due to patriarchal dualism and conceptions of rationality in classic Greek philosophy. There are connections in the philosophical thought of reason in Greek philosophy where women were thought to have a lesser reasoning ability with more of feeling and intuition than men.[233] Nature was thought to lack reasoning ability and was seen as thoughtless. Such philosophical developments perpetuated domination of women and nature. Other feminists placed the causal connection of the development of the domination over nature and women on the cultural and scientific changes that occurred in the scientific revolution of the 16th and 17th century when the old order of cooperation between humans and nature was replaced by the mechanistic worldview of modern science. This worldview sanctioned the exploitation of nature for production and economic competition. It

---

[232] Judith Mbula Bahemuka, "Status and Role of Women in African Societies: Suffering and Hope", in *Africa the Kairos of a Synod: Symposium on Africa*, Rome: Sedos, 1994, p. 35.

[233] Rosemary Radford Ruether, *New Woman/New Earth: Sexist Ideologies and Human Liberation*, pp. 204ff.

also sanctioned unchecked commercial and industrial expansion, and the subordination of women.[234]

The causal connection between the domination over nature and women was also seen in the symbolic associations and devaluations of women and nature that appeared in religion, theology, art and literature. There was often an association of the language that was used in describing women and nature. Human beings, consciously or unconsciously, associated women and nature linguistically. This betrayed what lied at the bottom of their heart and in the core of their reason. The language they used sometimes inferiorized women and non-human nature by feminizing nature and naturalizing women. It was not uncommon to hear people say, 'mother earth' or 'mother nature.' It was not uncommon to hear women described in animal terms like chicks, cows, serpents, cats, or bitches. Many more examples like these could be given. Things of the environment too sometimes were described in female and sexual terms, for example, 'virgin land,' 'virgin soil,' 'fertile soil,' or 'barren land.' So, some language expressions feminized nature and brought women more to the realm of nature. Such language expressions perpetuated the domination and inferiorization of women and the non-human creation. In this same particular vein, the use of language of 'family' for the Church in Africa and in the Archdiocese of Lilongwe perpetuated the inferiorization, domination, exploitation and oppression of not only women but also of nature. The African sense of family was laden with anthropocentrism, androcentrism, and patriarchy. With such conceptualization women and non-human nature were not treated and counted on the same rank with males, and had, hence, become objects of domination, exploitation and oppression.

The current African ecclesiology of Church as God's Family fell into the same trap of relegating the non-human creation. When the Church is defined as the 'family' what came quickly to peoples' minds were human beings and how special and unique they were in the sight of

---

[234] Carolyn Merchant, *The Death of Nature: Women, Ecology and Scientific Revolution*, San Francisco: Harper and Row, 1980, pp. 20-79.

God and in the history of salvation. There was no sufficient thought about the flora, fauna and everything that existed in this vast universe. Such self-understanding of the Church exalted the human beings as the closest to God and belonging to His family while the rest of nature was considered, consciously or unconsciously, as less important. Human beings were felt as if they were the sole beneficiaries of the redemptive work of Christ. With such concept there was little thought about the dignity of creation which eventually led to little thought about its place in the economy of salvation and its eventual destiny.

In the past four decades in both Church and society an enormous interest had been witnessed in both the women's movement and the ecological (environmental) movement. Many feminists argued that the goals of the women movement and the goals of the environmental movement were mutually reinforcing. In a world in which there was human-male-centeredness and in which there was the exploitation, domination, oppression of women and nature, the logical and natural aims of the movements were to acquire freedom and dignity for the oppressed beings. The causes and ultimate tasks of both of these movements were similar. The ultimate goals involved the development of worldviews and practices that were not based on male-biased models of domination.[235] Some women have argued that there could be no liberation for them and no solution to the ecological crisis within a society whose fundamental model of relationships continues to be one of domination. There was a need for a unification of the demands of the women's movement with those of the ecological movement to envision a radical reshaping of the basic socioeconomic relations and the underlying values of modern industrial society. Many eco-feminists defended that and essentially, they said that the environment was also a feminist issue.[236]

---

[235] Karen J. Warren (eds.), *Environmental Philosophy: From Animal Rights to Radical Ecology*, New Jersey: Prentice-Hall, 1993, pp. 253-267.

[236] Rosemary Radford Ruether, *New Woman/New Earth: Sexist ideologies and Human Liberation*, New York: Seabury, 1975, p. 204.

Human beings have to develop the ways of thinking about the non-human creation even in religious and theological terms. This would encourage them to reflect on how the non-human creation suffered as a result of evil. It would help them to reflect in detail on the depth to which evil and suffering reach into the biological world and become aware of the potential of Christ's redemption to effect the alleviation of such suffering of nature and creation. An eco-feminist stated that in such a reflection:

> We are reminded that the crucifixion did not just happen to one man in one historic moment, but that creation continues to suffer as a result of the evil and domination of humankind. I am making the case that creation is sometimes the victim of the same forces that crucified Christ. So, the creation-crisis theology and preaching must include the other-than-human beings within the scope of our moral consideration and proclamation of hope.[237]

Nature was often thought of in terms of what it not really was in the sight of God. It had even led to the tendency of humans to restrict salvation to themselves forgetting or deliberately choosing to think nature had no place in the realm of spirituality. It was important to reduce the tendency to confine the God-language (theology) to human categories. The conceptualization of the Church in terms which were very anthropomorphic was not good enough as the reality in question, salvation, encompassed much more than human beings alone. There was need to develop an ecological language usage in theology and ecclesiology. The exclusive use of human-centered language in theology and ecclesiology, like that of Church as Family, functioned to maintain patriarchal culture in the Church and in society, diminished and limited the view of God, Church and redemption, and enhanced the domination and inferiorization of women and nature. Ecclesiology had the task then of arguing against such exclusive use of male-centered language and foster the use of inclusive categories in understanding God and his creation.

---

[237] Leah D. Schade, *"Creation-Crisis Preaching: Ecology, Theology and the Pulpit,"* pp. 1-49.

Conclusion

In every age and in every part of the history of the Church there was need to critique the ecclesiology that characterized that epoch of Church history for the reason that such an exercise would help to make the Church relevant. The relevance of the Church in a particular season and epoch came when it was able to respond and speak to the experiences, challenges, and problems of its time.

Inasmuch as there were a lot of strengths with the African ecclesiology of Church as God's Family, the development and usage of the metaphor of family for the Church from the African perspectives had some genuinely challenging issues. The application of the new model of Church as Family of God posed a challenge to interreligious dialogue and ecumenism. The term family was sociologically exclusivist and when applied to the church there was the challenge of developing exclusivist elements in the understanding of the Church. The term excluded others who were from outside. When the members of the Church saw themselves from the perspective of 'family' they tended to exclude the others who are not Catholics. There were some Christians in the Catholic Church who did not consider themselves on the same level as the others Christians belonging to other Christian denominations and religious faiths. There were strong androcentric and patriarchal elements in the understanding of family of Africa, and when such a metaphor was applied to the Church, there was a substantial degree of transposition of such androcentric elements into a Church that was already male-dominated. Though in recent times the participation of women in the Church has gained some strides, largely the Church, even at the grassroots, is still male headed. Leadership, service, ordained ministry, and even the general ministry in the Church are male centered.

Furthermore, the application of the new ecclesiology of Church as God's Family, owing to how the concept of family was understood from an African cultural perspective, led to the inferiorization of women and the non-human creation. In many districts of the Archdiocese of Lilongwe the life of the people was still largely traditional even if there was also the mixing with some modern elements. In traditional societies and families, women were perceived as a lesser gender to the men. In families, life was still patri-centric. The roles were still given in favour of males. The term family was still a sociological and anthropological term and among illiterate Christian communities there was the tendency to literally understand the family as an anthropocentric reality. This eventually led to the inferiorization of the non-human part of God's creation.

In relation to the environment, the people at the grassroots thought first of the family as an anthropological and sociological term. The family for many of them was in reference to human beings. For them a family and consequently a society was composed of human beings. In the conceptualization of the Church as God's Family it was first of all understood to be about the human well-being brought about by solidarity and stronger bonds of cohesion, and not the environmental well-being. The environment was viewed as an object and raw material for human progress and development. The value of the environment was thought in terms of how beneficial it was to human life-support. Thus, the aspects of the proper intrinsic value, salvation and destiny of the non-human part of creation, were missing in some people. The people in this local Church understood the non-human part of creation as it exists in the environment as inferior to human beings and created to be at the service of man and woman. In this way the application of the model of Church as God's Family in the Archdiocese of Lilongwe contributed to the inferiorization of nature and this consequently contributed to its degradation and exploitation. It contributed to the diminished care and concern for the elements and systems of the environment as God's creation. In some way, thus, the concept of Church as God's Family (*familia Dei*) contributed to the degradation and destruction of the environment as did other Christian theological concepts like the dominion over nature, the *creatio ex-nihilo* (creation out of nothing), *imago Dei* (human creation in the image of God) and the *scala natura* (the scale of nature).

Chapter 7: Biblical and Theological Basis for Human Stewardship of the Environment

The inferiorization, degradation and destruction of the environment were not the ways human beings should have related to the environment. Human beings needed to protect and take care of the creation as it existed in the environment. The responsibility which human beings were to have over the environment has strong biblical and theological foundations. The chapter thus presents the biblical vision of the environment as a fundamental source of human stewardship for the environment.

It also goes on to look at an essential aspect that needed to trigger human respect, care and protection of the environment and this is the salvation and redemption that the environment was journeying towards. Hence this chapter looks and presents the biblical evidence for the spiritual and environmental salvation. The redemption of the environment is a theological concept that is alien to many Catholic Christians in the Archdiocese of Lilongwe and one that has been neglected in its catechesis. Finally, the chapter presents the general theology of the Catholic Church on the care of the environment and this among other ways is substantiated by a presentation of some prominent figures in Catholic theology and spirituality and what they said and taught, in agreement with mother Church, regarding the environment.

Biblical Vision of the Environment as Source for Stewardship

The Bible is not only one of the fundamental sources of theology but it is also the authority in understanding the origin, value, purpose and destiny of the environment. In it human beings find reasons why they have to respect and take care of the environment. Humanity depends on it, and if it is not cared for there are disastrous consequences which can fall on the people as well as the animate and inorganic elements of the environment itself.[238]

In the very first chapter of the Scriptures God instructed Adam and Eve to fill the earth and subdue it. God blessed them and said: "Be fruitful and increase in number; fill the earth and subdue it. Rule over the fish in the sea and the birds in the sky and over every living creature that moves on the ground" (Gen 1:28). This instruction did not give people the freedom to abuse the environment and its resources. The instruction needs to be well understood not only within the context of the book of Genesis but within the entire counsel of the Scriptures. People have a God-given responsibility to take care of the environment. This responsibility is not only because human beings are dependent on the environment, but also for the environment's own sake. Human beings are living in the same universe, on the same planet with the things of the environment and are ultimately dependent on the natural fruits of the earth for life-support. Hence every person has a stake in how elements of the environment and the natural systems are used and managed. People need to understand the value of the environment, develop the moral basis for practical actions for dealing with the environment. The Bible remains the fundamental source in developing the right attitudes and guiding concrete and practical actions in dealing with the things of the environment on which all people depend and which in turn also depend on human beings.

For human beings to accord the elements of the environment the value, respect, care and protection they deserve, one of the basic things was to understand how God looks at these things of the environment and what he teaches about them through the Scriptures. The human responsibility for spiritual and environmental salvation can best be understood following the God-given, inherent and intrinsic

---

[238] Herman Yokoniah Mvula, "Back to the Basics: Caring for Nature is Caring for Ourselves", in *Religion & Culture: A Journal of Religious and Cultural Studies*, Mzuzu University, Issue 2 (April 2015), Mzuzu: Mzuni, 2015, pp. 35-38.

value that is deeply imbedded in the things of the environment. The biblical vision of the elements of the environment is a very fundamental source for human stewardship of and responsibility for the environment. The catechesis on creation is of major importance. It concerns the very foundation of human and Christian life, as it makes explicit the response of the Christian faith to the basic questions that people of all times have asked themselves like: where did everything that has ever existed come from and where is it going? Where did human beings come from and where are they going? What was their origin and what is their end? The question about the origin and the one about the end, are inseparable. They are decisive for the meaning and orientation of people's lives and concrete actions.

The Environment as God's Creation

All that existed did not come to be on their own. It was not the product of any necessity, whatsoever. It was not a product of some blind fate or chance. It was neither a product of accident nor a product of some natural forces and processes. It was not a mere product or effect of the unmoved mover. Since the beginning, the Christian faith has been challenged by the responses to the questions of origins that differed from its own. Ancient religions and cultures produced many myths concerning the origins of the things that existed.[239] Some philosophers have said everything is God, or that the development of the world was the development of God (pantheism). Others said the world was a necessary emanation arising from God and returning to him. Still others affirmed the existence of two eternal principles, Good and Evil, Light and Darkness, locked in permanent conflict (Dualism, Manichaeism). According to some of these ideas, the world which possessed the things in the environment (at least the physical world) was evil, the product of a fall, and thus had to be rejected or left behind (Gnosticism). Some admitted that the world was made by God, but as by a watch-maker who, once he had made a watch, abandons it to itself (Deism), and remains no longer connected or related to it.

---

[239] John Paul II, *The Catechism of the Catholic Church*, Nairobi: Paulines Publications Africa, 1994, p. 96.

Others rejected any transcendent origin of the world but saw it as merely the interplay of matter that had always existed (Materialism). All these attempts bore witness to the permanence and universality of the question of origins. This inquiry is distinctively human.[240]

However, the Christian faith based on the Bible teaches that the universe, the world and the environment are God's creation: "In the beginning God created the heavens and the earth (Gen 1:1)." Therefore, human beings have the duty to take care of the environment basically because it is God's creation and his divine handwork. It is the product of the creative work of a personal God, a God who relates with what he has made. All that existed and exists in the environment has its origin in God. He created everything by his wisdom and love. He created out of nothing and this means that God did not need or use pre-existent material or help in order to create. If God had drawn the world from pre-existent matter, there would have been nothing extraordinary about that. Human artisans make from a given material whatever they want, while God showed his power by starting from nothing to make all he wanted. So, God created out of nothing. The Bible teaches that all that is, seen and unseen, was created by God: "and to make plain to everyone the administration of this mystery, which for ages past was kept hidden in God, who created all things" (Eph 3:9), and "in him all things were created, things in heaven and things on earth, visible and invisible" (Col 1:16). Based on the Scriptures, the Apostles' Creed states that God the Father is creator of heaven and earth, while the Nicene Creed says that he is the creator of all that is, seen and unseen.[241] Creation was the foundation of all God's saving plans, and the beginning of the history of salvation that culminated in Jesus Christ.[242]

---

[240] Vatican Council II, *Nostra Aetate (NA): Declaration of the Relation of the Church to Non-Christian Religions*, no. 2, 1965, pp. 738-742.

[241] John Paul II, *The Catechism of the Catholic Church*, Nairobi: Paulines Publications Africa, 1994, no. 219.

[242] John Paul II, *The Catechism of the Catholic Church*, no. 280.

Although God allows people to utilize elements or things of the environment, he retains ownership of all his creation. Though used mostly by human beings for their life support, they are still God's property. "The earth is the Lord's, and everything in it, the world, and all who live in it" (Ps 24:1). Three things are affirmed in these first words of Scripture: the eternal God gave a beginning to all that existed and exists outside of him; he alone is their creator. The totality of what exists depends on the One who gave it being. They proceeded from God's free will; he wanted to make creatures who share in his being, wisdom and goodness. God created by his free will, wisdom and love. The book of Revelation states: "For you created all things, and by your will they were created and have their being" (4:11b). The Psalmist exclaims in the same vein: "How many are your works, Lord! In wisdom you made them all; the earth is full of your creatures" (104:24), and "The Lord is good to all; he has compassion on all he has made" (145:9). The discoveries about the origins of the world, the dimensions of the cosmos, different forms of life and existence needed to invite human beings to a greater admiration for the greatness of the creator, prompting them to give thanks for all his works, respecting and caring for all that he created. Respect and care for the environment thus needs to develop from this fundamental understanding that it was God's work. It was God who gave human beings unerring knowledge of what existed, to know the structure of the world and the activity of the elements.

The Environment and Humanity Share a Common Origin and a Common Home

After God had created the natural environment he created human beings as the culmination of his creation. Then God said, "Let us make man in our image, in our likeness" (Gen 1:26). Creation in the image of God was not an act of conferring superiority but rather a mission for humankind to take care of the environment like God would have taken care of it as his. The same God who created the other creatures of the universe also created human beings. The environment and human beings are both God's creation. Human beings were put in the garden (the earth) full of elements of the environment. Thus, human beings and the environment, with its elements, share a common home. The earth and the universe are not only home to human beings. They are also home to the things of the environment; animate and inanimate. Therefore, human beings and the environment are to live and exist as neighbours. They are to be good neighbours who care for one another and between whom there is to be mutual dependence. Human beings need to live and exist in a fraternal relationship with the environment.

Thus, a factor that needs to bring about human responsibility for the environment is not only the fact that human beings are highly dependent on the things of the environment for their life-support, but also the fact that human beings share a common origin, a common home and a common destiny with the things of the environment. This sharing of a common origin needs to invite human beings to a sense of fraternity or brotherhood with the things of the environment. They have a common parent, the triune God himself, and a common home (the universe).

The Intrinsic Goodness and Value of the Creation

Another element about God's creation which invites human beings to respect and take care of the environment is the fact about the inherent goodness in all of God's creation. The works of God are ordered and good. Because God created through wisdom, his creation was ordered. God arranged all things by measure and number and weight. God made all creatures to share in his being, wisdom and goodness. Creation proceeded from God's goodness. Because creation came from God's goodness, it shares in that goodness. The creation story in the book of Genesis repeatedly states this goodness that God saw that what he had created was good (Gen 1:4, 10, 12, 18, 21, and 30). Nothing of God's creation as it exists in the environment is bad. The goodness of any being does not depend on how useful and beneficial it is to human beings. It does not lie on its utility to human life and support. It depends on the fact that God created and declared it good.

The qualities of being God's creation and of intrinsic goodness gives the creation great value. There is value in all God's creation, flowing from the goodness of its creator, and this calls for human responsibility for all the elements of the environment. Because God created, he therefore values all of his works of creation. There is a refrain of how God was pleased with what he had created and he found it to be very good. He created it in good order and for a purpose. He sustains all elements and systems in his creation, within particular orders to meet certain ongoing purposes.

The value of creation is also based on the fact that God loved and enjoyed all that he has made. The Psalmist exclaims: "You open your hand and satisfy the desires of every living thing. The Lord is righteous in all his ways and loving toward all he has made" (145:16-17). God places value on his creation as existing in the things and elements of the environment, independent of their utility to human use and human-centered values. This God-centered inherent value of the things of the environment presupposes that there is intrinsic value in everything that exists regardless of how useful or not it is to human beings. The value of a thing does not depend on how it can be used by humans. It exists for its own sake before it can be utilized by human beings.

The value of creation as it exists in the environment does not only lie in the fact that it is God's creation. It also lies on the fact that though God transcends creation, he is present in it. God's creative spirit is present in all of his creation. He is infinitely greater than all his works and he has set his glory above the heavens: "From the lips of children and infants you have ordained praise because of your enemies, to silence the foe and the avenger" (Ps 8:2). God's greatness is unsearchable: "Great is the Lord and most worthy of praise; his greatness no one can fathom" (Ps 145:3). But because he is the free and sovereign creator, the first cause of all that exist, God is present to his creatures' inmost being. Paul in his preaching to the inhabitants of Athens tried to make some links between their philosophical-religious tradition with the new faith he had come to preach and he stated: "For in him we live and move and have our being ... We are his offspring" (Ac 17:28). In the words of St. Augustine of Hippo, God is higher than the highest and more inward than a human being's innermost self. God fills all and is wholly present to all that he filled.[243]

God's Creation is for a Purpose

The creation of God, good and well ordered, was created for a purpose. Scripture and tradition never cease to teach and celebrate the fundamental truth that the world was made for the glory of God. Creation communicates the glory of its maker, God himself. The universe, created in and by the eternal Word (image of the invisible God), was destined for and addressed to human beings, themselves created in the image of God, and called to a personal relationship with God. The human understanding, which shares in the light of the divine intellect, can know what God said by means of his creation as it exists in the environment, though not without great effort and only in a spirit of humility and respect before the creator and his work. "There is no speech or language where their voice is not heard. Their voice goes out into all the earth, their words to the ends of the world" (Ps 19:3-4). In the same vein Job stated how difficult it was for human beings to understand the purposes of things that God created: "Who is this that obscures my counsel without knowledge? Surely, I spoke of things I did not understand, things too wonderful for me to know" (Job 42:3)."

God created all elements of the environment to fit and function in an orderly fashion within interrelated systems to meet certain ongoing purposes. The creative action of God did not end after the original creation described in the first chapter of Genesis. God did not abandon his creatures to themselves. He did not only give them being and existence, but also at every moment, upholds and sustains all things in being, enabling them to act and he brings them to their final end. This means accomplishing his intended order and purpose of all non-living and living elements of the environment and environmental systems. This is what is referred to as *creatio continua*. Recognizing this utter dependence, with respect to the creator, is a source of wisdom and freedom, of joy and confidence. God loves all things that exist and live.

---

[243] Silvano Borruso (trans.), *The Confessions of St. Augustine*, Nairobi: Paulines Publications Africa, 2014, no. 6, p. 11.

He detests none of the things that he has made, for he would not have made anything if he had hated it. How would anything have endured, if he had not willed it? Or how would anything not called forth by him have been preserved? He spared all things, for they all belong to him and are his.

Some of the reasons God created and continued to sustain the elements of the environment are for God himself to love and enjoy. He sustains them for his pleasure. He also sustains them to meet people's needs for things such as food, shelter, and life support. God placed human beings in the world and they would make use of the things in the environment by cultivating and guarding the things in the garden. "I give you every seed-bearing plant on the face of the whole earth and every tree that has fruit with seed in it. They will be yours for food" (Gen 1:29). In the same vein it was also stated: "The Lord God took the man and put him in the Garden of Eden to work it and take care of it" (Gen 2:15). In Genesis 9:1 God blessed Noah and his children and said: "Be fruitful and increase in number and fill the earth."

God did not create the universe only to support human life. The non-human creatures too depend on it. There is interdependence of all creatures and beings in the environment (see Gen 1:30). The natural environment is in so many ways, evidently, the indispensable basis for not only humans' material existence in this world but for the rest of the creatures of God. They all depend on the environment and all are dependent on one another. Therefore, in this kind of atmosphere of interdependence of all creatures there is a great responsibility for human beings to save the environment so that it is able to sustain the life and existence of all of God's creatures.

God also created and sustains his creation for it to glorify and reveal God to people everywhere. "The heavens declare the glory of God; the skies proclaim the work of his hands. Day after day they pour forth speech; night after night they display knowledge. There is no speech or language where their voice is not heard. The voice goes out into all the earth, their words to the ends of the world" (Ps 19:1-4). The scriptures never cease to teach and celebrate the fundamental truth that the world was made for the glory of God.[244] The heavens tell of the glory of God; and the firmament proclaims his handwork. The beauty and wonder of all creation has at all time filled human hearts with admiration and praise, fascination and gratitude. "For since the creation of the world God's invisible qualities—his eternal power and divine nature—have been clearly seen, being understood from what has been made, so that men are without excuse" (Rom 1:20). Mountains and seas, rivers and forests, plants and living creatures are never drying sources of joy and inspiration for human beings. The natural environment offers many values of emotional, spiritual, creative and esthetic nature which greatly enrich human beings.[245] Though this created world proclaims the glory of God it does not mean that God created all things to increase his glory, but to communicate it.[246]

So, God created and sustains all of his creation within particular orders to meet intended purposes. He gave the role to people as caretakers or managers of the elements of the environment and its systems. This is the understanding of dominion (Gen 1:28). People have dominion over the environment in the sense that they have responsibility to take care of it. People are God's creation, and they, too, are under the dominion of God. From the perspective of authority and control people and elements or resources of the environment are in the same class or order; all of creation including people need to submit to God's plans and ways.

The Environment Partakes of the Universal Redemption

Human beings have the responsibility to take care of the environment so that the divine will for the salvation of all the world becomes a reality in the lives of human beings but also in the life and existence of non-human creatures. The elements of the environment share in

---

[244] Dei Filius, Can. 5: DS 3025.

[245] Karl H. Peschke, *Christian Ethics: Morality in the Light of Vatican II*, Alcester: Goodliffe Neale, 1997, p. 745.

[246] St. Bonaventure, In II Sent. 1-2.

universal corruption and redemption through Christ: "For God was pleased to have all his fullness dwell in him, and through him to reconcile to himself all things, whether things on earth or things in heaven, by making peace through his blood, shed on the cross" (Col 1:19-20). All men and women have sinned and fallen short of God's expectations for a righteous life. They are all in need of the forgiveness of God and they require saving faith through a personal relationship with Jesus Christ: "If we claim to be without sin, we deceive ourselves and the truth is not in us. If we confess our sins, he is faithful and just and will forgive us our sins and purify us from all unrighteousness (1 Jn 1:8-9)."

The Bible also teaches that all creation was corrupted by sin. The effects of this universal corruption include not just separation of people from God, but also separation of people from themselves, from each other, and separation of people from the environment. The separation of people from God and the environment is due to the fall of humankind. The destruction of the environment is a consequence of sin. Prior to this fall there was close harmony between God, people and the natural environment. The introduction of sin into the world and its corrupting effects on all of God's created works shattered this harmony. For human beings, forgiveness and saving faith through Jesus Christ assures personal redemption of the believer before God and restoration of relationship and fellowship with God. The Bible teaches that God will also redeem the environment and restore the relationship and harmony between God, people, and the natural environment in the eternal world. God's plan for redeeming the natural environment is reflected in the Creation Covenant stated as follows:

> The creation waits in eager expectation for the sons of God to be revealed. For the creation was subjected to frustration, not by its own choice, but by the will of the one who subjected it, in hope that the creation itself will be liberated from bondage to decay and brought into the glorious freedom of the children of God. We know that the whole creation has been groaning as in pains of childbirth right up to the present time. Not only so, but we ourselves, who have the fruits of the Spirit, groan inwardly as we

wait eagerly for our adoption as sons, the redemption of our bodies (Rom 8:19-23).

The creation covenant is God's promise to redeem, restore, and renew the physical world including the environment in the new heaven and earth that he will create when the earth that human beings call home now, no longer exists. Peter states: "But in keeping with his promise, we are looking forward to a new heaven and a new earth, the home of righteousness" (2 Pet 3:13). Revelation 21:1 cements the same insight: "Then I saw a new heaven and a new earth, for the first heaven and the first earth had passed away, and there was no longer any sea." Such biblical evidence means that the physical environment is not destined for eternal destruction when the world comes to an end with Christ's return. The environment will also be redeemed and renewed.

In the new heaven and the new earth, the environment will also be restored to its pre-fall magnificence and perfection. Both people and the natural environment will be freed from the sufferings caused by the imperfections of the world we live in, including death and decay. This does not need to come as strange for in the Scriptures God was able to establish covenants or promises that even incorporated the natural environment. God said to Noah and his children: "I now establish my covenant with you and with your descendants after you and with every living creature that was with you—the birds, the livestock and all the wild animals, all those that came out of the ark with you—every living creature on earth" (Gen 9:9-10). The covenant clearly includes plants, animals and every living and existing creature on earth. So, it is clear that the Bible has precedents of God establishing covenants or promises that incorporated the elements of nature. In the new heaven and the new earth that God will one day create, in addition to the resurrection of the body, the environment will also be renewed. The mode of existence and renewal of creation in eternity is a mystery to the human mind.

It is, however, very important to avoid extreme positions in understanding the true picture of the environment when there is talk of its value and glorious destiny. One such extreme position that needs to be avoided on the value and importance of the physical world and nature as it exists in environment is that of improperly elevating the status of the elements of the environment to being equal or even above people, the so called deep ecology. The Bible teaches that although God values the elements of the environment and their systems, he placed a special higher value on people whom he crowned with glory and honour as the climax of his creation (Gen 1:26). Psalm 8:3-6, too, speaks about human dignity as it speaks of God's glory. This higher value that God placed on human beings is not only a gift but also a calling (vocation) and duty to take care of the things in the environment on which they depend in a spirit of interrelatedness.

Biblical Evidence for the Spiritual and Environmental Salvation

The created world as it exists in the environment, with its elements and systems, is not as simple as it appears in human eyes. It has a destiny in the sense of a glorious fulfillment. Creation does not only have value, a respectful beginning, as having been founded in the creator God, but it also has a glorious destiny. There is a promised future and hope reserved for creation. Paul the Apostle states that the whole creation has been groaning as in labour waiting with eager longing for liberation from the slavery to corruption and to be brought into the same glorious freedom of the children of God (Rom 8:22). Creation has hope of redemption, salvation and consummation. The destiny is the consummation of creation into the divine being of God from which it originated. Human beings have a moral responsibility to contribute towards the achievement and realization of God's own purpose for nature and the world. There is going to be recapitalization of everything in Christ. This is the destiny or glory of every creature that they will be reunited to God through Christ as the Gospel of John states: "But I, when I am lifted up from the earth, will draw all men to myself" (Jn 12:32).

One of the challenges that faces the Church today is that very few look at the elements of the environment as waiting in hope for redemption too. The understanding of salvation and redemption is too anthropocentric. The mission of the Church has concentrated on the redemption of human beings. The concept of the cosmic eschatology has not been well articulated and propagated to the people to develop a genuine sense of respect, care and protection of the elements of the environment and its systems. The majority of the people are only familiar with the concept of personal or individual salvation. The vocation and destiny of nature is not familiar to the Christians of the Archdiocese of Lilongwe.

The concept of cosmic eschatology or the theological concept of the redemption of the universe needs to be developed in the Church. The discussion of eschatology requires it to be universal, that is, all-reality embracing, not that which separates soul from the body, individual from the community, human history from the environment. The non-human part of God's creation needs to be taken seriously because the creator had a reason in the very beginning for the whole of creation, and a reason which he will see that it is fulfilled. The concept, discussion and evangelization of eschatology needs not be dominated by anthropomorphism. The coming of God into the world, the incarnation and the Parousia, have this non-anthropocentric sense of eschatology. They deal with the personal eschatology (eternal life for the believer), historical eschatology (the establishment of the kingdom of God), and the cosmic eschatology (the establishment of the new heaven and the new earth). These aspects are to be integrated by seeing eschatology as Theo-centric, modeled on the incarnation of a God who came to dwell in his whole creation. It is centered on God in his Trinitarian nature. This eschatology of the whole universe is necessary because it first of all contains the doctrine of creation. It accommodates the element of the understanding that the totality of creation, not only humanity and the earth, were created by God, but that they all have God as the source of their beginning through the act of creation. It is important because it puts emphasis on the unity and consistency of God's relationship to creation which requires that the new creation will be all encompassing and all things will be restored to their beginning.[247] The universal eschatology, in contrast to the personal eschatology which has been overemphasized, stresses the

---

[247] Jürgen Moltmann, *God in Creation*, 1996, pp. 255, 267-270.

interconnectedness of all things. All things in the universe, whether people are aware or not, depend on one another for survival.

Humans cannot be humans without the body, without the community, and further more without living in and depending on creation and the environment. All beings are interdependent and interconnected. All beings in the universe are dependent on each other. Even human life is dependent on the future conditions of the physical universe and the entire universe consequently needs to be included in the total picture of the treatise of redemption. This understanding needs to logically arrive at the conclusion that there is no redemption of humanity without the redemption of the environment. Human beings must recognize their being liberated in the context of their existence in the environment in the universe. While Moltmann, in his theology of creation, laid emphasis on an earth-bound eschatology,[248] I believe that the whole universe, thus far discovered and the part of it not yet discovered by humanity, is included in this realization of redemption. Hence it has to be understood in the sense of the universe bound eschatology. Neither the redemption of the world nor creation must be understood in the sense of the earth and its atmosphere but the whole universe which is a product of God's creative act. There is need for the rediscovery of this theology of the redemption of the totality of creation, universal eschatology, and this can spur the Church, local and universal, to further respect, care and protect the environment. Eschatology has to go beyond personal salvation and embrace the whole cosmos as creation that is also a beneficiary of the salvific works of Jesus Christ.

In such a context of the universal eschatology there is then the necessity of defining the proper vocation of humanity without which it will seem to render humanity irrelevant. Human beings are not irrelevant at all in this universal eschatology. They have a special vocation to answer to because of their capabilities and faculties of emotion, will and intelligence. They have to use these capabilities to make sure that the intentions of God in saving the whole world and

---

[248] Jürgen Moltmann, *God in Creation*, p. 260.

unite all things to himself are fulfilled. Thus, the human beings have a priestly vocation in respect to the redemption of all nature or creation. People are the agents for the redemption of the cosmos, not the sole purpose or beneficiary of its redemption.

There is a distinction to be made between eschatology of the individual, the human race and of the entire universe. The eschatology of the individual sets out from the doctrine of personal immortality which entails a certain form of survival after death. The rest of creation will be reunited with their creator through the divine recapitulation. There is going to be consummation of all things into God through Christ but their existence will possibly not be like individual entities of being enjoyed in this world. However, it is a mystery that is not easy to grasp how these things of nature will exist in God at their consummation. It is something that requires belief because the Scriptures have a lot of mention of the physical universe sharing in the general consummation. The Second Petrine letter states in this vein that: "But in keeping with his promise we are looking for new a heaven and a new earth, the home of righteousness (2 Pet 3:13), and this is in agreement to what Paul said about the future glory for all creation that: "The creation itself will be liberated from its bondage to decay and brought into the glorious freedom and of the children of God" (Rom 8:21). The last but one chapter of the Scripture begins with this vision of the future glory of all of creation: "Then I saw a new heaven and a new earth, for the first heaven and the first earth had passed away, and there was no longer any sea" (Rev 21:1).

Cosmic eschatology does not receive the much-needed attention in the evangelization task of the church as well as in Christology and theology as a whole. In Catholic theology and in the evangelization task in the Archdiocese of Lilongwe there is domination of individual or personal eschatology with its concern on death, judgment, heaven, (with purgatory as the intermediate state), and hell.[249] The redemption

---

[249] Many Christians in the Archdiocese of Lilongwe do not think and believe there will be redemption of the things of nature and the environment. The majority of them think and say salvation and redemption in Christ is only a privilege of humanity; thus, the catechesis has concentrated on the

of creation follows the corruption of creation. The origin and consequent actual sin impacted on the whole of creation, not only humans. However, many of the Christians in the Archdiocese of Lilongwe are very much at ease to say that the Fall of Adam has disastrous effects on humanity and the most evident symbol of these devastation is death, human death. But it is not only humanity which was affected by the sin of Adam and Eve. The environment too was damaged by sin and it continues to suffer the consequences of the evil of humanity.[250] It too waits for the transformation of the rest of creation by a divine act, the reversal of the damage caused by sin. God the Father reconciled the whole fallen world through the death of his Son and renewed it into a kingdom of God by spirit. The concepts of creation, sin or fallenness, reconciliation, renewal, the kingdom of God apply to the whole cosmos and not only to human beings. Since creation is real and very good, and the fall impacted all areas of God's creation, it should not be surprising that redemption is applied to all areas of God's creation as well.

It is the focus on individual redemption (which of course is foundational) in evangelization and in theology which has overshadowed the cosmic or universal redemption. Certainly, humans do not need to minimize God's works in human life. But they at the same time need not miss the reality and extent of Christ's work of redemption. It is high time human beings and Christians in the Archdiocese f Lilongwe realize this glorious destiny of the rest of creation which will be summed up in God through Christ. The book of Acts states about the cosmic redemption as contained in Peter's message in the temple: "He must remain in heaven until the time comes for God to restore everything, as he promised long ago through his holy prophets" (3:21). Paul, in his letter to the Colossians, states that this redemption of the

---

redemption of human beings through Christ and not necessarily of the whole of God's creation.

[250] The effects of the Fall of Adam and Eve are not difficult to grasp as there is for the Christians in the Archdiocese of Lilongwe very evident clue that the presence of evil, in the sense of the deprivation of the good, in this world must have its starting point.

whole of creation is an effect of the redemptive work of Christ on the cross: "And through him to reconcile to himself all things, whether things on earth or things in heaven, by making peace through his blood, shed on the cross" (Col 1:20).

This heaven and earth, in which the city of God is bridal imagery, recalls the Church in the place where God makes his home with humanity and lives among them, present in his fullness to creation and making all things new. Prophet Isaiah talks about the ecclesiological fulfillment characterized by peace between God and all of his creation. The biggest characteristic of the Kingdom of God is peace between God and his creation, and creation with one another: "The wolf will live with the lamb, the leopard shall lie down with the goat, the calf and the lion and the yearling together; and a little child will lead them. The will feed with the bear, their young will lie down together, and the lion will eat straw like the ox" (Isa 11:6-7). The church has to be seen as a vessel through which the incarnate works of God in Christ come to fruition, not only for humanity, but also through humanity for the rest of the cosmos.

The fall of Adam, whose effect not only affected and corrupted human beings but also the rest of nature, represents a failure of potential to unite creature and creator. This failure is redeemed ultimately in Jesus Christ and the whole of creation is included in the divine plan of salvation for the entire world. All creatures praised the lord: "And again they shouted: Hallelujah! The smoke from her goes up forever and ever. The twenty-four elders and the four living creatures fell down and worshipped God, who was seated on the throne. And they cried: Amen, Hallelujah!" (Rev 19:3-4). As the creatures share in praising God, they will also share in his ultimate life by being what it is called to be with order and purpose. The Pauline corpus is also awash with examples that nature in its existence also praises God and will also share in the ultimate life. In the first chapter of the letter to the Ephesians Paul presents a canticle praising God who is the Saviour of all creatures. The redemption of all creation is a plan which God, in his wisdom and insight, had purposed. He had made known this secret plan which he decided to complete by means of Christ: "To be put into effect when the times reach their fulfillment—to bring unity to all things in heaven and on earth under Christ" (Eph 1:10). Further, in his letter to the Colossians Paul presents a canticle that depicts Jesus Christ, the Son of the invisible God, as "the first born of all creation" (Col 1:15), and the first born from the dead. The resurrection of Jesus Christ had the effect of resurrecting the fallen creation.

Thus, there is need to return to the common usage of the word creation in reference to all beings (human and non-human) which came from God by a process of creation. Redemption has both an earthly and cosmic scope in Christ. In this the human being has a priestly (vicarious) role to play in the concretization of the redemption of nature. It is only when humanity is fully redeemed, when the priestly role is realized in its eschatological fullness that the New Creation will arrive. Scripture describes this as: "He will wipe every tear from their eyes. There will be no more death or mourning or crying of pain, for the old order of things has passed away" (Rev 21:4).

The inclusion of the natural environment in the divine plan of salvation and redemption has then to propel the faithful of Christ in the Archdiocese of Lilongwe to engage in the mission of the evangelization of the environment, bringing the good news to the creation of God. Creation has to receive, as it were, the good news that gave life not only to human beings but also to the rest of the environment. Evangelization of all creation and the ecclesial practice towards the saving of the environment are areas that need to be more developed in the ecclesial life and practice of the Archdiocese of Lilongwe.

The Theology of the Church of the Care of the Environment

One of the great personalities who understood this concept of the brotherhood with the natural environment and sense of neighbourhood with the environment and deserves mention was St. Francis of Assisi. He lived his understanding of human common origin with the natural environment in very concrete actions. He had a very concrete understanding and feeling of brotherhood with the things of the environment. Francis of Assisi (1182-1226) was an Italian Roman Catholic friar and preacher who lived in the middle ages. His concrete actions in his time showed his belief concerning the proper relationship that human beings needed to have with the things of the environment. His beliefs had their antecedents in the sacred scripture. There were however other environmental ideas and practices which appeared to be very original of him like nature mysticism and contemplation, and his extension of almsgiving to the non-human creatures.[251] He believed that the environment was the mirror of God. By this he meant that if humanity wanted to know God and his greatness the elements of the environment and its systems were capable of revealing that. With this he also meant that God spoke and communicated to human beings, among other means, through the things of the environment. He was filled with a deep sense of respect for the environment and had the belief that, with the common origin between human beings and other creatures, there was fraternity between people and the rest of creation. In this vein he called all creatures either as humanity's brothers or humanity's sisters. He even extended his preaching of peace and reconciliation to the animals like birds, dogs and wolves. The long history of ascetical life which he had joined to live was interpreted by him as a form of re-creation of the paradise which had been lost with the sin and fall of humanity, which now was to be symbolized by the peace and reconciliation of humanity with God and the rest of creation. He composed a canticle in which he preached how creation, as it exists in the environment, praises God and through the natural environment humanity can praise God, their maker. In stressing the common parentage, he addressed the things of the environment as brother or as sister. This is the Canticle of the Creatures and it flows like this:

> Most high, all powerful good Lord, all praise be yours, yours be the glory, and honour, and all blessing. To you alone most high, do they belong, and no human is worthy to mention your name.
>
> Praise be yours, my Lord, with all your creatures, especially Sir Brother Sun, who is the day and through whom you give us light.

---

[251] Roger D. Sorrell, *St. Francis of Assisi and Nature: Tradition and Innovation in Western Christian Attitudes Toward the Environment*, Oxford: OUP, 1988, pp. 1-134.

And he is beautiful and radiant with great splendor; and bears a likeness to you, most high One.

Praise be to you, my Lord, through Sister Moon and the sisters in heaven, you formed them clear, and precious and beautiful.

Praise be you, my Lord, through Brothers Wind and Air, and through air, cloudy and serene, and every kind of weather, through whom you give sustenance to your creatures.

Praise be you, my Lord, through Sister Water, so useful, humble, precious and pure. All praise be yours, my Lord, through Brother Fire, through whom you brighten up the night. How beautiful is he, how cheerful! Full of power and strength!

All praise be yours, my Lord, through our Sister, Mother Earth, who sustains us and governs us, and produces various fruits with coloured flowers and herbs.

All praise be yours, my Lord, through those who grant pardon for love of you, through those who endure sickness and trial. Happy are those who endure in peace, by you, most high, the will be crowned.

All praise be your, my Lord, through Sister Death, from whose embrace no mortal can escape. Woe to those who die in mortal sin! Happy those she finds doing your will! The second death can do them no harm.

Praise and bless my Lord and give him thanks and serve him with great humility.[252]

Thus, with his sense of universal fraternity and closeness to the elements of the environment, Francis of Assisi in this canticle called nature by human adjectives like Sister Moon, Wind and Water, and Brother Sun.[253] In his life as he experienced sickness and the stigmata that he received he called his illnesses his sisters. He had a deep sense

---

[252] www.appleseeds.org/canticle.htm/ [26.10.2015].

[253] www.en.wikipedia.org/wiki/Francis_of_Assisi/ [26.10.2015].

of brotherhood with all of God's creation. He considered himself not to be a friend of Jesus Christ if he did not cherish those for whom he died. Jesus Christ did not only die for human beings but for all of creation to heal it from the effects of the fall. He preached the teaching of the Catholic Church that the world that God created was good. But he went to say that creation concretely suffers a need for redemption because of the primordial sin of humanity. For him he wanted all humanity to believe that Jesus Christ died for all creation that they might enjoy being reconciled and at peace with God and attain their full nature again. Just as he preached to humanity and the non-human creation the universal ability and duty of all creatures to praise God, he also preached the rest of nature was called to redemption in Christ Jesus. He preached that there was a very special duty for men and women to protect and enjoy the environment as both stewards of God's creation and as creatures themselves. In this perspective he was against the philosophical and religious idea of the *scala naturae* which had separated humanity from the rest of nature. It was on this account that Pope John Paul II, on 29 November 1979, declared Francis of Assisi as the patron saint of Ecology in the Catholic Church because he had a great love for animals, the environment and indeed the rest of nature.[254] John Paul II often times in his pontificate reminded the Church in the world to take care of the environment following the example of Francis and that is why he was called by others as the Green Pope. During the commemoration of the World Environment Day in 1982 he said:

> Francis' love and care for creation was a challenge for contemporary Catholics and a reminder not to behave like dissident predators where nature is concerned, but to assume responsibility for it, taking all care so that everything stays healthy and integrated, so as to offer a welcoming and friendly environment even to those who succeed us.[255]

---

[254] John Paul II, *Inter Sanctos (Apostolic Letter AAS 71)*, November 29, 1979.
[255] www.w2.vatican.va/peace/documents/ [22.11.2015].

On the commemoration of the World Day for Peace on 1 January 1990, John Paul II said that the saint of Assisi, Francis, offered Christians an example of genuine and deep respect for the integrity of creation. Nature too honoured and praised God and hence all people were to be inspired by Francis of Assisi to keep alive in them a sense of fraternity with all of those good and beautiful things which God Almighty had created.[256] In this reflection he said that the lack for peace in the world was not only among humans. There was also lack of peace between humanity and the environment due to human activity.

Benedict of Nursia (480 – 547), regarded as the father and founder of western monasticism, taught about this purpose of God's creation. He said that through the things of the environment human beings could reach the knowledge of God. In the set of values deeply imbedded in the Benedictine Rule of Life there was the exhortation that the monks and nuns had to be aware of the presence of God in all things.[257] The nuns, monks and all Christians were to be aware of the divine presence in everything. Benedict exhorted the monks and nuns, and so all the Christians, to look for God in the ordinary things and events of each day. For him the realities of the environment and happenings of this world were means of getting closer to the knowledge of God. Without going to the extreme of pantheism, he taught of the immanence of God in all creation. Benedict also taught his followers and consequently desired the entire church to be aware of the dignity of work. He taught that a monk should not seek to live on begging but to live by the labour of their hands. They were to work not only to live but to appreciate the value of God's creation as it exists in the environment as well as its purpose. He developed a spirituality of work amidst a temptation in the world of his time to lofty life styles of seeking enjoyment and of looking at work as demeaning. In his spirituality of work, human activity of work was viewed as participation in the creative action of God, and from the human perspective to work was a divine activity assisting in sustaining

---

[256] John Paul II, (December 8, 1989), World Day for Peace Message of 1990.
[257] Rule of Benedict 19.1.

creation's order and purpose. This developed into his famous saying that "to work is to pray" (Latin, *laborare est orare*).[258]

The theology of the Church taught that the environment, being God's creation, deserved respect, love and care. Bonaventure (1217-1274), an Italian Franciscan friar, an accomplished philosopher and theologian, contributed to the development of a clear philosophy and theology of the environment that stood out among his contemporaries. It was a theology that promoted respect, care, protection and love of the environment because it is God's creation, fashioned with order and purpose, and deeply imbedded with inherent value. As Bonaventure went through his scholastic formation he felt called to fit into the love of creation and environmental spirituality of Francis of Assisi and into the Medieval Scholastic thought. It could be said that he Aristotelianized, philosophized and theologized the Franciscan spirituality of the environment. His theology was marked by deep and profound integration of faith and reason.

Bonaventure and Thomas Aquinas (an Italian Dominican) were 13th century colleagues, philosophy and theology giants at the University of Paris, France. They developed an extraordinary creation theology by the resources of faith and reason. In relation to nature they developed an understanding of Christ as the Incarnate Word, the concept of the Cosmic Christ (Christ being present in all of God's creation), and the understanding that Christ suffered along with the suffering world. The human being was part and parcel of the environment. They recovered a wholistic understanding of God, humanity and creation from some dualistic philosophies of the past which had separated humanity from the environment.[259]

The physical world that held all sensible things was designed for a purpose. In this physical world exist things which are signs that ultimately direct human beings to the divine art and wisdom. Through this wisdom all things have been made. The things that were seen in

---

[258] Benedictine Rule 48.1.

[259] Dawn Nothwehr OSF, *The Earth is the Lord's: Catholic Theology of Creation, Ecology and the Environment*, pp. 1 – 116.

the environment were real and not simply shadows. They were at the same time properties which pointed to God in some type of causality. All creatures had properties which pointed to God as a triple cause (efficient, formal and final). All creatures, from inanimate objects to angels, were signs and traces of God, for they all bore a relation of causal dependency upon God as their source.

The environment was very important as it was and still is home to God's creation. God was revealed through his creation. All creation was good and it was relational in character. All life and existence originated in God. Through him all finite reality found expression in the time and space of the created order. The ultimate destiny of all reality was their return to God. Bonaventure described the action of the incarnation of Jesus Christ as central to the manifestation of God's love for the world. Such was the metaphysical center that led all reality back and this was the sum total of nature's metaphysics. The metaphysics of nature was concerned with emanation, exemplarity, and consummation. Being was like illumination through spiritual radiations and returned to the Supreme Being. With emanation it meant that everything flowed from the Father, and exemplarity meant the conviction that all of the created reality was grounded in the divine archetypical reality, while consummation was the conviction, which he held, that all created reality ultimately returned to God. Thus, God is the origin, sustainer, and consummation of all created reality.[260] Such a concept of the created order (the environment) by Bonaventure stressed the divine origin or creation of all natural things, continued creative activity (*creatio continua*), and a divine destiny of all finite beings through their return to the infinite divine source. It was a profound picture of reality that respected the environmental created order and its purpose.

John Duns Scotus (1265 – 1308) was generally considered to be one of the three most important and influential philosopher-theologians of

---

[260] Zachary Hayes OFM, *The Cosmos, a Symbol of the Divine*, In *Franciscan Theology of the Environment: An Introductory Reader*, edited by Dawn M. Nothwehr, Illinois: Franciscan Press, 2003, p. 95.

the high Middle Ages. He was born in the county of Berwick, Kingdom of Scotland in 1265 and died in Cologne, Germany, on 8 November 1308. He was a Franciscan friar whose main interests were in metaphysics, theology, logic, epistemology and ethics.[261] He agreed with Bonaventure that the natural environment was very important because through it human beings were able to reach the knowledge of the existence of God. He said that all knowledge of God started from creatures. He developed an argument of the existence of God through which medieval philosophers and theologians called *quia argument* which meant from effect to cause. Knowledge of God started by and through creatures.

He was best known for his nature related philosophical doctrines which revealed the greatness of nature to command respect and care from humans. One of such doctrines was the 'univocity of being.' With this he argued that existence was the most abstract of the concepts that were there and which were applicable to everything that existed. Through this doctrine he denied any real distinction between essence and existence in finite beings. It was only in the infinite, God, where essence and existence could realistically be distinguished. He also developed the doctrine of 'formal distinction' as a way of distinguishing between aspects of the same things, and the doctrine of 'haecceity' with which he ascertained that in every being of nature there was a property that was supposed to be in each individual thing that made it an individual, different from this or that. This marked the beginnings of the principle of individuation. Such discussions on the nature of being were to imply respect of every being and respect accorded to every individual being for what it is as different from the other.

Other than the Franciscans, the Jesuits too had shown depth of interest in shaping the theology of the environment which had endeavoured to restore the human – natural environmental relationship. One influential Jesuit in this discipline was Pierre Teilhard de Chardin (1881-1955). He believed and taught that there was the

---

[261] www.wikipedia/wiki/Duns_Scotus/ [22.11.2016].

presence of God in all the things he had created. During his life time most of his works were not liked by the ecclesiastical officials and he was greatly censored by the Vatican. His view of creation as a living host or Eucharist species brought him into trouble with the ecclesiastical officials mostly because he was not understood within the context. However, the stand of the ecclesiastical officials had over time changed. Recently he was acknowledged for his contribution to the theology of creation by Pope Benedict VXI, who made extensive studies on him as a young theologian and later on as pope. He made references to him on many occasions too. Pope Francis also noted Teilhard's contribution to theology of the environment and its eschatological glorification in the encyclical that he published in May 2015 called *Laudato Si* which was on the care of the environment, humankind's common home.[262]

Teilhard's view of the cosmos was not of it as a finished building or a stationery container. He understood the cosmos as creation that was moving in history and itself was history. The cosmos was itself a movement which was moving from one beginning to one end. Creation was history. Teilhard liked to meditate on the Eucharist as the first fruits of the new creation. He viewed nature as it is in the cosmos as guiding towards the understanding of God but itself bearing the presence of God in the way Christ was present in the Eucharistic host. He identified the connection between the Eucharist, as the presence of Christ, and the glory of the cosmos as revealing God's presence. The final glorification of the cosmos lay in the fact that it too would be drawn back to the owner at the end of time. Human beings were existentially and even organically part of the environment and in their corporeality, they would be drawn back to their origin: "'But I, when I am lifted up from the earth, will draw all men to myself.' He said this to show the kind of death he was going to die'" (Jn 12:32-33).[263]

---

[262] Pope Francis, *Laudato Si: Encyclical Letter on the Care for our Common Home*, p. 61.
[263] www.en.wikipedia.org/wiki/Pierre_Teilhard_de_Chardin/ [3.12.2015].

The theology of the Church on the environment held that the plight, destruction and degradation of the environment and its resources were not a consequence of the biblical message. The Church however held that it was fundamentally and ultimately a result, effect or consequence of sin, as the separation of human beings from God. The primordial peace that reigned in the Garden of Eden came to an end when as a result of sin God pronounced judgment: "And I will put enmity between you and the woman, and between your offspring and hers; he will crush your head, and you will strike his heel" (Gen 3:15). Hatred, enmity, degradation and destruction of the environment did not mean that all those who continued to call themselves Christians displayed correct attitudes in dealing with nature. They too often have proved insufficiently acquainted with the true spirit of the biblical message and have been susceptible to the secularizing tendencies in society over the centuries of Christianity's existence. There was hence a need for a rediscovery of the theology of the care of the environment, based on the Bible, which had to guide the attitude and conduct of the Church and the world at large regarding the natural environment.[264]

The Church held that the human being was God's likeness not because they had the appearance of God. The likeness consisted in this that the human beings were representatives of God, who represented him to whatever existed and lived beside them on earth and in the entire universe. The inherent value, sustained order and purpose that were embodied in God's creation, from the biblical perspective, implied that human beings needed to respect and value the environment. They had the role of being caretakers or managers of the environment. The world and the entire universe were like God's household. Human beings were placed as stewards in charge of God's property. After God had created human beings in his own image, he put them in charge of the fish, the birds, and all wild animals, and indeed in charge of the whole of the environment (Gen 1:28). The people were hence to practice good stewardship over the environment.

---

[264] Karl H. Peschke, *Christian Ethics: Moral Theology in the Light of Vatican II*, Alcester: Goodliffe Neale, 1997, p. 748.

The words steward and stewardship are used, alluded to and implied in many examples in the Bible. Eliezer of Damascus was the steward of Abram's household. In the conversation about God's covenant with Abram there is the promise of the child. Not understanding what the Lord had in store for him Abram answered: "Sovereign Lord, what can you give me since I remain childless and the one who will inherit my estate is Eliezer of Damascus?" (Gen 15:2) While Joseph was in Egypt he rose to the rank of prime minister. He had a steward, a servant, in charge of his house. When his brothers from Canaan came to Egypt in search for food Joseph commanded the steward in charge of his house: "Fill the men's sacks with as much food as they can carry and put each man's silver in the mouth of his sack" (Gen 44:1b). When David made the decision to build a permanent home for the Covenant Box, he assembled all the leading men in Jerusalem and among them were the supervisors of the king's property: "David summoned all the officials of Israel to assemble at Jerusalem: the officers over the tribes, the commanders of the divisions in the service of the king, the commanders of thousands and commanders of hundreds, and the officials in charge of all the property and livestock belonging to the king and his sons, together with the palace officials, the mighty men and all the brave warriors" (1 Chr 28:1). The supervisors and officials in charge of the king's property were in fact the stewards of his property. In Jesus' parable of the workers in the vineyard hired at different times, a steward is alluded to in the person of the foreman who was told by the owner to pay the workers. "When evening came, the owner of the vineyard said to his foreman: 'Call the workers and pay them their wages, beginning with the last ones hired and going on to the first'" (Mt 20:8). Jesus in the Lucan gospel's parable of the watchful servants spoke of the need for Christians to keep watchful for the day of the Lord as servants. When Peter asked about the meaning of this parable, "The Lord answered: 'Who then is the faithful and wise manager, whom the master puts in charge of his servants to give them their food allowance at the proper time?'" (Lk 12:42). In the parable of the shrewd manager, Jesus said to his disciples: "There was a rich man whose manager was accused of wasting his possessions. So, he called him in and asked him, 'What is this I hear about you? Give an account of your management, because you cannot be manager any longer'" (Lk

16:1-2). St. Paul, preaching on the nature of true apostleship, exhorted the Corinthians to regard apostles of Christ as servants in the sense of stewards. He said: "So then, men ought to regard us as servants of Christ and as those entrusted with the secret things of God. Now it is required that those who have been given a trust must prove faithful" (1 Cor 4:1-2). So, the word steward could be interpreted as manager, caretaker, foreman, supervisor, one in charge of a household, or servant. In the Bible it refers to a person who is put in charge of taking care of something that does not belong to them. This is consistent with the Webster's Dictionary definition of a steward as one employed in a large household or estate to manage domestic concerns and property of another person.[265]

Human beings are to behave as stewards of the natural environment. The whole of creation is God's property. As such human beings were appointed by God to manage the domestic environmental concerns of the earth, their common home, and indeed of the entire universe. This role requires being faithful, wise and responsible. The steward needs to be concerned with meeting the daily needs of the household, he is not to abuse, exploit, or waste what they have been put in charge of managing. The steward needs to solve the problems of the household, maintain self-control, and follow the household or estate owner's wishes and instructions with respect to use and management of what had been entrusted to their care. The biblical texts which mandate the human beings to fill the earth and subdue it and have dominion over every living thing that moves upon the earth are to be understood in the sense of not the task of a master, but the task of a deputy, manager, servant, foreman or caretaker. As caretakers of the property of God human beings have the task to work on it and keep it. The land belongs to God, he cares for it and his eyes are upon it from the beginning of the year to the end. The book of Deuteronomy states: "It is a land the Lord your God cares for; the eyes of the Lord your God are continually on it from the beginning of the year to its end" (Dt 11:12). The human beings are not to pollute the land and environment in which they live. The book of Numbers exhorts human beings not to

---

[265] www.definition/steward/Merriam-Webster/dictionary/ [11.9.2016].

defile the land: "Do not defile the land where you live and where I dwell, for I, the Lord, dwell among the Israelites" (Nu 35:34). Human beings have to take care of the water and aquatic life for the sea is God's, he made it, and it is him too who formed the dry land. The Psalmist exclaims: "Come, let us sing for joy to the Lord. In his hand are the depths of the earth, and the mountain peaks belong to him. The sea is his, for he made it, and his hands formed the dry land" (Ps 95:1a, 4-5).

This right understanding of the responsibility of the human being over creation regards man-woman's dominion over creation as a charge to rule the world in holiness and righteousness and pronounce judgment in uprightness of soul. By his wisdom God made the human race to rule his creation, to govern the world with holiness, and to administer justice upon it with integrity. Therefore, in virtue of this assignment the human being is not to become an uncontrolled and unrestricted sovereign, who can do with nature and creation whatever they want. The earth and the entire universe is not the property of man and woman, so they can exploit it autocratically. Creation is and remains the creation of God. The human person is only the mandatory of God, to whom the dominion was merely entrusted in a vicarious (representative or deputy) way.

This theology of the Church regarding nature and the environment, however, stood different from the experience of the people in the Archdiocese of Lilongwe many of whom looked at nature as a mere source of raw material for their sustenance, survival and personal advancement. The common conception was that the world was created for man and woman and that was important only in the sense of its utility to the needs of humans. Human beings thought of themselves as above the realm of the natural environment and consequently its masters.[266]

The second chapter of the book of Genesis speaks of the Garden of Eden which God planted for human beings to till and keep. The fruits of all trees were at their disposal to serve them as their food. Only

---

[266] Int Matthew Sitolo, Mpherere, 4.5.2016.

from the tree of knowledge of good and evil they were not allowed to eat. This expresses the truth that God, the giver of all life and all its requirements and necessities, is the one who alone knows what is good for human beings. The values and purposes of human existence are not autonomous creations and decisions of man and woman. These have been implanted in reality by the superior wisdom of the creator. Unfortunately, the human beings did not remain close to God's guiding hand. Instead they pursued the delusion that they could know good and evil by themselves. The third chapter of the book of Genesis speaks of how human beings disobeyed the will and designs of God and ate from the forbidden tree. Human beings, living in the presence of God, sinned. The Catechism of the Catholic Church calls this disobedience the fall.[267] This disobedience brought curse, conflict and suffering not only on themselves but on all the creatures. Other books of the first testament share the same conviction that man-woman's sin and pride had detrimental and hazardous consequences for the whole of creation, although the immediate cause was not seen in the abusive exploitation of nature and creation but rather in people's disobedience and unfaithfulness towards God. The sin of humanity affected the environment. Prophet Joel states: "The fields are ruined, the ground is dried up; the grain is destroyed, the new wine is dried up, the oil fails" (1:10). The Prophet Amos also spoke about how the sin of humanity affected the environment as the sovereign Lord said: "I gave you empty stomachs in every city and lack of bread in every town, yet you have not returned to me. I also withheld rain from you when the harvest was still three months away. I sent rain on one town but withheld it from another. One field had rain; another had none and dried up (Am 4:6-7)." In the same vein prophet Hosea says: "There is only cursing, lying and murder, stealing and adultery; they break all bounds, and bloodshed follows bloodshed. Because of this the land dries up, and all who live in it waste away; the beasts of the field, the birds in the sky and the fish in the sea are swept away" (4:2-3). The sin of humanity affected the rest of creation.

---

[267] John Paul II, *The Catechism of the Catholic Church*, Nairobi: Paulines Publications Africa, 1994, no. 386-412.

Because of human sin, creation suffered too. The Prophet Isaiah states: "The earth dries up and withers, the world languishes and withers, the exalted of the earth languish. The earth is defiled by its people; they have disobeyed the laws, violated the statutes and broken the everlasting covenant" (24:4-5). The Church, basing itself on the Bible, thus held that the sin of man and woman affected creation. And ultimately the exploitation, degradation and destruction of nature and creation were results of sin.[268]

The Church holds that the sin or disobedience of man and woman is not the only thing that affected creation. The blessings which were called forth by the human being's faithfulness were also shared by the earth and all living creatures, the universe and all that existed. When humanity was faithful there would be peace and fecundity on the earth: "For you will have a covenant with the stones of the field, and the wild animals will be at peace with you" (Job 5:23). Environmental blessings would accompany obedience to the law as the book of Leviticus attested to: "If you follow my decrees and are careful to obey my commands, I will send you rain in its season, and the ground will yield its crops and the trees of the field their fruit. Your threshing will continue until grape harvest and the grape harvest will continue until planting, and you will eat all the food you want and live in safety in your land" (Lev 26:3-6). This blessing for obedience is even true of God's salvific action, especially at the end of time when joy and happiness between God and his creation will be restored.

Thus far articulated it clearly shows that the characteristic feature of the biblical Testaments' attitude towards the natural environment, which the Church hold and believe, is the admiration for its wonders and for the great wisdom of its design, which found expression especially in the prayers of the Psalms and other books of the wisdom literature. Such biblical texts of the Psalmist speak of the earth and all creatures as proclaiming the glory of God. The Psalmist states: "The heavens declare the glory of God; the skies proclaim the work of his

---

[268] Karl H. Peschke, *Christian Ethics: Moral Theology in the Light of Vatican II*, Alcester: Goodliffe Neale, 1997, p. 749.

hands!" (Ps 19:1). When human beings seriously contemplate on their being and existence they are prompted to praise their maker, revere and thank Him. In view of the wonders of creation the Psalmist exclaims: "How many are your works, O Lord! In wisdom you made them all; the earth is full of your creatures" (104:24). All of them depend on God for their sustenance. As they live and exist they display the glory of God.

The New Testament presupposes the Old Testament view of the origin and significance of creation and people's relation to it. It shares this fundamental view and retains it. Paul reflects upon man and woman's ties with the natural environment and their responsibility for it. He considers the inefficiencies of nature and sufferings of nature as a result of man-woman's sin. Its liberation from the bondage to decay accordingly stands in relation to man-woman's redemption. In Romans 8, it is very striking to notice how much creation and human beings are linked together in liberation. Both human beings and nature or creation are in the same situation; both groan under the distress of the present (8:22). Both are waiting for the adoption of the Christians as sons and daughters of God (8:19-23). Both are thrown on hope (8:20-24), and to both is held the promise of glorification (8:17-21). So there exists solidarity of origin, affliction, hope and redemption between human beings and creation. Creation will be redeemed if human beings were redeemed and became a new creation (2 Cor 5:17; Gal 6:15). Human beings have to change if the suffering of creation is to change. If human beings give honour to God, which is due to him, if the sinner becomes a new person, then a renewal of creation will come.

The Church's theology holds further, in this vein, that the process of reconciliation between God and creation has already begun in his Son Jesus Christ. According to the Pauline letters to the Colossians and Ephesians, God did not only create all things in Jesus Christ (Col 1:15-20), but it also pleased God to reconcile all things to himself, whether on earth or in heaven (Col 1:20; Eph 1:10). This reconciliation is a promise and also an offer. It began in Jesus Christ but is obviously not a yet and full reality. It is the here reality and the not-yet. It will become a reality to the extent that human beings live their lives in and with Jesus Christ and let themselves be guided by the spirit of love, respect, reverence and benevolence towards everything that lives and exists. And finally, this process of reconciliation between God and creation will reach consummation in eternity when all things will be recapitulated in God through Christ. The repeated assertion of the New Testament that all things were made through the Word, the *Logos* (Jn 1:3) and were created in and through God's son Jesus Christ (Col 1:16; Heb 1:2) gave expression to the truth that the *cosmos* is not the result of an anonymous energy, but of the love and wisdom of a personal God.[269] The creatures are not just products of materialistic determinisms and processes of natural selection, but they are a result of the creative love of a divine intelligence of infinite wisdom, imagination, beauty and benevolence. The Bible is very clear and unmistakably so that the universe is the handwork of God and therefore distinct from him. All creatures in the universe are his property and manifestations of his divine wisdom. All creatures are good. Being the property of God, it requires that human beings have the attitudes of appreciation, respect and care. The dominion granted to human beings over creation by the creator is not an absolute power, nor can one speak of a freedom to use and misuse, use and abuse, or to dispose of things as one pleases. This clearly means that when it comes to the world of nature, human beings are not only obliged to the biological laws, but also to the moral laws.[270]

Fundamentals for new lifestyles towards creation

While the creation story underlines the transcendence of God, the incarnation of God's Son in the person of Jesus Christ (Jn 1:14) also asserts an immanence of God in the world. God is present in nature and through it his glory is proclaimed. The doctrine of the incarnation, rightly understood, is a call to all peoples to love and cherish the earth

---

[269] John Paul II, *The Catechism of the Catholic Church*, Nairobi: Paulines Publications Africa, 1994, no. 51-53.

[270] John Paul II, *Sollicitudo Rei Socialis*, Vatican: Libreria Editrice Vaticana, 1987, no. 34.

and the entire universe and find the Divine therein.[271] There is a depth in all things, which makes them transparent for the presence of God. Serious observation, admiration, meditation and contemplation of the things of nature by human beings can reveal this divine presence in creation. When this is discovered, there is need for human beings to develop certain fundamental orientations for a proper conduct towards and treatment of nature with love and care, respect and protection. That includes love of nature, reverence for nature, moderation and self-limitation in the use of the resources of nature. God cares for and loves all his creatures, from the least things to the great events of the world and its history, and human beings have to love all that God created, loves and cherishes.[272] This love of nature is grounded in God's goodness, wisdom and amicability which every creature reflects. The Second Vatican Council in this vein said, "The human being is able to love the things themselves created by God, and ought to do so. They can receive them from God, respect and reverence them as flowing from the hand of God."[273] This love of nature is realized in the appreciation for the goodness and beauty of nature, and in respect for the purpose it is destined for by God.

The reverence for nature is another fundamental attitude needed to develop the right human conduct towards nature and the environment. This needs to be rediscovered because it is a virtue and attitude that got widely lost as a consequence of the mechanistic, materialistic and utilitarian approaches to nature. Not only human beings, but also animal and vegetative life as well as the inanimate nature merit appreciation, respect and protection. This attitude of reverence obviously presupposes that life and all that exists has its own goodness and value, not only extrinsically for the utility they may possess for humans, but also intrinsically on their own merit. Nature in its integrity

---

[271] Sean McDonagh, *To Care for the Earth*, London: Geoffrey Chapman, 1986, p. 119.

[272] John Paul II, *The Catechism of the Catholic Church*, Nairobi: Paulines Publications Africa, no. 303.

[273] Vatican Council II, *The Pastoral Constitution on the Church in the Modern World, Gaudium et Spes*, no. 37.

is not simply a reservoir of raw materials. It is a presence of values.[274] The intrinsic value of all things of nature and the environment is the truth that they were created by God and therewith are reflections of his goodness, beauty, wisdom and holiness. One of the main challenges in the local Church of the Archdiocese of Lilongwe was to view nature and the environment as having an inherent or intrinsic value i.e. this is to say that nature has its own merit internal without essential reference to how useful and beneficial it is to human beings. There was also need for moderation and self-limitation in the manner humans used resources of nature and the environment. There was need to counter the mere utilitarian use of nature and the environment with an attitude of respect, regard, care and protection. This attitude demands from human beings concern, self-limitation and self-control. Human beings cannot claim unbounded liberty of use of the resources of nature and the environment. They cannot claim unbounded liberty of, for example, scientific research, experimentation and use of nature for their survival. Human beings need to be prudent in the manner they use the resources of earth and the nature universe. Creation, as it exists in the environment, must not be abused. It has to always be remembered that God is the absolute proprietor and human beings are only the stewards of creation. The world is not only the property of God; it is also a presence of his wisdom and a communication of his divine spirit. So, in their dealings with nature and creation people are limited by a superior authority. Human beings have to respect the purpose and finality of nature which accorded with the will and intentions of its Creator. Man and woman have to care for their house (the world and the universe) so that it will remain a homestead favourable to their own life as well as to the subsistence of all the things that live, dwell and exist therein together with them.

With this kind of understanding of the theology of the Church regarding the environment concrete requirements are therefore made for very practical actions of humans towards nature and the

---

[274] Erazim Kohak, *The Ambers and the Stars: A Philosophical Inquiry into the Moral Sense of Nature*, Chicago: University of Chicago Press, 1984, p. 72.

environment. Such have to include responsible use of natural resources, care and protection of the world of nature, personal and corporate concern for everything that lives and exists, moderation and self-control in consumption, care for the animal world (Pr 12:10; Ex 20:10; Dt 25:4) and enactment of laws which are instrumental for environmental protection.[275] There is need for sanctions, imposts, controls, prohibitions and orders in the social market economy if the process of care, respect and protection of nature and the environment is to proceed. Nature and the environment have to be safeguarded.[276] It has to be realized at all times that the human being is something less than the measure of all things. They are not the sovereign of creation, but part of it. They live in communion with nature and ought to cherish it, just as they cherish their bodies and are to have good care for it. Human beings are to learn that they are part of a more comprehensive reality whose needs and claims they cannot ignore without doing harm to themselves.[277]

The environment is in so many ways, evidently, the indispensable basis for man and woman's material existence in this world. But of late this natural habitat, the 'house' of man and woman, is being threatened by the environmental and ecological crisis which is the result of either a too careless and wasteful exploitation of nature's resources or of environmental strains such as the land and soil degradation, pollution of water, land, and air, depletion of water, land and air resources, and excessive encroachment on nature which destroys the living space not only of human beings themselves, but also of animals and plants. The destruction of the environment is not something very new. It has already happened in times past in the history of humankind. But the damaging effects remained locally confined. Since the second half of the 20th century an enormous acceleration of environmental strains

---

[275] Louis Infield (tr.), *Lectures on Ethics*, New York: Harper & Row, 1963, p. 239.

[276] Pontifical Council for Justice and Peace, *The Compendium of the Social Teaching of the Church*, Vatican: Libreria Editrice Vaticana, 2004, p. 279.

[277] Karl H. Peschke, *Christian Ethics: Moral Theology in the Light of Vatican II*, Alcester: Goodliffe Neale, 1997, pp. 759-771.

occurred, propelled largely by a rapid expansion of industrialization and the vast increase of populations in many parts of the world. The menace for the environment was grave, with many species of animals and plants threatened by extinction. There was intensified agricultural activity, deforestation, overgrazing, to take care of the needs of the growing populations. There was exploitation of the forests, land, and atmosphere and water bodies. The Church was aware that more and more people were alarmed at the menace to nature and the environment.

The Archdiocese of Lilongwe witnessed a lot of the environmentally related disasters like change of the weather patterns, floods, dry spells, late onset of the rains, erratic rains, climate change, global warming, famine and many more. However, owing to the fact that many of the people in this territory were illiterate (in the sense of the modern usage of the term), slow to conceptualize that these disasters were caused by human beings because of their irresponsible conduct in dealing with nature and things of the environment. For a long time, they thought these were only natural disasters and nothing triggered by the actions of man and woman. In the least and owing it from their cultural beliefs, the people thought these disasters were a sign that God and the ancestors were not happy in the way people were living in their social-horizontal and vertical-spiritual relationships. This was and had not been in the sense of the modern understanding that the disastrous phenomena related to nature and the environment were a result ultimately of human sin. There was more and more awareness that the mundane actions of human beings, resulting from the globalization of the technocratic paradigm and effects of modern anthropocentrism, had affected nature and the environment.[278] This was leading to initiatives in the Archdiocese of Lilongwe to do a thorough examination of people's attitudes and actions towards

---

[278] Pope Francis, *Laudato Si: Encyclical Letter of Pope Francis on the Care for Our Common Home*, Nairobi: Paulines Publications Africa, 2015, pp. 59-67.

nature and creation.[279] The Catholic Church had now also gotten involved in this examination of the human attitude towards nature and creation. The Church embarked on the rediscovery and renewal of its teaching, vision, and theology on nature and creation.[280]

The Church's involvement in this examination of the attitude of man and woman was also triggered by some of the voices which held the opinion that the crisis was due to the influence of Christianity and in particular to the creation story of the Bible.[281] The initial chapters of the first book of the Bible, Genesis, appeared to give the human being a privileged position in the realm of created nature in such a way that man and woman seemed to be set off against the rest of creation and further more appeared to be invested with the authority of a total dominion over it. The voices which held this opinion that the environmental crisis was due to the influence of Christianity further argued that this had encouraged the misconception of the human being as the center of the world, while in reality human beings ought to have considered themselves as part of nature. The theology of the Church on this saw a certain irony with this accusation because the exploitation of nature and the environment had existed even where Christianity was not known. For example, the aborigines of Central America who lived from hunting had exterminated all large animals. A large part of North Africa, which was like the fertile garden of the Roman Empire, was transformed into a desert way back before the advent of Christianity due to imprudent cultivation. It was no better in Mesopotamia, which was the legendary garden of Eden, and parts of Arabia. The worldwide ravishment of nature through physics and techniques began at a time when the Bible was no longer the main guide for many intellectuals and the environment was no longer

---

[279] The Episcopal Conference of Malawi, Social Development Directorate: *Kusamalira Dziko Lapansi limene likutisunga Moyo tonsefe*, Balaka: Montfort Media, 2016, pp. 1-10.

[280] Karl H. Peschke, *Christian Ethics: Morality in the Light of Vatican II*, Alcester: Goodliffe Neale, 1997, p. 746.

[281] This charge is made again but in a restrained way by J. B. Cobb, *Is it too Late? A Theology of Ecology*, Beverly Hills: Bruce, 1972, pp. 1-76.

considered by then as God's creation. Instead the environment was viewed as a mere raw material with man and woman as their sovereign constructor, entitled to use the means at their disposal for whatever constructs and purposes they would find useful, challenging and pleasing according to their needs.[282]

Conclusion

The Bible is a fundamental source of morality for the believers. In discussing and presenting the theological basis for human stewardship and sense of responsibility over the environment the bible is a necessary resource. The things which exist in the environment, which human beings have seen and not seen, do not come about on their own or accidentally. They were all created by God. This calls for respect, care and protection by human beings who have been created in the image of God, *imago Dei*. The Bible views the things of the environment (God's creation) as sharing with human beings some things: a common origin (God), a common home (earth), a common finality or destiny (God), and this calls for a sense and commitment to universal fraternity. It also views everything participating in the act of 'being' as containing an inherent cum intrinsic goodness and value in being planted by the creator.

The value of the things participating in the act of 'being' does not depend on how beneficial they are to human beings. Human beings and the concept of beneficiarity to them are not the determinants of the goodness and value inherent in God's creation. Furthermore, all of God's creation, according to the Bible, is for a purpose. Thus, no matter how big or small the being is, all is created for a purpose by its creator to reveal the glory of God, for God to enjoy, to support human life, and for creation's own enjoyment in the participation in the life and being of God. Creation is groaning, like a woman labour, waiting for the revelation of the children of God (waiting for salvation).

---

[282] Karl H. Peschke, *Christian Ethics: Morality in the Light of Vatican II*, Alcester: Goodliffe Neale, 1997, p. 745.

The theology of the Catholic Church is largely based on this view of the Bible regarding the environment. It views the environment as God's creation, originating in God, and going back to God. Human beings and the rest of God's creation share a common origin, home, and destiny. Hence there is a sense of fraternity which should have developed in the ways human beings looked at the non-human part of God's creation. The environment contains the creative spirit of God and so God is present in it. The fact that human beings are created in the image of God is to be understood not as a conferral of human superiority over nature but rather as a call or vocation for human beings to take care of the world. The dominion is to be understood in the sense of responsibility and not in the sense of freedom to abuse and exploit the things of the environment. God remains the proprietor of his creation and human beings are only to behave as God's stewards (servants, foremen and women).

Chapter 8: Expressions of Church as God's Family and their Practices in Saving the Environment

A very important question that needed to be asked and answered was about what the Church in its different expressions as God's Family was doing to save the environment in the Archdiocese of Lilongwe. To approach this question is by looking at what the different ecclesial groups, which are the concrete expressions of the Church as Family, were doing to bring about the care, protection and respect of the environment, in other words, to save the environment. It is in these basic and local communities where the individual Christians experience the Church as Family. Connected to that, a detailed explanation was needed of how much this metaphor of 'family,' as applied in the Archdiocese of Lilongwe, was applied, and what were the actual mitigation practices of the Christians in relation to the environment. The purpose of this chapter is to explore if the ecclesiology of Family of God, which has brought closer links and interrelatedness among the Christians, has borne equal result in understanding, relating with, and taking care of nature.

The application of the African Ecclesiology of the Church as the Family of God in the Archdiocese of Lilongwe led to the formation and development of many ecclesial groups and communities where greater social cohesion was experienced. In these groups and communities, the members of the Church did not live simply as individuals but through these ecclesial social units the individual Christians were able to establish stronger human bonds or links of relationship among them.[283] Through these different groups they were able to live not as mere believing individual men and women but with stronger human relationships and a strong sense of belonging to the same family, the Family of God. In these groups they know each other and are responsible for one another. They share their joys and sorrows.

---

[283] Vatican Council II, *Lumen Gentium*, no. 9.

The believing community members were saving the environment through: the Diocesan Commissions and programmes (Education, Health, CADECOM, CCJP, Jesuit Centre for Ecology and Development, Primary Eco-Schools Programme), lay ecclesial organizations (CWO, CMO, DLCCY), Associations of Priests (ADCCOL) and Consecrated Women and Men (ARIMA, AMRIM, AWRIM), and Familial Movements (ME and CFM).

The Diocesan Commissions

The Small Christian Communities and other Church groups became tools through which environmental education and commitments were concretized. When the Christians met in these communities they, among other things, discussed issues related to the environment and how as human beings in their locality they were to take responsibility for nature in its diversity.

Policy and Technical Options to Stop Environmental Degradation

These communities provided institutional structures through which the diocesan commissions which were responsible for the social welfare of the people were able to penetrate the masses. Some of the commissions and centres in the Archdiocese of Lilongwe which were working in the area of the environment and ecology were the Catholic Development Commission, (CADECOM), Education Commission, Health Commission, the Commission for Justice and Peace (CCJP), the Jesuit Centre for Ecology and Development, Centre For Social Concern (CFSC), and the Primary Eco-schools Programme under the umbrella of the Commission for Justice and Peace.

The Catholic Development Commission (CADECOM)

The Lilongwe diocesan Catholic Development Commission (CADECOM) reached the rural communities through the structure of the SCCs with programmes dealing with environmental protection. It had programmes in many areas of the diocese including the traditional authorities of Chakhaza and Dzoole in the district of Dowa, and with these programmes they were working with the Small Christian Communities of Madisi, Mponela and Nambuma parishes. With funding from Caritas Australia, they had recently been involved in the area of food sustainability and nutrition with which they provided the rural communities with skills and means to grow crop varieties like maize, potato and cassava which did not require a lot of rain to mature. They also taught the rural agricultural communities modern techniques and environmental conserving methods of agriculture, planting of trees in gardens which increased the nitrogen content in the soils thereby improving the fertility of the land. They had programmes of providing seeds for legumes like groundnuts, soya and beans to these communities as a means to divert the farmers from the production of tobacco, as an income source, whose production required the use of a lot of wood and thereby contributing to the destruction of the trees or deforestation. The households were taught skills of planting woodlots to replace the green cover and contribute towards the reversal of the lost forests.[284] There was also advocacy among the rural communities not to allow anybody to engage in tobacco farming if they did not have woodlots. However, many people in these areas still indulged in the tobacco cultivation due to the traditional belief that tobacco was the back-bone of the economy and many of these by-laws regarding its cultivation were not adhered to because people needed a cash crop to be able to survive. Because of fear for one another the rural communities were not courageous enough to take to task those in their communities who grew tobacco even if they had no woodlots. In these parishes of Madisi, Mponela and Nambuma CADECOM instituted committees whose members were also representatives of the Small Christian Communities and through them the messages about saving the environment reached the grassroots communities.[285]

---

[284] Int Christopher Chiwandira, JTI technician, Madisi, 29.7.2016.
[285] Int George Nkhoma, CADECOM Coordinator, Mponela, 29.7.2016.

The Jesuit Centre for Ecology and Development

The Jesuit Centre for Ecology and Development has its headquarters in Area 9 in Lilongwe. It was a new social action, development and advocacy project of the Jesuit Fathers addressing environmental management and development issues in Malawi and in particular in the Archdiocese of Lilongwe. It used the SCC ecclesial structure as a springboard for reaching the communities at the grassroots level. It had the overall objective of promoting the dignity and fullness of life by working with women and young people to acquire skills that improved the quality of their livelihood while at the same time contributing to reversing environmental degradation. It promoted in the SCCs environmental management as a means of mitigating the impact of climate change through a commercial approach and public education to uplift the socio-economic status of vulnerable households. Their approach was to let communities adopt the energy efficient stoves through a door-to-door environmental campaign and public awareness campaign to bring about cultural and social transformation, and a grass-root participation in addressing deforestation and climate change at the household level. The centre, through this project, provided a meaningful economic activity and a means of earning income to unemployed women and youth in Likuni by making the energy efficient clean cooking stoves. It was these women and young people, unemployed, who were trained in the making of energy saving stoves in Mpampha (Likuni) which were sold to the various communities in the Archdiocese of Lilongwe.[286] According to the 2008 Population Census Report, over 90% of the population used biomass energy (charcoal and firewood). Cooking with too much wood contributes to deforestation. Another study revealed that the black carbon being emitted, mostly soot, was from the combustion of wood, and was the second most important contributor to climate change.[287] The majority of low-income households (constituting about 80% of the country's population), used

---

[286] Int George Notisi, Mbingwa, 23.7.2016.

[287] Atmosphere: A Journal of Geophysical Research, *Bounding the Role of Black Carbon in the Climate System: A Scientific Assessment*, 15.1.2013.

the traditional three stone open fires, which use too much wood fuel and emit a lot of black carbon.

The stoves, called *Chitetezo* ceramic stoves, were portable to allow indoor and outdoor cooking. They were made from clay readily available in Mpampha village in Likuni – Lilongwe. The stoves' life span was estimated to be around 3 years, with many stoves lasting as long as 7 years. The use of these energy saving stoves reduced deforestation. It was also cleaner and safer than the traditional three stone open fire. The stoves were energy saving and efficient as they reduced wood energy consumption by up to 70% as compared to the traditional three stone open fires. In this way its usage could significantly reduce the rate of deforestation.[288] These energy saving stoves reached all parishes in the Archdiocese of Lilongwe. The field officers of the programme conducted training with the catechists who in turn were to train community leaders on the environmental benefits of using these stoves. Then the catechists in the villages were provided with the stoves from where the village communities came to buy for household use. However, due to poverty and sheer negligence, not many households had these stoves because they could not manage to buy them. They were still using the traditional three stone open fires.[289]

The Primary Eco-Schools Programme

The Primary Eco-Schools Programme which was being carried out in the Archdiocese of Lilongwe was using the structure of the primary schools to reach the communities at the grassroots of the Church in order to provide environmental education. It was carried out in 165 primary schools in the diocese of Lilongwe: 115 schools in Salima district and 50 schools in Lilongwe district. With this programme the environmental education was being provided to SCCs belonging to the parishes of Salima and Benga in Salima district, and Chimutu-St. Patrick's, Nathenje, Mlale, Namitete, Nambuma, Chilinda and Kanengo

---

[288] Int Adamson Mnjowe, Ngooko, 18.7.2016.
[289] Int Katalina Kaziputa, Mwadyanji, and Mercy Chigwenje, Bowe, 18.7.2016.

parishes in Lilongwe district. The objective of the programme was to equip communities and schools with skills and competences to address the environmental problems and challenges in their neighbourhood. The programme used the schools as a springboard for reaching communities with environmental education. The field officers of this micro project who worked together with volunteers and eco-school committee members provided the environmental education. In the so called eco-committee where the programme was being implemented there were two members from each SCC. The two members were preferably members of the CCJP in the SCCs because the issue of the environment was also a moral, justice and peace issue with God's creation. The purpose of their presence in the committee was to provide linkage between the programme and the Small Christian Communities. The issues being tackled and the environmental education provided reached the communities through these members. In the area where the programme was being implemented there were a number of environmental challenges which had surfaced: climate change, unpredictable rain patterns, the decreasing water levels of Lake Malawi, acute deforestation in the Dzalanyama area and in the Dowa-Salima highlands, soil erosion, scarcity of water in rivers where water would run throughout the year like Lilongwe, Linthipe and Lifidzi etc.[290]

The programme's education encouraged the communities to plant trees wherever possible. It provided environmental education to the children in the schools so that they grow up with respect for the integrity of creation through concrete actions as well. Some of the actual activities included planting of woodlots near the schools and in their homes. They were told to plant trees and fruits in the school area and the same had to be repeated around their homes. The communities were educated to plant trees along the river banks of Linthipe and Lifidzi so as to hold the water and reduce siltation of the lake. The communities were also trained in livestock production. They were provided not only with training but also with starter packs for the

---

[290] Int Steven Matemba, micro-project field officer of the Eco-schools programme in Salima, Katakungwa, 20.8.2016.

livestock production. Some of the animals kept were pigs, goats, poultry, and guinea fowls. This livestock production was connected with the environmental management because the whole idea was to provide alternative sources of income for the grass roots communities which would have otherwise indulged in charcoal burning and selling which destroyed trees. When the poor communities which saw charcoal burning and selling as a source of income were economically empowered through other means then the forests were saved.[291]

The programme had also a very special focus on women. They trained women in these communities who were charged with the work of in turn training other women in issues of the environment. These were called Eco-Women in their communities. The women in the communities where this programme was being implemented were trained in natural resources management. They were told not to be wasteful in energy use and food preparation. They were taught how to plant and take care of trees. They were taught fruit tree planting and were encouraged to have home and kitchen gardens where they could grow vegetables. The women were also encouraged to use the energy saving stoves for cooking in their household. However, there was not much progress with the usage of the energy serving stoves because many of the rural women still preferred the traditional way of three stones open fires and also because the energy saving stoves were found to be expensive to buy by some poor people.[292]

The programme also carried out among women and the rest of the rural communities advocacy of human rights. Among the women there was special advocacy by the programme for the right to education for the girl child so that they would in the long run be economically empowered. There was also a lot of advocacy against forced marriages which still took place in these communities. Often parents, due to poverty, gave their daughters in marriage when they were still young. The purpose was to get rid of them from their homes assuming doing so would reduce the pressure of the parents in taking care of them.

---

[291] Int Matthews Kalimanjira, eco-committee member, Msumba, 21.8.2016.
[292] Int Steve Matemba, Katakungwa, 20.8.2016.

The parents did this in order to get money or monetary items (cows and goats) from the daughters given by the sons-in-law as bride price. They also wanted to enjoy the financial and psychological support of the sons-in-law. Through the advocacy programme the field officers and the eco-women encouraged the girl children to go to school. The parents and guardian were encouraged not to give their daughters in marriage when they were still young. Education was deemed the only way to transform the communities.[293]

The project also ran an advocacy programme against over-population. The population of the country was growing at an alarming rate. Then it stood at 17 million and if the trend continued it was expected that by the year 2030 there were going to be about 30 million people in the same land mass of Malawi. The programme reached the communities with messages for people to plan their families to smaller and manageable sizes. As a church programme it encouraged the women to use the natural family planning also known as the Billings Method. However, on such very personal issues people still used their conscience. Some Church women were already using the artificial methods of birth control promoted by the government of Malawi and by some Non-Governmental Organizations involved in health and population control such as *Banja la Mtsogolo* (a local subsidiary of the Population Services International - PSI).[294]

Lay Ecclesial Organizations

The African ecclesiology of the Church as the Family of God was also applied in the Archdiocese of Lilongwe through formation of ecclesial groups based on gender and generation with the intention of bringing the people of God close to one another and fostering a family spirit among the different groups. The establishments of the Catholic Women Organization (CWO), Catholic Men Organization (CMO) and the Diocese of Lilongwe Council for Catholic Youth (DLCCY) are examples of the concrete expressions of the model of Church as God's

---

[293] Int Amina James, eco-women member, Mtemeiti, 21.8.2016.
[294] Int Bernadette Abraham, Mtiya, 21.8.2016.

Family among the women, men and youth in the Archdiocese of Lilongwe.

The Catholic Women Organization (CWO)

In Lilongwe Archdiocese the Catholic women began to gather together in 1974 with the aim of fostering among them unity, fraternity, mutual spiritual and social support, encouraging each other to be more available in the Church and participate in its services of evangelization and development. This was a year after the commencement of the Lilongwe 1973-1975 Mini-Synod that decided on the creation of the Small Christian Communities. The development of the Catholic Women's Organization was part of the implementation of the Vatican II theology of the local Church and the ecclesiology of Communion that developed from it. These meetings of women were also a way of living the ecclesiology of Church as the Family of God. This coming together of the women in the Church to form associations and groups, in the diocese of Lilongwe, was also influenced by the same movement among women in other churches who had begun to come together to pray and discuss issues of spiritual and development importance.

The aim of the Catholic Women, as they began coming together fostering strong bonds of fraternity, was to contribute towards establishing the Kingdom of God in this locality through their unity as Jesus said: "That all of them may be one, Father, just as you are in me and I am in you. May they also be in us so that the world may believe that you have sent me" (Jn 17:21). They sought to support one another in development issues too. Through their organizational meetings the women wanted to teach each other good behaviour based on the Gospel values, teaching each other prayer and Bible sharing or reflection, and deepening their faith. They also wanted to support one another in alleviating their poverty and uplifting their identity in the family, in the church and in society.[295] CWO embraced all the Catholic women in the diocese, and in the other Catholic dioceses in Malawi. The CWO began from the SCC where it gathered together all the

---

[295] Bungwe la Amayi Achikatolika, *Constitution*, Balaka: Montfort Media, 2004.

women in the particular Catholic Christian community and the organization went up through all the ecclesial structures of the Church in the Archdiocese of Lilongwe. The women in the SCC elected every three years their own executive committees for leadership. This meant that there was leadership of CWO at the SCC, outstation, zone or centre, parish, deanery, and diocesan levels. The members of the executive committees were the chairlady and her deputy, secretary and her deputy, treasurer and her deputy, and four committee members. The Catholic Women Organization at the parish, deanery and diocesan levels had in addition priests as chaplains and religious sisters as matrons.[296]

The naming of these women groups and gatherings in the diocese of Lilongwe had been one of the controversial issues in the development of the organization. In the CCAP there developed in Malawi the association of women one of whose aims was to foster unity among women and they were called *Azimayi Achigwirizano*. When the Catholic women in the diocese of Lilongwe began to gather together in the mid-1970s for prayer, meetings, discussions of spiritual and social development issues, they did not use the technical name of Catholic Women Organization (CWO). Instead they were also loosely called by the name used for the association of women in the Presbyterian Church, *Achigwirizano*. Even in some official documents of the Church in the diocese of Lilongwe this word appeared to describe the association of women. The Pastoral Secretariat of the diocese of Lilongwe in 1978 issued a document titled *"Maudindo mu Mphakati ndinso Msonkhano wa Bungwe la Mphakati"* in which the diocesan authorities sought to articulate how the SCC leadership and meetings were to be organized. The document mentioned the chairlady of the women group in the SCC to sit among the executive members of the Christian community. In this document the word used for the organization of the Catholic women was *Achigwirizano,* a repeat of the term used for the women organization in the Presbyterian Church of

---

[296] Int Bridget Chinkhandwe, Catholic Women Organization member, Ngooko, 30.5.2016.

Central Malawi.[297] In the typical rural communities this usage of this word of Presbyterian origins for the organization of women in the Church has continued.[298] So even though the coming together of women in the diocese of Lilongwe began in 1974, the coinage of the phrase Catholic Women Organization (CWO-*Bungwe la Azimayi a Chikatolika*) developed later, actually from the late 1980s. The idea of naming it differently was to differentiate it from similar organizations of women existing in other churches. With the increasing levels of literacy among women the usage of the term Catholic Women Organization, with its Chichewa synonym *Bungwe la Azimayi a Chikatolika,* has become more and more common among the Catholics. In modern times the usage of the term *Bungwe la Azimayi Achikatolika* also raised some questions. Some Catholic women in the diocese tended to think that it was optional for them to join the organization. Bungwe would mean it being an association where one was free to join or not. But the CWO leadership together with the ecclesiastical authority in the diocese held that by virtue of being a Catholic woman, through baptism, one became automatically a member of this organization. This meant that it was a must to belong to this organization for any and all women in the Catholic Church in the Archdiocese of Lilongwe. In this case there was a growing proposal that the Catholic Women Organization had in vernacular to be called *Gulu la Amayi Achikatolika* (mandatory to join and no option) and not *Bungwe la Amayi Achikatolika* (which entails an option to join).[299]

The Catholic Women Organization was a member of the World Union of Catholic Women's Organization (WUCWO) which represented 100 Catholic women organizations worldwide. WUCWO was established in 1910 and it comprised Catholic Women Organizations from over 100 countries. It currently has a membership of over 5 million women. In

---

[297] Pastoral Secretariat of the Diocese of Lilongwe, *Maudindo mu Mphakati ndinso Msonkhano wa Bungwe*, Lilongwe: Likuni, 1978, p. 20.

[298] Int Crispin Kambwembwe, member of St. Philomena SCC, Mphalawe, and Laurent Salatiyere, Catechist for Sungeni Zone, Sungeni, 17.5.2016.

[299] Int Mrs. Anita Kaliu, Lilongwe Archdiocesan Chairlady, Catholic Women Organization, Bwaila - Lilongwe, 16.5.2016.

2006 the Pope accepted it as a public international organization of the faithful. This canonical status honoured the efforts of faithful Catholic women active in the union at the parish, diocesan, national and international levels. WUCWO promoted the presence, participation and co-responsibility of Catholic women in society and Church, in order to enable them to fulfill their mission of evangelization and work for human development. It promoted the formation of women to meet contemporary challenges, foster awareness and respect of cultural diversity, networking with other international organizations and faith communities for the respect of human rights, especially for women and children. The World Union of Catholic Women's Organization had also consultative status with the United Nations Economic and Social Council (ECOSOC), the Human Rights Council (based in Geneva), FAO (based in Rome), participatory status at the Council of Europe (based in Strasbourg), and was an official partner of UNESCO (based in Paris-France). WUCWO had member organizations from five (continental) regions namely, Africa, Asia-Pacific, Europe, Latin America/Caribbean and North America. Its General Secretariat was based in Paris, France. In November 2009 the Catholic Women Organization in Malawi was accepted as member of WUCWO. This acceptance was ratified in 2010 in Jerusalem, Israel.[300]

Policy and Technical Options to Stop Environmental Degradation

The women formed the major church group in the Catholic Archdiocese of Lilongwe. They were present in many ecclesiastical structures of the diocese: SCCs, out station, zone, parish, deanery and the diocese. In their group meetings, other than meeting for prayer and devotions, they also discussed issues related to the environment. The leadership of the women groups time and again came up with agenda items which aimed at creating awareness of how they, as

---

[300] This information is from the Working Paper for the African Region Conference of WUCWO prepared for the WUCWO Conference in Malawi in Lilongwe from 30th -5th September 2016. The theme is: "Women, proclaimers of God's Mercy" based on Jn 4:9, "Come and see who told me everything I did. Could this be the Messiah?"

women, had contributed to the degradation of the environment and how in turn they had to participate in reversing this. They encouraged each other to improve in the areas of home sanitation to keep the air clean and this would often be through making sure that in their homes they had the sanitation fundamentals of the toilets, kitchen, bathrooms, and lines for drying clothes, rubbish pit and traditional tray for drying kitchen utensils commonly called *thandala*.[301] They participated in planting trees as a source of energy, to beautify their places and contribute towards the maturation of the hydrological cycle. Some women were indeed planting the trees near their homes every growing season. During their 2016 annual national conference, held in Karonga, the women leadership made a resolution that every Catholic woman had at least to plant one tree every year.[302] However many complained that the growth of these trees was not assured as there wasn't enough water to keep them strong and growing given the recent history of dry spells in the area. Goats and cows, let loose, were also known to be destroying the trees when they were still young.[303] The women also encouraged one another to use the energy saving cooking stoves which in turn would save the environment (the trees and the air). With these stoves they could even use alternative sources of fuel like maize husks and animal dung. Despite creating awareness among each other on the environmental benefits of the *Chitetezo mbaula* (energy saving stove) women in many households were still using the traditional three stone open fires because these ceramic stoves were found by many poor communities to be expensive to buy.[304] They encouraged each other to practice land conservation methods to improve the fertility of the soils because the chemical fertilizers did not only destroy the natural fertility of the soils but they also pollute them through the process of soil acidification, and the chemical fertilizers too were expensive to manage. Though the women

---

[301] Int Killiness Kaphamtengo, CWO member, Malufu, and Maria Zimba, CWO member, Chinkhwiri, 19.8.2016.

[302] Int Agnes Kachiwala, CWO vice chairlady, Madisi Parish, Natola, 13.1.2016.

[303] Int Klara Soko, Mtanila, 17.8.2016.

[304] Int Mercy Paskazio, Kabulungo - Dzoole, 19.8.2016.

taught each other to take care of their food resources and practice food frugality, there was little progress in some areas. For example, in many households, the women still prepared food more than the family could eat leading to a lot of it being thrown away. The remains, commonly called *mkute*, were wasted. A few households would reuse the food items left over from the previous day.[305]

The women also encouraged each other to change their life styles and plan their families because the increase in the population exerted a lot of pressure on the resources of the environment. Even though there was creation of awareness of the dangers of over-population there wasn't much progress in this area as the rural communities continued to multiply. Many women in the Catholic Archdiocese of Lilongwe found it hard to follow their cycles in terms of the church promoted and preferred Billings Method of birth control. There were no enough experts to teach the rural women how to follow the Billings Method to prevent conception and the explanations given by a few were not easy to follow.[306] Other women, though Catholic, went for the artificial birth controls provided in private and government hospitals like the taking of pills, the loop and the no-plant. However, there was slowly growing resentment from the men to have their wives use these artificial methods of birth control due to claimed side effects. Some men claimed that their wives who were taking these artificial methods of birth control were not exciting in bed and did not easily have the sexual desire resulting in refusing their husbands the conjugal rights. Others claimed that the users of these artificial methods of birth control developed heart and blood complications, continuous joint pains, as well as continuous menstrual emissions.[307]

---

[305] Int Agness Jossam, Chiweza (Kalumo), 19.8.2016.

[306] Int Dofa Divaison, Prisca Jester, Sophret Panganani, and Veronica Kazula, Chakhaza, 19.8.2016.

[307] Int Devison Chandanda, Bisai Mwale, Killiness Kaphamtengo, Maria Zimba, Madisi, 19.8.2016.

The Catholic Men Organization (CMO)

In the recent times, there emerged in the Archdiocese the Catholic Men Association. Though it was still in its infancy and on a small scale, its growth is still worth mentioning. The Catholic Men Association (CMO) formally existed so far in five parishes in the Archdiocese of Lilongwe and these were in St. Francis-Kanengo Parish (where it was established in 2008), St. Patrick's Area 18 Parish (2012), Chilinde Parish, Kawale Parish and Mtima Woyera Parish (2015). This is not to say that the men in the various ecclesial communities and parishes did not meet. They could meet if there was a need and a task to be undertaken. The CMO was not just an imitation or a carbon copy of the Catholic Women Organization. Where it exists, the CMO exists in its own right. The CMO were being established upon the realization that the participation of a lot of men in the Catholic Archdiocese of Lilongwe left a lot to be desired. Apart from the leadership roles which were mostly taken by men, the general services of the Church in Lilongwe were carried out with more commitment by women. The participation of men in the activities of the Small Christian Communities was less compared to that of women. The Catholic Men Organization in the five parishes, so far where it had been established, served to pull together men at all levels of the Church structure (SCCs, outstation and parish) to raise interest in them for active prayer life and more involvement in the life of the Church like the women did.[308] The Catholic Men Organization embraces all Catholic men in the parishes where the organization has been established and it was expected to embrace all catholic men in the Archdiocese. The organization aimed at evangelizing and reaching out to all men and indeed all of God's people through services guided by the Gospel values. It existed especially also to raise spiritual consciousness among men for the things of God and the Church.

When the men gathered in these religious groups, formally as CMO or informally as belonging to the same community (SCC), they also

---

[308] Int Dalitso Sambo, chairperson of the Catholic Men Organization, St. Patrick's Parish, Area 18-Lilongwe, 16.5.2016.

discussed issues related to the environment. There was creation of awareness among them to be catalysts of sanitation in their homes by making sure they provided for the household the necessary sanitary items like toilets, bathrooms, kitchen and rubbish bins to safely dispose of wastes. They worked together with the commissions to empower themselves to take care of the environment by planting trees, using energy saving cooking stoves, planting *vetiva* grass in their fields to prevent soil erosion, and cultivate in their fields legumes which had the benefits of not destroying the environment but by addition of nitrogen restoring the soils' fertility.[309] They also discussed the importance of family planning. The town ecclesial communities, knowing the economic difficulty of raising big families, were improving their family sizes. They are aware that the population increase does not only exert pressure on the family and government, but also on the resources of the environment. There were still problems with the rural communities because some men did not allow their wives to follow either natural or artificial family planning methods.[310] One setback for the spiritual growth and the numerical growth of the CMO membership was that in some communities and parishes there was the taking of alcohol after their meetings. This did not go down well with some Christians who felt that it was a contradiction in aim and term. However, some people argued that it was better for the men to consume alcohol together after their meetings and then head home, instead of consuming it in indecent places like bars.

The Diocese of Lilongwe Council for Catholic Youth (DLCCY)

Since the establishment of the Catholic Church in the Archdiocese of Lilongwe, the Church paid particular attention to the young people through youth apostolate and catechesis. The children and youth were given instructions in preparing them for the reception of the sacraments of initiation like baptism, confession, Eucharist, and confirmation. When they reached puberty, there were lessons or instructions aimed at deepening the faith of the young people and also

---

[309] Int Adam Mnjowe, Chika, 19.8.2016.

[310] Int Laurent Salatiyere, Mkokoko, 20.8.2016.

preparing them for adult life and marriage. Normally these instructions were given by the counsellors, *Alangizi*, who regularly convened the young people in the Small Christian Community for these instructions. However, with the ecclesiology of the Church as the Family of God, since the 1970s young men and women in the Archdiocese of Lilongwe had been coming together to foster links of fraternity among them at all levels of the Church beginning from the SCCs, outstations, zones, parishes, deaneries up to the diocesan level. But it was in the 1990s and 2000s that the youth movement became better organized in the diocese of Lilongwe in all its structures. These youths who met at these different levels of established in 2010 a Diocesan Youth Council, at the initiative of their youthful chaplain, Fr. Louis Malama, a Salesian priest. The council embraced all Catholic youths of the diocese and it aims at bringing the Catholic youths close to one another and instilling a family spirit among them. It also aims at evangelizing all youths in the diocese in their mission of reaching out to all God's people through various roles carried out and guided by the Gospel values and the social teaching of the Church. The mission statement of this youth movement is: "Sir, we want to see Jesus"; that through youth catechesis, they might take the Gospel to the young people and the young people might come to the Gospel of Jesus Christ. The youth movement has a number of objectives. Some of them are to deepen the faith of the youths and help them to judge their life experiences according to the Gospel values. It also has the objective of ensuring effective communication and promote co-operation and networking among the youths at all levels in the diocese thus enabling them an exchange of ideas and experiences with other youths and other members of the society.[311]

In the SCC there exists a basic Catholic Youth Council which comprises all Catholic youths in this particular community. The youth in the SCC comes together and elects their own leaders (i.e. chairperson, secretary and their deputies, treasurer, and two other committee members). The youth group members in the Small Christian Community were meant to meet on their own at least once a week

---

[311] Diocese of Lilongwe, *Youth Constitution*, Likuni Press, 2010, pp. 5-11.

and preferably on Sundays. This kind of leadership went up the ladder of ecclesial structure.[312] In their activities the youth in the SCC are assisted and accompanied by three men and women as patrons and matrons. The chairperson and secretary of the youth group in the SCC represents the youth on the parish youth council meetings. The youth group at the parish level is assisted by youth coordinators and a priest who serves as their chaplain. At the deanery and diocesan levels there is a youth executive that is assisted by a diocesan chaplain.[313] The coming together of the Catholic youth at the SCC, outstation, zone, parish, deanery and diocesan level inculcates among the youth a family spirit and a sense of fraternity. They met often to strengthen this familial spirit among them. Parochial exchange visits among the youths were encouraged to help them interact, share spiritual experiences, and develop their sense of togetherness.

Policy and Technical Options to Stop Environmental Degradation

The young people in the Church in the Archdiocese were involved in taking care of the environment. In their groups they discouraged one another from being involved in the actions of deforestation and to be more involved in the conservation and preservation of the environment. In the annual programmes of some parish youth groups they included a tree planting programme in their communities at the household, SCC, outstation and parish level. The youth also participated in the planting of woodlots.[314] Planting of the trees was one thing; taking care of them remained another. This was so because even in such communities there was no tangible and conspicuous replacement of the forest cover. Furthermore, the number of trees planted did not tally with the amount of destruction and so the effect of their programme was not seen much. In those places where the communities had managed to plant some little forests the young

---

[312] Int Mayamiko Chimwaye, Chairman of the parish youth, Madisi Parish, Lungu, 20.8.2016.

[313] Int Fr. Thomas Kasiya, Youth Chaplain, Archdiocese of Lilongwe, Likuni, 28.5.2016.

[314] Int Damiano Raphael, Chaponda, 20.8.2016.

people were involved in securing them through provision of oversight and preparation of firebreak paths. When the young people gathered in their meetings the topics for discussion included also issues of family planning. They encouraged each other that when they would get married they were to decide with their spouses on a small family size because big families resulted in overpopulation and this consequently put a lot of pressure and demand on the natural and environmental resources.[315]

The youth in the Church were also involved in saving the environment through their culinary services in their households. In many of the families household chores including cooking were done by women and young people (mostly girls and young ladies). There was a growing usage of *Chitetezo Mbaula*, the ceramic stove, in cooking at the household level. This ceramic stove has a lot of environmental advantages, as it uses very little firewood and produces minimum-smoke combustion. It preserves the heat for a long time even after the wood has burnt out and it directs the heat upwards to the bottom of the pot sitting on the pot-rests. With this ceramic stove there were also alternative sources of energy. Some young people in their household even used other materials like animal-dung and maize straw, *gaga*, for fire on these stoves which worked equally well.[316] In this way the trees were saved. Some of the young people interviewed mentioned that they were using solar power in cooking. The solar gadgets were even finding their way into the rural communities through the week day or mobile markets. The usage of solar power in cooking reduces deforestation and the pollution of air in the environment through combustions.[317] Even if there was growing usage of ceramic stoves in cooking designed to save energy, the majority of the population were still using the traditional three stone open fires in cooking and this was very energy wasteful.

---

[315] Int Evance Moyo, Mkanda, and Linley Kapachika, Ntchisi, 19.8.2016.

[316] Int Selina Daniel, Kalumo-Ntchisi, 20.8.2016.

[317] Int Griffin Kachitsa, Silumba, and Kingsley Lameki, Malenga, 20.8.2016.

Many of the young people in the Archdiocese of Lilongwe live in the rural areas. Whilst pursuing their studies they were also involved in a lot of farming activities. In the rural parishes of the Archdiocese of Lilongwe many of the people are involved in tobacco farming and the youths of this area are involved in this industry. Tobacco farming was a major source of income for them. The young people in some of their group meetings, related to the environment, encouraged each other to maintain the tobacco shades to avoid cutting down trees every year in preparing new shades for the industry. They also participated in the saving of the environment by planting the family woodlot which they used in the processing of tobacco. However, given the scarcity of land in most of the communities, they did not have enough place where they could plant trees good enough to match the number of trees which were in turn used in the processing of tobacco. They also participated in campaigning against the cultivation of flue cured and dark fired tobacco, because these varieties of tobacco demanded heavy usage of wood in its raw processing.[318] They discouraged those in their communities who did not have woodlots to cultivate these wood energy wasting varieties of tobacco.

In the youth groups they also taught each other good farming methods such as cultivating across the slope to prevent erosion of the soils in the hilly areas like those of Ntchisi, Salima, Nkhotakota and Dowa, and not burning crop residues after harvest. They also discouraged each other from using bad fertilizers like those containing Ammonium sulphate.[319] In some of their meetings they encouraged each other at the village level to use or apply manure in their fields so as to bring back the lost fertility in their pieces of land. They created awareness among their peers that chemical fertilizers were not only expensive but also dangerous to the natural life of the soil as they increased its acidification. They pollute the soils and the water in the ground. When water is polluted the human population too gets bad effects in their health.[320] In their communities and especially at household level they

---

[318] Int Joseph Phiri, Mkanda Trading Centre, 20.8.2016.

[319] Int Juliet Mapulanga, Kalumo-Ntchisi, 19.8.2016.

[320] Int Griffin Kachitsa, Silumba, and Pemphero Khisi, Chiwembe, 20.8.2016.

kept livestock such as cows, goats, and sheep. The youth in some of their group meetings, on the environment, discouraged each other from over-grazing. They created awareness among themselves that overgrazing was not good as it laid the ground bare exposing the land. When the land is bare it becomes prone to soil erosion. They encouraged the shepherds to keep shifting their animals to pasture them and not being in the same place for too long to let the grass grow. The youth also, through their leadership, were able to approach the traditional doctors to plant more trees, as through their profession they used a lot of parts of trees which could lead to the drying up e.g. bulk, leaves, roots and stems. When they use the roots for the production of their traditional medicines, it impacts negatively on the environment as many trees dry up and die when their roots are exposed.[321]

In the rural communities other than through agriculture there were other sources of income for the young people. Some of them are through small scale businesses like charcoal burning, brick molding, and mice hunting and selling. The youth in the Church through their groups encouraged each other to envisage small scale businesses which were environment friendly. They encouraged one another not to be involved in charcoal burning and to burn bricks for constructional purposes only if they had a woodlot. They needed not rely on the natural trees growing in the gardens and hills for their industry. In construction the ideal would be to use cement blocks instead of burnt bricks which required a lot of wood to be processed. But cement blocks were very expensive. The lesser evil was to let only those with a woodlot burn bricks and replace their woodlots annually. They also encouraged each other to take care of the remaining resources by not setting bushfires for hunting mice or as a way of land preparation.[322]

---

[321] Int Vincent Kaponda, Mkangu, 21.8.2016.

[322] Int Cathereen Sadzu, Malomo, Victor Banda, Chiwembe II, and Martha Phiri, Makuka-Kabudula, 20.8.2016.

Associations of Priests, and Consecrated Women and Men

Another concrete expression of the model of Church as the Family of God was the development of the Associations for Diocesan Catholic Clergy of Lilongwe (ADCCOL), for Women Religious (AWRIM) and for Men Religious (AMRIM).

Associations for Diocesan Catholic Clergy of Lilongwe (ADCCOL)

Through ADCCOL the individual diocesan priests working in different parts of the diocesan were brought closer to one another to live a life of fraternity, unity, mutual support and solidarity. The local Church in the Archdiocese of Lilongwe, being part of the universal Catholic Church, had the presence of missionary clergy since its inception as the Vicariate of Nyasa in 1897.[323] In the early days of the presence of the Church in this territory there was a strong presence of foreign missionaries most of whom belonged to the Missionaries of Africa, a congregation (founded in Algiers by Cardinal Lavigerie) that had been assigned the task of evangelizing the people of this territory by Rome, and the Montfort Missionaries who were later called to help in this task especially in the South of the Vicariate of Nyasa. The missionaries committed themselves also to the development and formation of an African clergy with the aim of making the Church more African even in leadership. They sent young men to Kipalapala Seminary in Tanzania where they were trained to become priests. The first Malawian priest was ordained in 1937 and this was Fr. Cornelius Chitsulo who later became bishop of Dedza until his death in 1984. In 1939 another Malawian priest was ordained and this was Fr. Laurent Mangani. Both

---

[323] When the Holy See created the Vicariate of Nyasa in 1897 it included the territories of the whole of Malawi (then called Nyasaland) and three Zambian dioceses of Chipata, Mansa, and Kasama. With the growth of the Church in this area more and more dioceses were later created. But it is the Lilongwe territory that kept the name of Nyasa Vicariate. The name Nyasa Vicariate was changed to Likuni Vicariate in 1951. It then it became Lilongwe Vicariate in 1957. The Lilongwe Vicariate was raised to the status of Diocese in 1959. Lilongwe became an Archdiocese on 10.2.2011.

of these were from the Mtakataka-Mua Lakeshore area where the White Fathers had established strong missions. In the 1940s and 1950s the numbers of ordinations to the priesthood were steadily growing and these decades saw ordinations of some young men from the western and central parts of the vicariate. These included Fr. Chikufenji, Fr. Tobias Sam Banda (1942), Fr. Selvero Sepere (1952), Fr. Nyongani, and Fr. G. Chisendera (who became bishop of Dedza in 1984). In the 1960s and 1970s there was a sizeable group of Malawian men who were ordained to the priesthood. Guilleme, Kachebere, Ludzi, Namitete, Nambuma and Likuni parishes deserved special mention as most of the Malawian clergy in Lilongwe came from these parishes. This somehow showed the maturation of the Church in these missions and good fruits of the work of the missionaries.

These Malawian or local priests, working together with the foreign missionary priests, were also living in the same houses or priestly communities (rectories) with them. This cultural differences and perceptions created problems. Some of the missionary clergy looked down upon some of the Malawian priests. There were occasional feelings of superiority and these few local priests were sometimes isolated in the missions and parishes where the missionary priests were in charge. The Malawian priests started to feel that they needed to support one another in their priestly vocation amidst the challenges of working with and living together with white clergy where the cultural differences brought some problems. Since the missionary priests were united because of their common spirituality and congregational vows and values, the local priests felt they needed to build strong bonds of solidarity, unity, and brotherhood among themselves. In this pursuit they were encouraged by the ecclesiology of the Church as the people of God and as a communion which had developed from the Second Vatican Council.[324] These marked the origins of the Association of the Diocesan Catholic Clergy of Lilongwe (ADCCOL) which eventually became a member association of ADCOM (Association of Diocesan Clergy of Malawi). The development of the Small Christian Communities in 1973 in the diocese of Lilongwe made

---

[324] Int Fr. Alberto Samson, Mpherere, 20.5.2016.

the fraternal interactions among the priests even stronger because it made them visualize themselves as constituting one family through their ordination and common spirituality of attachment and commitment to their diocese. In 2015, the diocesan priests who were in ADCCOL numbered 66 and were working in 19 parishes in the Archdiocese: Kachebere, Mkanda, Ludzi, Guilleme, Namitete, Likuni, St. Patrick's Area 18, Mtima Woyera, Maula, Kawale, Chilinde, Mlale, Nathenje, Salima, Lumbadzi, Mpherere, Mponela, Nambuma, and Madisi. The rest of the 37 parishes in the Archdioceses were served by priests belonging to Congregations and Societies of Apostolic Life.[325]

Through this association the local priests in Lilongwe lived the ecclesiology of Church as Family of God. There was a strong sense of fraternity and sense of family among them through their allegiance to the association. They met regularly to encourage and support one another. They met three times per year for their ordinary association's meeting. An extraordinary meeting could be called if there were urgent issues to be addressed and sorted out. The objectives of the association were to foster unity, brotherhood, solidarity, support, and inter-personal relationships among the diocesan priests. The members of ADCCOL, saw themselves as a family of diocesan priests supporting each other in vocation, spiritual life and pastoral work. The association fostered unity and fraternity among them. Such unity, brotherhood, and solidarity is shown in celebrating life together as children of the same family, the family of God. They visit each other and celebrate things like birthdays, patron saint and feast days together. They mourn together when one is bereaved and they are there for one another providing support. The leadership of the association also moves around to support and encourage priests going through some spiritual and vocational crisis. They also have the duty to provide moral support for those priests who might be under disciplinary action.[326]

The Lilongwe diocese's application of the model of the Church as a communion, emanating from the ecclesiology of Vatican II, and the

---

[325] Int Fr. Matthews Sitolo, Fr. Francis Ngalande, Mpherere, 20.5.2015.
[326] Int Fr. Martin Mthumba, Mtima Woyera Parish, 5.5.2016.

consequent African ecclesiology of the Church as the Family of God also led to the formation of associations of consecrated women and men (Nuns and Religious Priests and Brothers) in the diocese. These religious women and men were consecrated to God and the Church through the evangelical vows of poverty, chastity-celibacy, and obedience to the ecclesial authorities. These different women and men congregations and societies of apostolic life working in the Archdiocese did not live as mere individual communities. The sense of the Church as the Family of God made them come together and create associations. Through the creation of such associations they were brought closer to one another, living a sense of family, for sharing of the ministry and for their mutual support in the evangelization work of the Church in the diocese of Lilongwe.

There was a good number of, about 14, congregations of nuns working in the diocese and these were: Canossian Sisters (CS) with a community in Kanengo; Carmelite Sisters (CM) with communities in Namitete, Msamba/Area 36; Carmelite Missionary Sisters (CMS) with communities in Kapiri, Chiphaso and Mtengowanthenga; the Congregation of the Mother of Carmel (CMC) with a community in Lilongwe's Area 49; Franciscan Sisters of the Sacred Heart of Jesus and Mary (FCJM) with a community in Madisi; the Little Servants of Mary Immaculate (LSMI), also called the Blue Nuns, with communities in Nkhotakota and the Catholic Secretariat in Lilongwe Area 11; Medical Missionaries of Mary (MMM) with a community in Lilongwe Area 47; Missionaries of Charity Sisters (MC) with a community in Kawale-Lilongwe; Missionary Sisters of the Immaculate Conception (MIC) with a community in Lilongwe Area 10; Missionary Sisters of Our Lady of Africa (MSOLA) with communities in Lilongwe Area 2 and 3; the Poor Clares with a monastery in Maula; Sisters of Charity of Ottawa (SCO), also called the Grey Nuns, with communities in Kachebere, Guilleme, Ludzi, and Mkanda; Sisters of Mary Mediatrix (SMM) with communities in Mlale, Area 49 and Chezi; Sisters of St. John the Baptist (Baptistine) with a community in Lilongwe's Area 47; Teresian Sisters (TS) with communities in Lilongwe's Area 2, Benga, Likuni, Mpherere, Malambo, Maula, Mlale, Msamba, Mtima-woyera, Nambuma, Lilongwe's Area 18, and Salima; and Franciscan Sisters (FS) with communities in Likuni and Nathenje. Among these Sisters' Congregations working in the Archdiocese of Lilongwe only the Teresian Sisters (TS) are a locally founded congregation and the rest are of international origin and membership. Only the Poor Clares are cloistered and spending their whole life in Prayer through monastic life. The rest of the sisters' congregations are contemplatives in action and hence are involved in pastoral, health, education, social, charity and administration work.

There are in the Archdiocese of Lilongwe 12 different Congregations of Consecrated Men, who through the evangelical vows of poverty, chastity and celibacy, and obedience, dedicated themselves to God and the ministry of the Church. These are: the Comboni Missionaries (MCCJ) with communities in Msamba and Lilongwe's Area 47; Discalced Carmelites (OCD) with communities in Kamelo, Chiphaso and Kapiri; Franciscan Capuchin Friars (OFM.Cap) with communities in Kaggwa and Padre Pio Area 49; Missionaries of Africa (M.Afr.) with communities in Maula, Chezi, and Kanengo; Salesians of Don Bosco with communities in Nkhotakota and Don Bosco Area 23; the Society of Jesus (SJ) also called the Jesuits with communities in Area 9, St. Joseph Kasungu; St. Patrick's Missionary Society with communities in Mtengo wa Nthenga and Chigoneka in Area 47; Franciscans OFM with a community in Nanthomba-Dowa; Missionaries of St. Paul with a community in Kalembe-Chamama, the Community of St. Paul with a community in Benga; Brothers of St. John of God with a community in Area 10; and the Marist Brothers with communities in Area 9 and Likuni. The priests and brother in these congregations and societies of apostolic life are involved the pastoral, health, social work, administrative and education domains of the human and ecclesial activity.

These different Religious institutes of men and women started to come together after the conclusion of the Vatican Council II (1965), in its spirit, for their mutual support and also for closer collaboration with the bishop and the rest of the pastoral workers in the diocese:

> Care must be taken that the union of major religious superiors, men and women, should have access to some council attached to

the Sacred Congregation of Religious and should be able to be consulted by the said council. It is of utmost importance that the national unions of major religious superiors, men and women, should cooperate with confidence and reverence, with the Episcopal conferences. To this end, it is desirable that questions having reference to both bishops and religious should be dealt with by mixed commissions consisting of bishops and major religious superiors, men and women.[327]

The Association of Religious Institutes in Malawi (ARIMA)

The wind of forming associations to bring together the religious women and men spread to most of the dioceses in Malawi. The Lilongwe diocesan coming together in form of an association of the consecrated women and men in these years following the Vatican II contributed to the formation of the Association of Religious Institutes in Malawi (ARIMA) in 1966 and the first bishop chairperson was Bishop Jobidon (M.Afr.). Bishop Jobidon helped with the drafting of the first ARIMA constitution. The first chairperson was Sr. Jacques Denise, a sister of the Missionaries of Our Lady of Africa, who served from 1964 (when the first meeting was convened) to 1970. Sr. Mary Laurentia, a sister of the Missionaries of the Immaculate Conception, served as Secretary during the same term. The association existed as a mixed religious group of Religious women and men up to 1990 when this association gave birth to two associations drawn on gender lines: AWRIM (Association of Women Religious in Malawi) constituting of only consecrated women and AMRIM (Association of Men Religious in Malawi) constituting of only consecrated men. At the local level the men and women religious came together as local or diocesan chapters of these associations, AWRIM and AMRIM.[328]

The executive members of AWRIM and AMRIM met three times a year to evaluate the plenary session, to monitor and see the progress of the

---

[327] Vatican II, *Decree on the Up-to-date Renewal of Religious Life, Perfectae Caritatis*, 1965, nos. 42-43.

[328] Int Sr. Jennifer Machemba SCO, Mkanda, and Sr. Bernadette Densani SCO, Ludzi, 1.6.2016.

activities done and not done and evaluate all the activities planned within the year and plan for the coming year. In these meetings, the Superiors of the congregations, the Nuncio of Malawi and Zambia, the bishop responsible for religious, member of Association of Men Religious Institutes of Malawi (AMRIM) were usually present. Owing to their numerical strength, AWRIM (association of women religious) was more active than AMRIM (association of men religious). Statistically in Malawi, there were about 1000 sisters (nuns) working in eight dioceses of Malawi namely: Karonga, Mzuzu, Lilongwe, Dedza, Mangochi, Zomba, Blantyre and Chikwawa. The Association of Women in Religious Institutes of Malawi (AWRIM) was a member association of Religious Institutes and Societies of apostolic life in Malawi. It had a membership of 29 congregations composed of 4 local and 25 international religious institutes (of which 2 were cloistered) which carried out numerous activities across all dioceses in the country. The apostolate of AWRIM included all levels of education, health care, social work, agriculture, family apostolate and other pastoral and religious initiatives. The sisters had a common call to mission, being ever ready to go wherever they were needed. They lived in community where they shared its supports as well as challenges. They were committed to the spirit of dedication, of free giving, of joy in duty, of freedom of spirit and of mutual charity.[329]

Through these associations they were fostering among the religious women and men the spirit of being Church as Family, close to one another, networking, mutually supporting one another and living in solidarity. The associations also fostered a harmonious and efficient collaboration among the different women and men Religious Institutes in the Archdiocese. They also dealt with questions related to the promotion of religious life in general, in order to deepen their spiritual and religious life according to the constitutions and spirit proper to each Institute, and in accordance with the directives of the Holy See. The associations also studied and solved apostolic problems common to all Religious Institutes working in the country and in the

---

[329] Strategic Plan 2014-2018, *Association of Women Religious in Malawi*, 2014, pp. 1-2.

Archdiocese. They worked as conduits of cooperation with the diocesan bishop and with the Episcopal Conference of Malawi (ECM) and dialogue with the other National Commissions and Associations, including but not limited to, the Association of Diocesan Clergy in Malawi (ADCOM), in order to promote greater unity and efficiency in the apostolate. The associations also provided an official representation with the Congregation for Institutes of Consecrated Life and Societies of Apostolic Life (CICLSAL) and the Apostolic Nunciature. They maintained communication with the International Union of Superiors General (IUSG), the Association of Consecrated Women in Eastern and Central Africa (ACWECA), the Association of Member Episcopal Conferences in Eastern Africa (AMECEA) and Episcopal Conference of Malawi (ECM).[330]

Policy and Technical Options to Stop Environmental Degradation

These groups of consecrated life, consolidating the living of Church as God's family between priests, religious sisters and brothers did not only bring the members closer to one another, but had also become tools and springboards for enhancing the promotion of the care for the environment. As religious ministers and workers they understood themselves to have the daunting task of explaining and propagating the integrity of the environment as God's creation. They used their platform to bring messages, based on the Scripture, which aimed at transforming the conduct of the people of God in relation to the environment. The official Catholic Church produced a lot of material on the care of the environment, God's creation, including the most recent encyclical by Pope Francis, *Laudato Si,* which was on the care of the earth (our common home). Many of such publications remained unknown to the ordinary Christians. The clergy and religious women and men saw that it was their responsibility to make such publications and teachings on the care of the environment became known to the ordinary Christians.[331]

---

[330] The Episcopal Conference of Malawi, *Malawi Catholic Directory 2011*, Balaka: Montfort Media, pp. 16-27.
[331] Int Emmanuel Diliwo, Mchinji, 21.8.2016.

The clergy, religious women and men in the Archdiocese of Lilongwe were encouraged to take care of the environment. Following the spirituality of the monastic life of old they were encouraged by the church leadership and the leadership of their different congregations to fall in love with their surrounding in their communities in their parishes and institutions. They were encouraged to take care of their surrounding environment.[332]

The clergy, women and men religious were involved in practical issues and actions related to the environment. As church leaders they encouraged the parish communities to plant trees in the parishes and institutions which they ran in order to maintain the environmental beauty left by the early missionaries. In parishes in the Archdiocese of Lilongwe trees were being planted to keep the green cover of the premises. Examples could be given of Kachebere, Likuni, Chezi, Nanthomba, Ludzi, Guilleme, Mlale, Mpherere, Nkhotakota and Namitete parishes where there were large trees being well taken care of, and others being replanted.[333] However, the challenge remained of seriously taking this initiative to the premises in the rural areas where the people were living like in the Small Christian Communities, outstation centers, and zone centers. In some of these areas the places were bare.

Another challenging area regarding the care of the environment for the clergy, women and men religious groups was in advocacy and the raising of the prophetic voice in defense of creation. These groups, organizations and association of AWRIM, ARIMA, ADCCOL, ADCOM were big organizations which, if they raised their voices loud enough, would have helped the government to seriously consider some of policies that it put in place in endeavouring to alleviate the poverty of the people. Some of the programmes being implemented by the government were not friendly to the environment. The farm subsidy programme, through which the Malawi government provided fertilizer

---

[332] Archbishop Tarsizio Ziyaye, Archdiocese of Lilongwe, homily for final profession mass for religious women, Ludzi parish, 21.8.2016.
[333] Int Raphael Piringu, Guilleme, 23.8.2016.

subsidy to the poorer people, was good in intention but the means remained to be improved. With this programme there were a lot of chemical applications into the soils which in turn polluted the soil and the ground water, leading to their acidification. These ecclesial groups of women and men religious should have raised their voices to speak on behalf of God's creation and prevent it from the utilitarian abuse by humanity. The promotion of organic fertilizers should have been an alternative.

Another government programme the ecclesial groups of men and women religious should have been critical of was the provision of affordable housing to the poor people through the government providing building materials such as cement and iron sheets to the poor so that they would build good and decent houses for themselves. The poor people were to do their part by moulding bricks. A lot of trees were destroyed by this programme because people molded bricks and burnt them using firewood. These ecclesial groups of influence, in a prophetic role for promotion of justice with nature, should have spoken out in support of such a programme but with better means which were friendly to the environment and which should have protected the trees and forest cover. They should have advocated putting a stop to the construction of buildings using bricks burnt using firewood and the promotion of building using either cement blocks or clay blocks.[334]

Development of Family Movements

Since the development of the Catholic Church in the diocese of Lilongwe there has been particular attention by the catechists, marriage counselors, *alangizi*, and clergy towards the instruction of boys, girls and young people in preparation for married life. Meetings of boys and girls, and young people with their *alangizi* monthly in the communities were not rare. There was keen interest by the Church to instruct those in married life, as families, to consider themselves as

---

[334] Int Francis Damaseke, Mlale, and Noel Mtonza, Coordinator, Catholic Commission for Justice and Peace, Likuni, 24.8.2016.

domestic churches since the inception of the Church in Lilongwe more than a century ago. Bishop Mathias Chimole, bishop of Lilongwe, co-signed a pastoral letter together with other Malawian bishops in 1994, the same year the ecclesiology of Church as Family of God was adopted, which was an appeal to the families to be sustained in their efforts to bring marriage and the family to the level which God intended them to realize when he instituted marriage (Gen 1:26-28). The bishops considered the importance of love between the spouses as an expression of love of Christ for his Church (Eph 5:21-33).[335] The Church gave catechetical instruction on the importance of good families which, as domestic churches, became first schools of social values, virtues, prayer, and became the seed bed for vocations to marriage, to the priesthood and the religious life.[336]

The development of the ecclesiology of the Church as the family of God, emanating from the Vatican II ecclesiology of communion, had seen the growth of movements in the Archdiocese of Lilongwe which aimed at fostering the spirit of love and sense of responsibility towards each other in the families. These family movements were also enhancing in the families the spirit of being a domestic church between the spouses and with their children. They served to foster close ties between the spouses and together in the service of church and society. There were two marriage and family apostolate movements in the Archdiocese of Lilongwe which stood out in fostering this love and closeness among the spouses and collectively closeness in the Church. These were the Christian Family Movement (CFM) and Marriage Encounter (ME).

---

[335] The Episcopal Conference of Malawi, *Caring for Our Families: Pastoral Letter to the Catholic Faithful in Celebration of the International Year of the Family*, Balaka: Montfort Media, 1994, p. 3.

[336] Vatican II, *Decree on the Church's Missionary Activity: Ad Gentes Divinitus*, 1965, no. 19.

Marriage Encounter (ME)

Marriage Encounter in the Archdiocese of Lilongwe was part of the movement World Wide Marriage Encounter (WWME), which was the largest pro-family movement that was active in over 90 countries. In 1962, a Spanish priest, Fr. Gabriel Calvo, started the movement with the motto, "love one another; as I have loved you" (Jn 13:34). Over 2.5 million members had become encountered since the movement started. Couples, priests and religious brothers and sisters joined the movement by attending an initiation time which was called an Original Week End (OWE). During the OWE the couple or couples were taken through a series of talks by ME presenters in which they participated towards the arrival of the experience or encounter of a new way of communicating with each other as husband and wife in their lifetime relationship. They discovered this new way of communicating with each other through questions and dialogue in a spirit of love and understanding in a new way that they never encountered before.[337] The Original Week End encouraged the discovery of good communication in order to keep the relationship vibrant and strong. Marriage Encounter provided right communication tools between the spouses, and together in the Church community, to help the relationships at both levels; family and SCCs. The movement taught a simple yet highly effective communication technique that allowed them together to explore important areas in their relationships in a spirit of love, understanding and forgiveness.[338] Thus Marriage Encounter enlivened the spouses in their relationship and it increased love and even romance in the family. It brought the encountered spouses closer to each other and together brought them closer to the Church. It

---

[337] Int Gaudencia Ngala, Robert Ngala, ME leaders, Nkhotakota Circle, Dwangwa and Rosaline Lockie, Davie Lockie, ME leaders, St. Patrick's Circle, Area 12, Lilongwe, 26.6.2016.

[338] Int Grace and Hastings Chiudzu, ME Regional Couple, Central Region, Lilongwe, 27.6.2016.

fostered the deepening of their lifetime commitment and together to enjoy and make their good marriages even better.[339]

It was not only the ones who had taken matrimonial vows, those in blessed marriages, who were allowed to become encountered and consequently members of this movement. Priests, religious brothers and religious sisters could also attend these Original Week End talks where they became encountered and consequently became members of Marriage Encounter. The reasoning behind this was that through their priestly and religious vows they were spiritually and intimately bonded to their Church of Christ which they had to serve with commitment. But they needed to enter together with a person as their spiritual partner who had to be of the same gender; a sister had to attend and carry out the dialogue questions with a fellow sister, and a priest could enter and follow the talks with a fellow priest or religious brother. The understanding was that the commitment of the priests and religious brothers and sisters to the Church was similar to the commitment of husband and wife. The Original Week End helped one to connect more meaningfully to those that one was called to serve with commitment.[340]

Marriage Encounter in the diocese of Lilongwe came at the initiative of Bishop Matthias Chimole. In the mid-1980s he developed keen interest in how WWME couples played roles in the Church as couples in other countries. He desired to have the movement begin in his diocese where he was bishop. In April 1985 he sponsored 2 couples, 2 priests and 4 sisters to attend an Original Week End in Ndola diocese in Zambia. Later on, he invited and sponsored 2 couples and a priest from Lusaka Archdiocese in Zambia, and a couple from the Archdiocese of Harare in Zimbabwe to give the very first Original Week End at Msamba Catholic Conference Centre in the diocese of Lilongwe from 25 to 27 July 1985. During this OWE five couples were encountered as members of this movement and among them were Joseph and Florence Das, Charles and Aline Melleke, and Bishop Chimole

---

[339] www.wwme.org/ [17.5.2016].
[340] Int Sr. Jane Machemba, Mkanda, 18.5.2016.

himself attended the weekend to demonstrate how serious he was to bring ME to the diocese of Lilongwe. When he became encountered his partner was Fr. Silvester Maliseni. The second Original Week End was held the following week from 1 to 3 August where five couples were encountered, some of them being Francis and Esther Namarika, and Zachary and Stella Mullewa.[341] From the diocese of Lilongwe ME reached Mzuzu diocese in 1990 when Fr. Gerald Grimonpoint, French, piloted its introduction in Nkhata-Bay. In 1992 ME reached Blantyre with the efforts of Fr. Montfort Sitima, at the time of writing, bishop of Mangochi diocese, who, after attending an Original Week End, developed the desire to bring the movement to his home diocese and center of ministry Blantyre. The first National Ecclesial Team responsible for the activities of the entire family of ME in Malawi served from 1988 – 1992 and these were Charles and Alinafe Melleke with Fr. Lawrence Chuwa. Joseph and Florence Das with Fr. Marcel became the next National ecclesial team. The movement grew bigger and bigger and by 2016 it prided in having over 700 encountered families in Malawi, plus 19 priests and 18 Sisters.[342] At the time it was Godfrey and Selina Mwenelupembe, who succeeded Frank and Sheila Chinkhandwe, with Fr. Jos Kuppens who were serving as the National Ecclesial Team responsible for the activities of the ME movement at the national level.[343]

In the countryside the movement was divided into regions and circles. There were so far only three regions for ME in Malawi: ME Northern Region, ME Central Region and ME Southern Region. The Marriage Encounter Region for the Centre which comprised the Archdiocese of Lilongwe had more than 250 encountered couples and these were present in 13 circles namely Nkhotakota, Kasungu, St. Francis-Kanengo, Kaggwa, St. Patrick's-Chimutu, St. Kizito-Chigoneka, Maula,

---

[341] Int Ester and Harry Lozo, ME regional treasury couple, Central region, Area 23, Lilongwe, 18.5.2016.

[342] www.mwnation.com/marriage-encounter-clocks-30-yrs-in-malawi/ [13.5.2016].

[343] Int Grace and Hastings Chiudzu, St. Patrick's Circle, Area 12, Lilongwe, 17.5.2016.

Likuni, Mtima-woyera, Msamba, Banja Loyera-Chilinde, Don Bosco, and Mchinji.[344] Since 2014, the leadership team responsible for the Central region (in the Archdiocese of Lilongwe) comprised Hastings and Grace Chiudzu (regional couple), Maxwell and Evetarita Kalulu (facility couple), Harry and Esther Lozo (finance couple), Angella and John Magalasi (liturgy couple) with Fr. Maximian Khisi as the regional team priest. This team's term of office should have expired in 2016 but due to the National Ecclesial Team's uncomfortable feelings and conduct with the leadership team for the centre it was terminated and replaced by a new team on 22 May 2016. The new leadership team for ME Central Region (Archdiocese of Lilongwe) comprised Paul and Kondwani Kulemeka (Regional couple), Mike and Esther Masika (Facility couple), Bon and Rhoda Banda (Finance couple), Macdonald and Mary Mumba (Liturgy couple).[345] Depending on the size of the community membership in the parishes, the members were organized into circles and served by a circle leadership. The leadership positions at all levels (circle, regional and national) were for a renewable term of three years. The movement had a number of challenges including leadership wrangles between the regional team and some circle leadership, between the regional team and the national ecclesial team, clash of powers between the National Board of Marriage Encounter and the National Consultative Board which, instead of playing the advisory role to the ME at the national level, became a decision maker in the process. There were also financial problems which made it difficult for couples which were poorer to attend the OWE as they had to pay for themselves for their lodging and attendance of an Original Week End at a designated conference centre. There was also the language problem as up to 2016 the talks which were presented in the OWE were still in English and not in the vernacular. This made it difficult for those who did not speak English to

---

[344] Int Evetarita and Maxwell Kalulu, ME Facility Couple, Central Region, Lilongwe, 23.5.2016.

[345] Int Grace Chiudzu, Area 10, Lilongwe, 22.5.2016.

attend the OWE, become members of ME and participate in the movement.[346]

The Christian Family Movement (CFM)

Another lay family movement active in the Archdiocese of Lilongwe was the Christian Family Movement (CFM). It was a member of the International Confederation of Christian Family Movements (ICCFM). The Christian Family Movement began in 1940 in South Bend, Indiana and Chicago, Illinois. It was started by Burnie Bauer and his wife Helene with the mission of promoting Christ-centered marriage and family life, helping individuals and their families to live the Christian faith in everyday life, and to improve the society through actions of love, service, education and example. The movement was introduced in the diocese of Lilongwe for these intentions in 1980 during the time of Bishop Matthias Chimole. The CFM was a concrete expression of the family as 'domestic church' in which members lived their faith actively. It was a movement of parish small groups of Catholics and their families who met in one another's homes or in parish centres to reinforce Christian values and encourage Christian parents through active involvement with others. Membership comprised families who sought to promote Christian values and work together with all other church groups to promote growth of the Church and families. During their meetings the members practiced the See (Observe)-Judge-Act method.[347] In 2016, the diocesan leaders of CFM in the Archdiocese of Lilongwe were Mr. and Mrs. Saizi. There were other smaller groups of the lay family apostolate in the Archdiocese of Lilongwe such as the Pro-Life Movement, Focolare Movement, Teams of Our Lady, and Couples for Christ. The pro-life movement getting its roots in the Archdiocese of Lilongwe steadily was part of Human Life International. It had members in Madisi, Mponela, Lumbadzi, Mtima Woyera, Salima and Likuni parishes. The leadership of the movement provided pro-life

---

[346] Int Hastings, Chiudzu, St. Patrick's Circle – Area 12, Lilongwe, 17.4.2016.

[347] "See (Observe)-Judge-Act" is a method of reflection, group discussion and action identification which was founded by Joseph Cadjin, the founder of the Young Christian Workers in Belgium. It is also called the Jocist Method.

education programmes and trained couples and families in Natural Family Planning (NFP) as the Catholic Church's accepted method of population control amidst the growing understanding that the growth in population exerts pressure on the environment and leads to the exploitation of its resources.[348] The pro-life movement strengthened the institution of family in and outside the Church as the foundation of society. It engaged couples from the grassroots of the Church to appreciate the gift of human life based on the Bible, take care of it, and resist the growing attempts of government and parliament to legalize abortion as a means of population control and reducing the pressure on the environment.[349]

These Catholic Christian family movements fostered the concretization of the understanding of the Church as the Family of God. Such movements were also present in other dioceses of Malawi and because of this a need was felt to coordinate the activities of these movements at the national level of the Catholic Church in Malawi and also to foster good relationships between movements. In May 2016, the National Pastoral Directorate at the Episcopal Conference of Malawi (ECM) spearheaded and concluded the work that led to the formation of the Association of Catholic Family Movements with the purpose of advancing the family apostolate both in the Church and in society.[350]

The members of these family movements as a must belonged to the grassroots ecclesial groups of the Small Christian Communities, Catholic Women Organization, Catholic Men and Catholic Youth organizations so much that they participated in these different groups' initiative in taking care of the environment: through improved sanitation, planting of trees, saving energy, practice of conservation agriculture and attempts at population control. On a very deeper level

---

[348] Int Alphaeus Zikomankhani, diocesan director, Pro-Life Movement, Likuni, 30.8.2016.

[349] Int Klara, Sambakunsi, Madisi, Peter Sambakunsi, Pro-life Movement members, Madisi, 4.9.2016.

[350] Int Vincent Mwakhwawa, Acting Coordinator, ECM Pastoral Directorate, Area 11, Lilongwe, 10.5.2016.

these family groups helped the couples to create more awareness on responsible parenthood as a means of reducing undue pressure on the environment and its resources.

Conclusion

The great advantages the application of the concept of Church as God's Family is that it has brought greater bonds and links of fraternity among the members of the Church and fostered the engagement of believing communities towards saving the environment. Christians in the different expressions of the Church as God's Family in Lilongwe Archdiocese took part to save the environment.

The different Archdiocesan Commissions and Centres involved in the environmental salvation were doing something with the people at and through the grassroots communities (SCCs) to mitigate environmental destruction rampant in the territory. The Education Commission, Health Commission, Catholic Development Commission (CADECOM), Catholic Commission for Justice and Peace, the Jesuit Centre for Ecology and Development, the Primary Eco-Schools Programme, Center for Social Concern were in some important ways involved in this task. The different gender, age, and vocation based ecclesial organizations were also involved towards saving the environment, and these included: Catholic Women Organization, Catholic Men Organization, and the Diocese of Lilongwe Council for Catholic Youth, the Association of priests (ADCCOL), and the Association of Religious Institutes in Malawi-Lilongwe Chapter. Other specific family movements in the local Church of Lilongwe also took part in the care of the environment. These specific familial movements were the Marriage Encounter (ME) and Christian Family Movements (CFM).

The imbalance between the policy and technical options to stop environmental degradation in the Archdiocese of Lilongwe, emanating from the usage of the ecclesiology of Church as God's Family, was unearthed. The environmental and ecological commitments did not match the gravity of the problem. They were sporadic and little effect was seen on the ground in terms of environmental mitigation. Much as the ecclesiology of Church as God's Family was lived in the Archdiocese of Lilongwe, had managed to do was to bring the believers closer together, and not closer to nature. The Christians in the Church no longer lived as mere individual women and men without links, but now they lived with stronger human relationships and a strong sense of belonging to the same family, the Family of God.

Whilst being involved in some ways in saving the environment, the expression of the new ecclesiology in the Archdiocese of Lilongwe did not bear significant results on the environment and God's creation. God's creation as existing in the environment remained so much alienated. People still largely looked at nature as an object and raw material to be exploited for human support, progress and development. There was not much sense of universal fraternity with the rest of God's creation. The people looked at themselves as above, not as part of, God's creation and almost at liberty to do anything they wanted to with nature and the environment. With such mentality and actuality, the environment, being God's creation, has been used and abused by people for their selfish ends. The model of Church as God's Family managed to bring people closer to one another but alienated them from the rest of God's creation (nature). It contributed more towards the protection of human life and not much to the protection of the world of nature. With the goodness and richness contained in the model of Church as God's Family, there was a need for a development and usage of a complementary ecclesiological concept which would be a source of religious convictions for sensitivity and responsibility for God's creation. There was need for a discovery of a concept from where an ecclesiology of inclusion for nature would emerge; a concept which would bring more awareness and actuality about the salvation of the environment and the consequent human responsibility for the earth and its resources.

Chapter 9: Church as New Creation, a New Concept for Saving the Environment

Having looked at the imbalance between the protection of human life and the protection of the world of creation brought about by the self-understanding, expressions and applications of the Church as God's Family in the Archdiocese of Lilongwe, there was need to propose a complementary ecclesiological concept. This proposed new ecclesiological concept, if reclaimed, adopted and used, would augment the strengths and richness contained in the other models of the Church including that of Church as God's Family. It would help in the salvation of the environment. Such a proposal was the reclaiming and development of the ecclesiological concept (self-understanding) of Church as New Creation, *Nova Creatio*.

The recommendation of this new ecclesiological concept, of Church as New Creation, is not a denial of the validity of the self-understanding of Church as God's Family but that, with the problem raised about the Church's self-understanding of being Family of God and its implications and mitigation in the Archdiocese of Lilongwe, this reclaiming of the self-understanding of Church would complement the other models and lead to an ecologically sensitive and inclusive ecclesiology which would provide a powerful ethos for convictions about environmental care and mitigation.

The Church, though having its transcendental origins, cannot be a real Church independent of its history. The phenomenon and experience of the people (with its problems and challenges) is to influence the way of being Church in a particular epoch. The historical experience of the people in their part of the world provides the *fora* for definition and mission of the Church. This process is a must for the Church if it is to remain relevant. Ecclesiology from its own perspective, like other forms of art, science, education and wisdom, has to contribute towards addressing the ecological and environmental crisis.

Openness to the Present Situation

There is an urgent need for the Church in the Archdiocese of Lilongwe in its self-understanding to be attentive to the present situation with its problems and challenges. The Church cannot not be real church without being attentive to the challenges and problems of its history. History shapes the way of being church and the experiences of the world provide the *locus* for the mission of the Church. The Church is to strike a balance between the beauty of the applications of the values in the model of Church as God's Family and the requirements of the Church today amidst its challenges. The Church does not exist in a vacuum. It exists in history, in time and space and has hence to be defined, in part, by its historical context. This openness to the needs of the present situation is important, if not necessary, in order for the Church to remain relevant. There is certainly a lot of meaning, goodness and beauty with the model of Church as God's Family which has been the driving force in African ecclesiology in modern times. It is a model highly founded not only in African sociology and anthropology, but also with a rich biblical and theological basis. However, given the natural environmental challenges of our present situation in Africa in general,[1] and in the Archdiocese of Lilongwe, there is need to tilt the ecclesiological understanding of the local church towards one which will assist in the provision of answers to the needs of the present time. This in no way is to mean the model of Church as God's Family is no longer relevant, but that there is need for a complimentary understanding that will assist in dealing with the problem and challenge of the destruction of the natural environment.

The current image of the Church in the Archdiocese of Lilongwe of Church as God's Family has a lot of advantages. In being so, the Church is conscious of one of the most striking features of today's world; the intense development of interpersonal relationships which is seen in the advancement of genuine fraternal dialogue and human fellowship that has led to the promotion of deeper understanding of the laws of

---

[1] Benedict XIV, *Africae Munus*, nos. 79-80, p. 40.

social living among human beings.² This is in tandem with the design of God who willed to accord a communitarian nature to the human vocation. The human being is not a solitary being. From the beginning God made them male and female: "It is not good for the man to be alone. I will make a helper suitable for him" (Gen 2:18). This partnership between man and woman at the very moment of their creation constituted the first form of communion between persons. By their innermost nature human beings are social beings. And if a person does not enter into relations with others they can neither live nor develop their gifts and potentials. There is interdependence between human beings and their society, and interdependence between the personal growth and the growth of society. The person needs society and the society needs the person. Through their dealings with others, through mutual service, fraternal dialogue, human beings develop their talents and are able to rise to their destiny. In the present time these mutual relationships and interdependence have increased from day to day giving rise to a variety of organizations and associations, both public and private. This socialization is not without its dangers. But it certainly brings with it many advantages for the strengthening and betterment of human life and qualities.

God, in his fatherly care for all, desires that all human beings form one family and deal with each other in a spirit of fraternity or brotherhood. All of humanity is in fact destined to the very same end just as it has the same common origin.³ Just as God did not create human beings to live as individuals but to come together in the formation of social unity, so he willed to make them holy and save them, not as individuals without any bond or link between them, but rather to make them into a people who would acknowledge him and serve him in holiness.⁴ At the very outset of the history of salvation as

---

[2] Denys Turner (ed), *The Church in the Modern World*, Dublin: Scepter, 1968, p. 100.

[3] The Second Vatican Council, *Pastoral Constitution on the Church in the Modern World, Gaudium et Spes, GS,* no. 24.

[4] The Second Vatican Council, *Dogmatic Constitution on the Church, Lumen Gentium,* no. 9.

enlightened by Scripture, God chose a certain people as members of a given community, not as individuals, and revealed his plan to them, calling them his people. In sending Moses to lead the Israelites out of the Egyptian slavery, God calls them his people: "I have indeed seen the misery of my people in Egypt" (Ex 3:7). "And now the cry of the Israelites has reached me, and I have seen the way the Egyptians are oppressing them" (Ex 3:9). God then made a covenant with his people on Mount Sinai to which his people agreed saying: "Everything the Lord has said we will do" (Ex 24:3b).

Human beings need one another and rely on each other. Love of God and love of neighbour is the first and greatest of all the commandments. The Scripture teaches that the love of God cannot be separated from the love of one's neighbour. Therefore, love of one's neighbour is the fulfillment of the law: "Let no debt remain outstanding, except the continuing debt to love one another, for he who loves his fellowman has fulfilled the law" (Rom 13:8), and "whoever claims to love God yet hates a brother or a sister is a liar" (1 Jh 4:20). It goes without saying that it is of utmost importance that in the world today human beings are coming to rely more and more on each other. The world, as it were, is drawing together every day. Furthermore, the Lord Jesus Christ prayed to his Father for his disciples requesting that the disciples may all be one, even as the Father, the Son and the Holy Spirit are one (Jn 17:21-22). This opened new horizons to human reason by implying that there is a certain parallelism between the union existing among the divine persons and the union of the sons and daughters of God in truth and love. It did promote the spirit of interdependence.

The communitarian nature of the Church is perfected and fulfilled in the work of Jesus Christ, for he, the Word made flesh, willed and liked to share in human fellowships. For example, he was present at the wedding in Cana. Jesus and his disciples had also been invited to the wedding (Jn 2:2). Jesus visited the house of Zacchaeus. He stayed at Zacchaeus' house that day (Lk 19:6) and sat down with publicans and sinners. In his preaching he clearly outlined an obligation on the part of the sons and daughters of God to treat each other as brothers and sisters, hence making up a family. He prayed for them to be united. As redeemer of the world he delivered himself even unto death for the sake of all. No one has greater love than Jesus who laid down his own life for his friends (Jn 15:13). His command to the apostles was to preach the Gospel to all peoples in order that the human race would become the Family of God. As the first-born of many brethren, Christ established by the gift of the Holy Spirit a new brotherly communion among all who received him in faith and love. This is the communion of his own body, the Church, in which everyone as members of the other should render mutual service in the measure of the different gifts bestowed on each. This solidarity among all the believers is to constantly increase until the day when it will be brought to fulfillment.[5] Thus, it can be seen that it is very right to envision the Church as the Family of God and such a vision has such afore-seen advantages.

However, in as much as there are some constants in the nature of the Church, the Church is not a static-reality. It evolves and responds to the challenges of its time and space (historical context). It keeps, as it were, changing the goal posts according to the needs of the time. As it does so, the Church does not discard the old, but builds on it to envisage the new so as to be relevant and responsive to the challenges and problems of the day. The Church is always encouraged to be open to the needs of the time. There is need for the Church, universal or local, to be in solidarity with the whole human family including the challenges it is going through. The Second Vatican Council's pastoral constitution on the Church in the modern world, *Gaudium et Spes*, states that the joy, hope and anguish of the present time, especially of those who are poor or afflicted in any way, are the joy and hopes and grief and anguish of the Church as followers of Christ. The Church cannot stand aloof from the problems and challenges of the people of its time. It is composed of people who are united with Jesus Christ and guided by the Holy Spirit pressing onwards towards the kingdom of God and they are bearers of the message of salvation which is intended not only for the world of humans but for the entire universe

---

[5] The Second Vatican Council, *Pastoral Constitution of the Church in the Modern World, Gaudium et Spes*, no. 32.

which is God's creation. This is the reason why the Church needs to cherish a feeling of solidarity with the world, the human race and its history (past, present and future).[6]

In today's world, understood as the theatre of human history, it is also always imperative for the Church to think of how it would remain relevant. The Church needs to think about how it is going to be present in the contemporary situation of the world and nature and function in this atmosphere. This world, bearing the marks of its travail, triumphs and failures, has been created and is sustained by its Creator. It is freed from the slavery of sin by Jesus Christ so that it might be fashioned anew according to God's design and finally brought to its destiny and fulfillment. At all times the Church carries the duty to read the signs of the time and to interpret them in the light of the Gospel. The Church needs to respond to the problems and challenges of the present time. The questions that bother the world and human history call for answers and the Church, among other institutions, is to respond to the promptings of the Holy Spirit. It is imperative for the Church to do this in a language that is intelligible to every generation according to its needs and questions. The Church is to speak in its theology and practice of a social and cultural transformation whose repercussions are felt, too, on the religious-ecclesiological level.[7]

To the problem and challenge of the degradation of nature and the environment as experienced in the geographical confines of the Archdiocese of Lilongwe, which the ecclesiology of Church as God's Family did not address much, there is need for the local Church to revisit its ecclesiological self-understanding. While not neglecting this ecclesiology of Church as Family of God, the local Church in Lilongwe has to embark on the theological development of another model of Church that would help bring about the much-needed sensitivity and concern for creation and the care and protection of the environment.

---

[6] The Second Vatican Council, *The Pastoral Constitution on the Church in the Modern World*, no. 1.

[7] Denys Turner (ed), *The Church in the Modern World*, Dublin: Scepter, 1968, pp. 83, 84.

Importance of and Relatedness to 'Laudato Si'

In May 2015, Pope Francis published an encyclical titled '*Laudato Si*' on the need for care of the environment which is humanity's common home. It is not only addressed to the believers but also to all people of good will. The title of his publication, '*Laudato Si, mi Signore* (Latin for Praise be to you, my Lord),' was taken from the very first words of the Canticle of the Creatures, a prayer, reflection and song composed by Francis of Assisi (1181-1226) in which he reminded all that the earth was a common home and like a sister with whom humanity and all nature shared life and like a beautiful mother who opened her arms to embrace all reality. Pope Francis, in this encyclical, bemoaned that the earth was being harmed and exploited by human activity, and that this cannot be indifferent to humanity's life. The destruction humanity has caused to sister and mother earth (nature) is beginning to bite back. He said:

> This sister now cries out to us because of the harm we have inflicted on her by our irresponsible use and abuse of the goods with which God has endowed her. We have come to see ourselves as her lords and masters, entitled to plunder her at will. The violence present in our hearts, wounded by sin, is also reflected in the symptoms of sickness evident in the soil, in the water, in the air and all forms of life. This is why the earth herself, burdened and laid waste, is among the most abandoned and maltreated of our poor; she groans in travail (Rom 8:22). We have forgotten that we ourselves are dust of the earth (Gen 2:7); our very bodies are made up of her elements, we breathe her air and we receive life and refreshment from her waters.[8]

This effort being presented herein agrees with Pope Francis in *Laudato Si* that the effects of environmental degradation like global warming, climate change, intermittent rain patterns, dry spells, floods, storms, decline in the quality of human life resulting from the pollutions of the water, land and air among others, were not simply natural disasters.

---

[8] Pope Francis, *Laudato Si: Encyclical Letter on the Care for Our Common Home*, 2015, p. 7.

There is a human cause to these scenarios; there are human roots to the environmental and ecological crisis.

In this encyclical, as unfolded in its six chapters, Pope Francis drew the attention of the people of good will and believers to what was happening to mother earth, humanity's common home. There is pollution (of the land, soil, air and environment) some of whose forms are part of people's daily experience. This pollution, among others, happens due to the use of atmospheric pollutants, transport and industrial fumes, use of substances that contribute to the acidification of water, soil and air, poor waste management and the throwaway culture. Such things produce a broad spectrum of health hazards, especially among the poor. They also lead to climate change, loss of biodiversity, decline in the quality of human life and the breakdown of society. It also leads to global inequality since the human environment and the natural environment deteriorate together.[9] The deterioration of the environment and of society affect the most vulnerable of the planet. Both everyday experience and scientific research show that the gravest effects of all attacks on the environment are suffered by the poorest.[10] For example, the depletion of fishing reserves especially hurts small fishing communities without the means to replace those resources; water pollution particularly affects the poor who cannot manage to buy bottled water; and the rise in the sea level mainly affects impoverished coastal communities or populations who have nowhere else to flee to.

While there are natural causes to the ecological crisis, Pope Francis, in *Laudato Si*, acknowledged like many others, that there are also human roots to the ecological crisis. A certain way of understanding human life and activity has gone awry, to the detriment of the world surrounding people. Such human roots include the creativity and power brought by technology, the globalization of the technocratic

---

[9] Pope Francis, *Laudato Si*, pp. 16-29.

[10] Bolivian Bishops' Conference, Pastoral Letter on the Environment and Human Development in Bolivia, *El Universo, don de Dios para la vida*, 2012, p. 17.

paradigm, and crisis and effects of modern anthropocentrism. Humanity has entered a new era in which the technical prowess has brought people to a crossroads. Science and technology are wonderful products of a God-given human creativity.[11] Technology has remedied countless evils which used to harm and limit human beings. This includes the advances in the areas of medicine, engineering and communications. These are worth appreciating. However, there is a problem that the contemporary persons have not been trained to use the technological power well, because the immense technological development has not been accompanied by a development in human responsibility, values and conscience. Human beings are so much focused on their freedom, immediate needs, self-interest, security, and consequently creation is viewed largely as a utility or raw material for human development and progress.[12] This attempt has established among others the utilitarian approach that human beings have in the Archdiocese of Lilongwe towards nature or the environment. The application of the Church in the concept of being the Family of God has led to the objectification and subordination of nature. Human beings and material objects which exist in the environment no longer extend a friendly hand to one another. The relationship has become confrontational.

The globalization of the technocratic paradigm has made it easy to accept the idea of infinite or unlimited growth, so attractive to economists, financiers and experts in technology. This is based on the lie that there is an infinite supply of the earth's goods, and this has led to the planet being squeezed dry beyond every limit. It is a false notion that an infinite quantity of energy and resources are available, that it is possible to renew them quickly, and that the negative effects of the exploitation of the natural order can be easily absorbed.[13] There is need to realize that science and technology, from the beginning to the

---

[11] John Paul II, *Address to Scientists and Representatives of the United Nations University*, Hiroshima (25 February 1981), 3: AAS 73 (1981), p. 422.

[12] Pope Francis, *Laudato Si*, p. 61.

[13] Pontifical Council for Justice and Peace, *Compendium of the Social Doctrine of the Church*, p. 464.

end of the process, are not neutral. There is need to slow down and look at reality in a different way.

Modern anthropocentrism has paradoxically ended up prizing technical thought over reality, since the technological mind sees nature (God's creation) as an insensate order, as a cold body of facts, as an object of utility, as raw material to be hammered into useful shape; it views the cosmos similarly as a mere 'space' into which objects could be thrown with complete indifference. Modernity has been marked by an excessive anthropocentrism which in modern times, under another guise, continues to stand in the way of shared understanding and of any effort to strengthen social bonds. An inadequate presentation of Christian anthropology has given rise to a wrong understanding of the relationship between human beings and the world. Often what is handed down is the vision of mastery over the world which gives the impression that the protection of nature is something which the faint-hearted care about. There is need to realize that everything in the world is interrelated.

Since everything is interrelated and interconnected, the current problems call for a vision capable of taking into account every aspect of the global crisis. Hence, it is not possible to talk of only environmental ecology without a fair consideration of the other aspects of the global reality. Since ecology studies the relationship between living organisms and the environment in which they develop, the care of the earth and the entire universe has to take into account all its ingredients: environment, people and society, economics, and cultures. In summary there is need for an integral ecology, one that clearly respects its material, human, social, and cultural dimensions. Authentic development should include efforts to bring about an integral development in the quality of human life, and this entails considering the setting in which people live their lives. Human ecology has to be sensitive to the notion of the common good, a central and unifying principle of social ethics. In the human approach and relation to the world there is need to show sensitivity and solidarity with the poor who too are endowed with basic and inalienable rights ordered to their integral development. There has to be sensitivity of justice between the generations. The goods of the earth are not only meant for the people living today, but also for those coming in future when even the present generation will be long gone. This must limit the modern people's models of production and consumption.[14]

Laudato Si acknowledges the variety of opinions which are there regarding environmental degradation and these lay the basis for the different approaches and lines of thought which have emerged regarding this situation and its possible solutions. At one extreme are those who uphold the myth of progress and say that the ecological and environmental problems will solve themselves simply with the application of new technologies and without any need for ethical considerations or radical change by human beings. At the other extreme are those who view people and their interventions and activities as the big threat, jeopardizing the global ecosystem, and consequently the presence of human beings needs to be reduced and all forms of interventions prohibited. Pope Francis said that viable future scenarios would have to be generated between these extremes, since there was no one path to a solution to any problem, let alone this one of environmental degradation.[15] Hence a variety of proposals is possible to redress the problem of the ecological crisis, all capable of entering into dialogue with the intention of developing comprehensive solutions to the problem. In this view, an honest debate of ideas is encouraged but not in the abstract way but aimed at reaching good proposals for the redressing of the issue of environmental degradation. There must be a way out, which can redirect the human steps so that they can do something to solve the problems.

Pope Francis, in *Laudato Si,* proposes a number of approaches and actions, and such included an honest dialogue on the environment in the international community, dialogue for new national and local policies, dialogue and transparency in decision-making, politics and economy in dialogue for human fulfillment, and religions in dialogue with science.[16] To achieve this integral ecology he proposes an ecologi-

---

[14] Pope Francis, *Laudato Si*, pp. 79-89.
[15] Pope Francis, *Laudato Si*, p. 36.
[16] Pope Francis, *Laudato Si*, pp. 92-109.

cal education and spirituality which would mark a movement towards a new lifestyle, educating for the covenant between humanity and the environment and the need for an ecological conversion in human beings. This conversion entails a new way of relating between human beings and the world. This will be possible if human beings avail themselves to be enlightened by the light of faith and to understand the gospel of creation. This gospel of creation, as articulated by the Scriptures, means understanding the need of respecting everything that shares in 'being' and 'existence' for they are all good: "God saw everything that he had made, and behold it was very good" (Gen 1:31). This means everything that shares in being bears the spark and spirit of the Supreme Being and Good, God himself. Human beings, created, are endowed with dignity for they are created and made in God's image and likeness. This shows the immense dignity of each person, "who is not just something, but someone. They are capable of self-knowledge, of self-possession and of freely giving themselves and entering into communion with other persons."[17] This being created in the image of and likeness of God is not a conferral of superiority with unlimited freedom to plunder the resources of the world at will. It is rather a conferral of a mission to take care of the things that God has made. This is the understanding of the mandate of 'dominion' (Gen 1:28) over the earth and of 'tilling it and keeping it' (Gen 2:15) which people had before it was distorted by sin. This gospel of creation means the understanding that there is nothing in the created world that is free of ownership. The created things of this world are God's. God is their proprietor: "For they are yours, O Lord, who love the living" (Wis 11:26). Human beings have to relate with them with the sense of universal communion and deal with them with the highest sense of stewardship. They have to care for nature knowing that the earth is essentially a shared inheritance, whose fruits are meant to benefit everyone, including the future generations,

Many things have to change, but it is above all human beings who need to change. The new lifestyle means for human beings to make a new start, capable of rising above themselves, and choosing again

---

[17] John Paul II, *Catechism of the Catholic Church*, no. 357.

what is good. It should involve changes in human models of production and consumption. The human beings need to develop the awareness of their common origin, of their mutual belonging, and of a future to be shared with everyone. They must be capable of going out of themselves towards the other. Unless they do this, other creatures will not be recognized for their true worth. This basic awareness will enable the development of new convictions, attitudes and forms of life. Ecological education, aimed at creating an ecological citizenship, should not be limited to providing information only and fail to instill good habits. There is a nobility in the duty to care for creation through little daily actions and in this way the ecological education could bring about real changes in lifestyle. In this vein Pope Francis said:

> Education in environmental responsibility can encourage ways of acting which directly and significantly affect the world around us, such as avoiding the use of plastic paper, reducing water consumption, separating refuse, cooking only what can be consumed, showing care for other living beings, using public transport, planting trees, turning off unnecessary lights, or any number of other practices. All of these reflect a generous and worthy creativity which brings out the best in human beings. Reusing something instead of immediately discarding it, when done for the right reasons, can be an act of love which expresses our own dignity.[18]

Given the complexity of the ecological crisis and the environmental problem and their multiple causes, there is need to realize that the solutions will not emerge from just one way of interpreting and transforming reality. Respect has to be shown for the various cultural riches of different peoples, their interior life and spirituality. If people are truly concerned to develop an ecology capable of remedying the damage they have done, no branch of the sciences and no form of

---

[18] Pope Francis, *Laudato Si*, p. 116.

wisdom can be left out, and that includes religion and the language particular to it.[19]

In this vein, theology, including the discipline of ecclesiology, cannot be left out. It has to be deployed in the search for provision of answers which will redirect human steps in dealing with nature and the environment. It has to be deployed in the search for the provision of an ethos which will trigger radical change in human beings on how they view and related to nature, and one which will spark off a new style of life in terms of relation, production and consumption. Pope Francis mentioned, in *Laudato Si* that the ecological commitments for the believers, which will in turn influence other human beings around them in the world, will among other things develop from their convictions.[20] They will stem from their convictions of who they are as Church.

Since the greater social cohesion (human fraternity) among believers in the Archdiocese of Lilongwe largely stemmed from the concept of Church as God's Family, there is need for the development of a new concept of being Church which will generate the required ecological commitments. In this pursuit the book proposes the reclaiming of the ecclesiological concept of Church as New Creation, *Nova Creatio*. This will reignite in them the sense of what the believers have become through their conversion, faith and commitment to the way of Christ, as well as re-awaken in them the awareness of their mission to renewing the face of the earth. This concept will contribute from the religious point of view towards providing an ethos for a renewed view of nature (creation), renewed Christian anthropology, change in the relationship to nature, change in lifestyles, and change in the models of production and consumption.

The Church as New Creation

There is need for the Church in Lilongwe to get more involved in the promotion of care and respect for, and protection of the natural

---

[19] Pope Francis, *Laudato Si*, p. 38.
[20] Pope Francis, *Laudato Si*, p. 39.

environment. Environmental mitigation is much more than mere planting of trees since the ecological and environmental crisis is much more complex. The Church together with the other populace in this region has to resist the evident temptation of the diminishing concern for the environment. One of the ways the Church can do this is to renew its ecclesiology and promote human radical change in lifestyles, habits, models of production and consumption. There is need to rediscover ecclesiological concepts which will include the whole of God's creation in the understanding of the redemptive and salvific mission of the Church. One such way is to promote the understanding of the Church as a New Creation, *Nova creatio*. The concept of Church as New Creation will bring back human beings to the realm of God's creation and bring about more sensitivity towards caring for the rest of life and being. The self-understanding of the Church as Family of God has promoted human feelings of superiority over nature. The concept of Church as new creation, bearing the feeling of universal fraternity, can shape the practices of the Church in favour of saving the natural environment. This reality and expectancy of the new creation can spur on the people in the Archdiocese of Lilongwe to participate in renewing the face of the earth. The Second Vatican Council's document, *Gaudium et Spes*, speaks about the new earth and the new heaven, and it states that there is no knowledge of the moment of the consummation of the earth and of human beings: "It is not for you to know the time or dates the Father has set by his own authority" (Ac 1:7).Tere is also no knowledge of the way the universe will be transformed. But one thing is sure, that the form of this world, distorted by sin, is passing away: "For this world in its present form is passing away"(1 Cor 7:31b), and God is preparing a new earth in which righteousness dwells: "Meanwhile we groan, longing to be clothed instead with our heavenly dwelling" (2 Cor 5:2), and Peter wrote, "But in keeping with his promise we are looking forward to a new heaven and a new earth, the home of righteousness" (2 Pet 3:13). The happiness of the new creation will surpass all the desires of peace arising in the hearts of people: "No eye has seen, no ear has heard, no mind has conceived what God has prepared for those who love him" (1 Cor 2:9). Then with death conquered, the sons of God will be raised in Christ and what was sown in weakness and dishonor will put on the imperishable (1 Cor 15:42, 53), and all of creation will be set free from its bondage to decay (Rom 8:19-21).[21] This is the kingdom of God. Here on earth the kingdom is mysteriously present; but when the Lord returns it will enter into perfection and consummation.

The proposal of the concept of Church as a New Creation which the Archdiocese of Lilongwe should utilize to bring about more and more concern for nature and creation has rich biblical and theological foundations. The Bible is the story of salvation. In this story, the introductory chapters occupy a unique place and they speak about creation and all that exists. There is a solemn expression of the truth of creation and how it originated and how it will end. Creation originated and ends in God, and he is the source of its order and goodness. There is the pronunciation that in the beginning God created the heavens and the earth (Gen 1:1). These introductory chapters also speak about the vocation of man and woman in propagating what was created, and then they speak about the drama of sin. The profession of the Catholic faith took it up from there that God the Father Almighty is the creator of heaven and earth (Apostles' creed), of all that is seen and unseen (Nicene Creed).[22] The biblical story is one and its events are necessarily connected. It is about God the creator, then creation, the fall into sin and its consequences on humanity and nature, then about Jesus Christ, the Son of God, who came to raise up the fallen world. Thus, creation is the foundation of all of God's saving plans.[23] If there was no creation, there would have been no need of a plan of salvation by God. Creation is the starting point of the salvation history that culminates in Jesus Christ. The mystery of Christ casts conclusive light on the mystery of creation and reveals the end for which, in the beginning, God created the heavens and the earth.

---

[21] The Second Vatican Council, *The Pastoral Constitution on the Church in the Modern World, Gaudium et Spes*, no. 39.

[22] German Bishops' Conference (Translated by Stephen Wentworth), *The Church's Confession of Faith: A Catholic Catechism for Adults*, San Francisco: Ignatius, 1985, p. 10.

[23] John Paul II, *The Catechism of the Catholic Church*, no. 280.

From the very beginning God envisaged the glory of the new creation in Christ. With the fall of humanity, the whole cosmos was held accountable to God: "Now we know that whatever the law says, it says to those who are under the law, so that every mouth may be silenced and the whole world held accountable to God" (Rom 3:19). Through human sin the whole world became subject to God's judgment: "When we are judged by the Lord, we are being disciplined so that we will not be condemned with the world" (1 Cor 11:32). Through sin human beings became by nature children of wrath: "Like the rest, we were by nature deserving of wrath" (Eph 2:3), and the world was in the power of the evil one: "We know that we are children of God, and that the whole world is under the control of the evil one" (1 Jh 5:19), and the devil is the prince of this world. The devil is the source of this situation in the world which needs salvation.

However, the Bible is equally conscious of the other side of the coin, namely that God nonetheless loved this world that he gave his only Son, not to condemn the world, but to pronounce liberation over it: "For God so loved the world that he gave his one and only Son, that whoever believes in him shall not perish but have eternal life" (Jn 3:16), and Jesus Christ speaking about this great love and mercy of God said: "For I did not come to judge the world, but to save it" (Jn 12:47b). God has compassion over this world which needs to be saved. In Jesus Christ, God entered into the world, where the devil ruled in order to redeem it. Jesus Christ overcame this alienation from God. The entry of God himself into the world, incarnation, brought meaning and sense into the world of humanity and the result of this redeeming entry of God into the world in the person of Jesus Christ went to the very root of human existence.[24] In this context, Paul explicitly said that if anyone was in Christ, he was a new creation: "Therefore, if anyone is in Christ, he is a new creation; the old has gone, the new has come!" (2 Cor 5:17). This means that not only has the person acquired a new reality through grace, but also the person, as a person in the universe

---

[24] Edward Schillebeeckx, *World and Church*, London: Sheed & Ward, 1971, pp. 5-7.

(world) has been renewed in and through grace in Christ. The redeemed world becomes a new creation and a kingdom of God.

The articulation of the theology of new creation is very important in the development of this concept of Church as New Creation. The new creation is a concept found in the New Testament (though prefigured in the Old Testament), related to the new life, new man and new woman. The newness refers to the spiritual rebirth through Christ Jesus. There are two biblical verses where the actual phrase, the new creation, is found and these are Gal 6:15[25] and 2 Cor 5:17.[26] But the language of the new creation is also contained, included and alluded to in other verses in the Pauline Corpus. 2 Cor 5:14-19 speaks about the ministry of reconciliation by Christ. Since he died for all, he was also raised again for all. So, those who live do not live for themselves only. The Church is called not only to live for itself, but also for others and for the rest of God's creation that it attains its fulfillment. In Eph 4:17-24, Paul gave the Christian community in Ephesus some pertinent instructions for Christian living having being made new through their faith in Jesus. As new creatures they were to be different from the Gentiles. Christians needed not be full of greed. They were not to indulge in every kind of impurity. He reminded them that they had put off the old self, corrupted by its deceitful desires, and were to put on a new self, created to be like God in righteousness and holiness. In Eph 2:11-22, Paul instructed them that Christ had destroyed the enmity between humanity and God and brought back the peace that reigned, as it were, in the Garden of Eden. Humanity has to be seen as one and creation as one, without any hostile boundaries. Through Christ, all are now reconciled. In Col 3:1-18, Paul spoke about the new nature that the believers possessed and put on. He told the Colossians to clothe themselves with compassion, kindness, humility, gentleness and patience. These texts, too, present the teaching on new creation even

---

[25] "Neither circumcision nor uncircumcision means anything; what counts is a new creation" (NIV).

[26] "Therefore, if anyone is in Christ, he is a new creation; the old has gone, the new has come! (NIV)

though without the exact phrase.[27] Other references include Eph 2:10. In such Pauline texts, the apostle Paul was dealing with one of his favourite themes, the death and resurrection of Jesus. He was arguing that the death upon the cross was not an end in itself, but the necessary step towards the resurrection, and that the new life which was manifested in that wonderful victory over the grave, was to be imparted to all who, through faith in Jesus Christ, partook in the same experience. For Paul it meant that in the *hic et nunc* (here and now) situation, in the life human beings lived in the flesh, the whole drama of the cross and of the open grave (the resurrection) was destined to be re-enacted, and a death to sin meant for any person who sought it a resurrection to righteousness.

Other than these Pauline texts, there are references also that allude to the idea of a new creation with a *double entendre* in Matthew's word *genesis* between the meaning of origin (Genesis as the first book of Moses) and Genealogy. Genesis is the book of creation, and Matthew begins his Gospel with an account of creation, genealogy, of Jesus: "A record of the genealogy of Jesus Christ the son of David, the son of Abraham" (Mt 1:1). There are also allusions of the new creation in the Gospel of John. John, the evangelist, starts his Gospel with the words, "in the beginning" (Jn 1:1). This mirrors the beginning of the book of Genesis which starts in the same way: "in the beginning" (Gen 1:1). The passion, death and resurrection of Christ is the heart of his redemptive work. This marks the re-creation of the world that has been corrupted by sin. They are events that establish the new creation. When Jesus was dying on the cross, his final words were, "It is finished" (Jn 19:30) and this reflects the word "completed" found in Ge 2:1: "Thus the heavens and the earth were completed in their entire vast array." These were words used by God when he had finished the work of creating the whole universe. Furthermore there is emphasis twice in the Gospel of John that the resurrection of Jesus happened on the first day of the week: "Early on the first day of the week, while it was still dark, Mary Magdalene went to the tomb and saw that the stone had been removed from the entrance" (Jn 20:1),

---

[27] www.en.wikipedia.org/wiki/new-creation-theology/ [10.3.2016].

and Jesus appeared to his disciples on the first day of the week: "'On the evening of that first day of the week, when the disciples were together, with the doors locked for fear of the Jews, Jesus came and stood among them and said, 'Peace be with you'" (Jn 20:19). The resurrection of Jesus, according to the structure of the Gospel of John, is the eighth sign (after the seven signs in the Gospel of John) and this indicates a week of creation, and then a new creation beginning with the resurrection of Jesus. Matthew and Luke just like John, name the day of Jesus' resurrection as the first day of the week. The early Christians saw this as signifying the first day of the new creation. The old creation came about through the symbolic six days of creation. Now, the new creation had only one day, what the Gospel narratives refer to as the first day of the week. This single day for the new creation, in contrast to the six days for the old creation, hints that the new creation has only just begun. God began the work of the new creation with the resurrection of his Son Jesus Christ. A new age had begun. Those who believe in Jesus Christ, conforming their lives to him, take part in the new creation. The risen Christ, after his apparition to Mary Magdalene (Jn 20:11-18), appeared to his disciples late Sunday evening (the first day of the week) and he breathed on them and imparted upon them the gift of the Holy Spirit (Jn 20:22). The action of the risen Jesus breathing upon the disciples mirrored the action of God in the Old Testament breathing into Adam and giving him life: "Then the Lord God formed the man from the dust of the ground and breathed into his nostrils the breath of life, and the man became a living being" (Gen 2:7). So, the disciples were given new life by the resurrection of Jesus and they became a new creation.

Many ruins of ancient churches had a baptistery, often with three steps that led into a small pool, and three more steps going out on the opposite side. The Catechumens, those chosen for baptism, would strip off their clothes before descending into the water. After being baptized, they would robe in a white garment. The disrobing signified the putting off of the old Adam of sin (the old nature) and the enrobing signified the putting on of Christ, the new Adam, the new man and eventually the new nature. Today this baptismal symbolism of the old and the new continues to take place. The baptismal rite in the Archdiocese of Lilongwe has a part in which the *baptizandi*,[28] especially the infants, after the water has been poured onto their foreheads in the Catholic form of baptism, have their shirts or dresses taken off and they are dressed in new white shirts or dresses. For adult male catechumens, on the day of their baptism they come to church carrying a white shirt which ritually they will put on after baptism. For the female catechumens they have to put on a white head-dress commonly called *duku* in the local tongue. The putting on of white dress, shirt and head-dress, for those who are newly baptized, is a symbol of their putting on of Christ, the new Man and the new Adam. Thus, they become a new creation by participation in the paschal mystery of the death and resurrection of Jesus Christ.

If any person is in Christ, they are a new creature and there is a new creation. There is a new creation within and without. There is a new creation that is already in part accomplished but waiting its blessed consummation when the great Creator returns in glory to complete his handwork within and without, in soul and in body, in heaven and on earth. It is the great characteristic of the New Testament that it demands a new creation, through conversion (*metanoia*),[29] and faith in Jesus. This is its specific message. Other systems that seek to change character and society insist on education, training, amelioration, reformation or revolution. The New Testament has little to say about these, but it demands that through conversion the person becomes a new creature or a new creation. Nothing is sufficient except a definite change in the spirit of the person. It has to be a change that is so complete and radical that it can be considered as a creation, an act of supernatural grace, which makes the creation new, and all life and

---

[28] The word *baptizandi* is a catechetical and liturgical term which properly means those about to be baptized.

[29] *Metanoia* is a transliteration of the Greek word that sounds the same and bears the meaning of repentance and conversion. The word represents the message of the New Testament as derived from the preaching of John the Baptist who proclaimed the baptism of repentance (Mk 1:4) and the first preaching of Jesus Christ who called on people to repent for the kingdom of God was at hand (Mt 4:17).

existence new with it. The Cross of Christ impacted every realm of God's creation. On the cross Jesus defeated Satan, and sin was dealt with. On the cross he brought a new creation into being. But this new creation brought about by the resurrection of Jesus Christ from the dead is not a finished product. It will be completed in eternity. Meanwhile, as human beings live in this earthly life, in a vicarious way they are to participate in the act of renewing the face of the earth.

The new victory won in the resurrection of Jesus Christ is not simply a new exodus from sin, but even more grandly, a new creation. The centre of the start of the passion of Jesus was set in the garden of Gethsemane, just at the foot of the Mount of Olives, where Jesus went to pray: "Jesus went out as usual to the Mount of Olives, and his disciples followed him" (Lk 22:39). The early fathers of the Church saw the garden of Gethsemane as an echo of Adam in the Garden of Eden. The tomb of Jesus, too, was in a garden. This reference points to a new creative action of God who, through the passion of Jesus Christ, brought a new creation, reconciled with him, into being. Furthermore, the picture of a new Eden crowns the Bible story in the book of Revelation. The heavenly Jerusalem coming down to earth is described as having a river running through the midst with the tree of life beside it, bearing the twelve kinds of fruit leaves for the healing of the nations: "Then the angel showed me the river of the water of life, as clear as crystal, flowing from the throne of God and of the Lamb down the middle of the great street of the city. On each side of the river stood the tree of life ..." (Rev 22:1-2). Thus, this text from the last chapter of the book of Revelation mirrors, through the resurrection of Jesus Christ, the restoration of Eden. The symbol of the river of life in the new city mirrors the river of life in the book of Genesis: "A river watering the garden flowed from Eden ..." (Gen 2:10). However, the resurrection of Jesus itself is the central and most powerful image of the new reality.

This new creation involves a new standing before God, a new relationship with God, a new way of relating and dealing with the rest of nature and creation, and a new way of life by getting rid of sin. The new creation within will influence the new without and change the person, and the person will change the world. The new self will have the capacity to make all around them good and new again. When this great change takes place, even the face of the natural environment will have a different appearance. There will be a new glory in the heavens and a new beauty on the earth. The old things will pass away and they will become new (2 Cor 5:17).[30]

Advantages of the Image of Church as New Creation

In the current problem of the serious damage that has been and continues to be done to the natural environment in the Archdiocese of Lilongwe, evidenced in worrisome rates of deforestation, throwaway culture, land, air and soil pollution and erosion, depletion of flora and fauna, leading to diverse environmental consequences such as unpredictable weather patterns, climate change, famine, droughts, dry spells and floods, I recommend a development and accommodation of the ecclesiological concept of Church as a New Creation to complement the model of Church as God's Family.

The concept of the Church as a New Creation has the advantage of addressing the problem of the inferiorization of the earth, with its resources, systems and elements. The usage of the term 'new creation' in defining the Church's nature and mission is ecologically sensitive and ecclesiologically inclusive. It avoids the weaknesses and abuses which go together with the concept of family in its sociological and anthropological confines from the African perspective. The usage of the concept of New Creation for the Church does not subordinate the created world and its resources. Even if human beings were created in the image of God, the concept of Church as New Creation is very considerate of the non-human part of God's creation. It does not put human beings in a privileged position as does the concept of Church as God's Family when there is the transposition of sociological and anthropological family structures into the Church. It becomes a Church for all people, open to all and responsible for all the whole of God's creation. The male centeredness of the Church can be avoided at least through the concept of the Church as a New Creation.

---

[30] www.blog.spu.edu/lectio/pauls-vision-of-the-new-creation/ [15.3.2016].

The usage of the concept of New Creation for the Church has the advantage of getting rid of all anthropocentrism, ethnocentrism, excessive particularism, and the diminished idea of the individual characteristic of the African sociological and anthropological concept of family. The concept of Church as New Creation has the capacity to open new forms of dialogue for human beings in the Church with those of different faith affiliations and new forms of dialogue with the non-human part of God's creation. The emphasis on the concept of Church as Family has the weakness of breeding exclusivism, like the exclusion of others from one's particular group that one thought was the Family of God. The concept of new creation defeats this challenge to interreligious dialogue and ecumenism and opens the church to new relations with others and the rest of creation. Thus, the Church, understood as New Creation, can better understand its role as being an agent and instrument of reconciliation not only between people and God, but also of reconciliation between people and the natural environment. With this concept the Church can understand much better the earth as being among the 'poor' that need to be saved.

The understanding of the Church as a New Creation has the potential of avoiding the distortion of the concept of salvation and liberation as if human beings were the only beneficiaries of the effects of the Cross and Resurrection of Jesus Christ. The poor that Christ came to save will include the suffering earth, with its elements, resources and systems: "The Spirit of the Lord is on me, because he has anointed me to preach good news to the poor" (Lk 4:18).The Church will be able to see itself as having the mission of proclaiming the good news for the salvation of the suffering mother earth.[31] The androcentric connotation of salvation and liberation in the concept of Church as God's Family is defeated in the concept of Church as a New Creation. The concept is not restrictive but inclusive of the rest of creation and nature as beneficiaries of the salvific works of Christ. Through Jesus Christ, God reconciled all things to himself: "For God was pleased to have all his fullness dwell in him, and through him to reconcile to himself all things, whether things on earth or things in heaven, by making peace

---

[31] Pope Francis, *Laudato Si: On the Care for Our Common Home*, nos. 62-95.

through his blood, shed on the cross" (Col 1:19-20). Thus, the concept of Church as New Creation is attentive to the cosmic eschatology and it fosters the three-fold communion of God with human beings and the rest of nature. The self-understanding of the Church as New Creation has the capacity to conscientize the people and the Church of their duty (mission) towards the care, protection and sustenance of nature so that it gets reunited with its creator and its destiny fulfilled.

This model can spur the Church for more concern and action towards respect, care and protection of nature and the environment. The concept of the Church as the New Creation can be a relevant vision of the Church which is based on and backed by the Scripture and sound theology. This model is contrary to the other models which are too platonic, idealistic, and spiritualized. This model of Church as the New Creation, on top of the spiritual aspects of the Church, also includes emphasis on the physical, social, political and geographical aspects as providing the context and mission of the church. It is conscious of the need for renewal of the world for both humanity and nature. And it is the responsibility of human beings to renew the face of the earth. It stresses the dawning of a new age when there will be renewal of earth, the universe, the resurrection, and socio-political interactions among the redeemed.

The new creation concept expects that the ontological order and scope of eternal life is essentially continuous in the rest of God's creation and nature. The absence of sin and death will be the final sign. This approach of understanding what the Church is does not reject physicality or materiality but affirms them as essential both to wholistic anthropology and to the biblical idea of a redeemed creation. The approach has strong scriptural backing (in texts such as Isa 25, 65, 66, Gal 6, 2 Cor 5, Rev 21, Ro 8) which speak of the renewal of the universe and others that speak of the effects of the redemptive work of Christ on humanity and creation as a whole. The model emphasizes the relevance of matters such as the renewal of the world and the universe, nations, economics, agriculture and other socio-political issues.

This concept of Church as a New Creation, inclusive of all creation (not only human beings), has the advantage of bringing the human being back to the realm of God's creation; not above and not below God's creation. It brings human beings back to the web of life with its intrinsic interconnectedness. In this web of life and existence, everything in the world depends on others.[32] Despite the fact that the human beings were created in the image of God, they still remain God's creation. The theology of the Church has, at times, overemphasized the unique place of man and woman as created in the image of God, different from others, and considered as the summit of all creation. The New Creation ecclesiology insists on the circular model of existence where all beings of nature, including human beings, are interdependent. This appears to be against the traditional pyramidal model where human beings are considered as unique, next to the spiritual beings and the summit of God's creation. The particular place of the human being as created in the image of God needs to be understood in the sense of a mission. Human beings share the spirit of God and from this they are commissioned to take care of God's creation. This sharing in the spirit of God is not to be understood selfishly by human beings. They need to discover God in all the beings of his creation and find his life-giving spirit in the community of creation that they all share.

Practical Applications of the New Concept

There are some proposals of rediscoveries and new fundamental orientations, attitudes and concrete requirements which have to be applied in the Archdiocese of Lilongwe in order to curb the destruction of the environment, which in part has been a consequence of an incorrect application of the African Church's self-understanding as God's Family. Though promoting the sense of fraternity among people in the believing community, this ecclesiology did not deal sufficiently with the problem of a diminishing concern for the environment. For

---

[32] John A. Ryan, *Science and Spirituality*, Mzuzu: Mzuni Press, 2011, p. 33-37; David Kirchhoffer, *Saving Our World: Approaches to Ecology*, Germiston: Lumko, pp. 1-3.

the impact of this new proposed ecclesiology of Church as New Creation to be felt, the rediscovery of these fundamental attitudes, orientations and concrete applications regarding nature and the environment need to permeate the structures of this local Church. This means there is need for an ecclesiological formation that has to be felt at the household, SCC, out-station, zone (center), parish, deanery and archdiocesan level. They have to be mainstreamed in the programmes and activities of the entire ecclesial structure. All levels of the Church are to understand themselves as a New Creation and a missionary servant of the new creation, wherever people exist. This will lead to the salvation of the environment and the consequent renewal of the face of the earth.

With the new self-understanding of Church as New Creation, the Christian community needs to develop a practical attitude of love for God's creation as it exists in the environment. This attitude of love for the things of the environment is not to be simply based on how beneficial they are to humanity. This love for the things of the environment needs also to be grounded in God's goodness, wisdom and glory which every creature in heaven and earth reflects. There is need for the Church and people in this territory to develop a sense and practicality of reverence for creation for human beings depend on it and through it humanity is able to know God. Reverence for nature is a basic feature for an ecological consciousness. It is a value that people have lost and need to rediscover. The world, since medieval times, has been too much influenced by the mechanistic and materialistic approaches to nature which became prevalent in the train of René Descartes (+1650) and Isaac Newton (+1727).[33] Without this return to

---

[33] Rene Descartes in his doctrine of nature draws a sharp division between the human being as the subject of cognition, the *res cogitans*, and nature as the object of cognition, *res extensa*. By this he means and implies that the essence of the human being consists in his cognition (reasoning), and this is the prime reality. He even says, cogito ergo sum, I think, therefore I am. Nature on the other hand, to which the essential constituent of the human being does not belong but only his insignificant body, is the object, which stands at the human being's disposal. It is a composition of mechanical parts,

the reverence of creation, in terms of all that lives and exists, no correction of the modern attitudes towards nature will be possible and its consequences will ever be disastrous.[34] This return to the sense of reverence for nature, fundamental for ecological consciousness, requires a spiritual formation which goes beyond a concept of science that limits itself to the methods of mathematics, physics, chemistry, and regarding the material world only as home to objects to be dominated and used to the advantage of the human being. This attitude of reverence for nature presupposes that life and all that exists have their own goodness and value, not only extrinsically for the utility they might possess for humans, but also intrinsically in their own merit. Not only humans, but also animal and vegetable life as well as the inanimate nature merit appreciation, respect and protection. Furthermore, human beings need to exercise moderation and self-limitation in the way they approach and use the things and resources of the earth. This is a categorical demand and obligation on the part of human beings, a dread before the unscrupulous use of human power over the resources of the earth. Humans have to counter the merely utilitarian use and replace it with an attitude of regard and protection for the things of the environment. It demands from human beings concern, self-limitation and self-control. This is not to say that nature can be considered a partner on equal footing with the human being. This is shown by the fact that nature is not capable of respecting any right of others and in particular the rights of human beings. The obligation, however, for humans to respect nature and to guard its values, does not entail that it is necessary that nature should possess rights.

In the catechesis of the Church in the Archdiocese of Lilongwe in ecclesiological understanding, while appreciating the importance of interpersonal relationship among the Christians with a sense of being children of God, there is need to review the position of human beings from the misleading consideration of them as the centre and summit of creation. Human beings, while appreciating their uniqueness and

---

subject to mechanical necessity. In this mechanistic model, nature is the construction material for the human being, who is the constructor.

[34] G. Friedrich, *Ökologie und Bibel*, Stuttgart: Kohlhammer, 1982, pp. 29-31.

their being created in the image of God, are to be presented in catechesis and theological understanding as also being within the interdependent web of life and creation. There has to be a development of this sense of interdependence between all beings in creation from the smallest to the largest, the wisest to the unintelligent, and from animate to the inanimate beings. Human beings depend on the things of the environment, and they, too, depended on human beings.

In the application of the new ecclesiology of Church as New Creation, the non-human part of God's creation as it exists in the environment is to be considered as human beings' neighbour, in obedience to the greatest commandment, of love of God and love of neighbour, has to be loved: "Love your neighbour as yourself" (Lk 10:27). The environment means the total surroundings of a person, given by the creator, shaped by him and on which the human being has influence. The continuing pollution of the natural environment and degradation of nature is a far-reaching problem. Everyone needs to contribute to its protection.

Through the application of the new ecclesiology of Church as New Creation, there is need for proactive action in the Church to remove in human activity the selfish and utilitarian approaches to nature and creation. People are not to look at the environment as a mere resource for their livelihood and survival nor take care of it for fear of environmental disasters and in consideration of only future generations. In as much as human beings have the earth as their common home and are deeply dependent on it for their life and survival, it has to be understood that the world is not only created for man and woman. The value and goodness of nature and creation does not lie in their utility to the life and existence of human beings. Nature has intrinsic goodness and value, independent of human beings, and this is derived from the value and goodness of its maker, God. It exists in itself, and only in God. If God had willed, he would have ended his creation without human beings. There was nothing impossible with God: "For no word from God will ever fail" (Lk 1:37).

The Archdiocese of Lilongwe needs to come up with various programmes, using its existing institutional structures of the Small

Christian Communities, Outstations, Zones, Parishes, Deaneries, Commissions and Centers, which will bring about the awareness and concrete action in pursuit of the protection of the environment. Such concrete actions to be applied include the re-forestation, restoration of green cover wherever possible, moderation and self-limitation in the use of the resources of the environment, reduction of fume emissions, and promotion of conservation agriculture through which the land and the soils will be preserved and protected. There is need for responsible use of the natural resources and this requires personal concern, critical conduct and restraint in consumption. There has to be an understanding of the subordination of technology to the comprehensive good of all of creation. The chemical wastes in the cities and towns are not to end up in rivers and the lake resulting in killing life therein. There is need for special care for the animal world. This is because animals regarded collectively as a species or individually are capable of feelings and sufferings. There is need for prevention of cruelties towards animals. Such initiatives are very important on the part of the Christians if indeed they are to understand themselves as part and agents of the new creation brought about by the resurrection of Jesus Christ.

In applying the new concept of Church as New Creation, the Church needs to play the advocacy role, too, offering environmental education by defending and speaking in defense of the world of creation. The provision of environmental education alone is not enough. From this education has to emerge environmental commitments. The local Church in the Archdiocese of Lilongwe in its prophetic role is to include issues of nature and the environment. In exercising the prophetic role in the past, the Church has concentrated on issues of human rights, liberation and freedom of self-expression. Now is the time for this prophetic role of the Church to include issues of nature and the environment, for creation is also suffering and it is among the world's poor. The Church needs to speak for nature and creation which is going through terrible suffering. It has to speak for the world of nature which is weeping due to destructive human activity. It is to develop a sense of justice and peace for the natural environment. In this pursuit there is need for the commissions in the Archdiocese of Lilongwe to spearhead lobbying for enactment of laws and sanctions for the protection of the environment as human beings pursue their personal and corporate development through settlement, business, agriculture, and development in general. Laws should be very instrumental in the protection of the environment. Human beings are to exercise responsible stewardship over creation. By creating them in his image, God entrusted the world to human beings as his stewards. The earth needs to be taken care of and developed; it is not to be exploited and destroyed.[35] The natural environment is God's creation and therefore belongs to him. Only he is the absolute proprietor. The human being is only the steward of God's creation.

Conclusion

As the issues of the environment are increasingly receiving mention and attention in the public sphere, the Church in Africa needs not remain indifferent. Nothing in this world is indifferent to humanity and unconcerned to the Church. The historical milieu becomes the ground and theatre for the practice and mission of the Church. Having discussed the self-understanding of the Church in Africa as God's Family, with its strengths and challenges, and its implications on the care of the environment in the Archdiocese of Lilongwe, the book proposes and recommends a new concept that would complement the model currently defining the Church in Africa. This new concept has to augment and complement the efforts of the model of Church as the Family of God in Africa saving the environment. Such a concept needs to be biblically based, among other bases, if it is to qualify as an ecclesiological model. For this new ecclesiological model to address the problem of the destruction of the environment, its perception of Church and salvation is not to be one-eyed: it is not to be articulated in the interest of human beings only, but it has to include rather the rest of God's creation.

---

[35] German Catechetical Association, *Credo: A Catholic Catechism*, London: Geoffrey Chapman, 1983, pp. 257-264.

Thus, book recommends the development of the ecclesiological model of the Church as New Creation. The self-understanding of the Church has to include the biblical values of new creation. This new concept would seek to restore the full vision of the nature and mission of the Church and redemption. It would correct the fragmentary circle of Christian vision and change its narrow and biased perception of the world and God. This new model would generate new theological insights and concrete ecclesial practices in the care of the environment. It has the possibility of preaching the gospel of creation[36] and liberate humanity and the environment from human violence.[37] It is high time that the Church needs to define itself, in nature and mission, further in ways that are sensitive to the rest of God's creation as it exists in the environment. The Church is to see itself as having a primary role, too, being an instrument of bringing reconciliation between humanity and the rest of the creation. The people in the Church have to recognize that they are called to serve, not only humanity, but the whole of God's creation that it gets fulfilled and reunited with its creator. Creation's purpose is to be accomplished and in this the Church has a mission.

With this new ecclesiological model, the Church in Africa is to mainstream the issues of the environment in its theology, ecclesiology, missiology and concrete actions. The Church cannot afford to remain outside the challenges associated with the environment. The Church, as an application and expression of the people's religiosity, has a great influence on the practical and moral life of the people. The teaching of the Church is a fundamental source of the people's ethics. The way the Church defines itself in terms of its nature and mission will certainly influence the concrete commitments and actions of its people and the wider society in how humanity can relate to the environment because the practice of the Church is shaped by the way it is structured and defined. It is the self-understanding of the Church that propels its outward action and practice within its ecclesial community, *missio ad*

---

[36] Pope Francis, *Laudato Si*, nos. 62-82, pp. 38-49.

[37] Elizabeth Schüssler Fiorenza (ed), *The Power of Naming: A Concilium Reader in Feminist Liberation Theology*, New York: SCM Press, 1996, pp. 1-37.

intra, and in the external society, *missio ad extra*. Thus, the issues of climate change and the environment need to receive particular attention in the area of theology and specifically in ecclesiology. Relevant and new ecclesiological models have got the potential and capability of transforming the mindsets of the people of God in terms of who they are and how they ought to relate to the elements and resources of the environment. In the wake of the challenge of the destruction of the environment, I recommended that the self-understanding of the Church as God's Family is to accommodate the values in the new ecclesiological concept that the book proposes of the Church as New Creation.

Since Malawi is largely Christian (80% of which 20% are Catholics), the renewal and redefinition of the Catholic Church will help a lot in the enhancement of the respect for, care of, and protection of the environment. The proposed new self-understanding of the Church as New Creation will help in environmental mitigation. This will be, among others, through: the rediscovery of the environment as God's creation, an active awareness that humanity has a lot in common with creation (origin - God himself, home - earth itself, and finality - in God himself), an awareness of the intrinsic and inherent value and goodness in creation, the awareness of each being's purpose (from the smallest to the largest, the animate and inanimate beings), and a deep Christian conviction that creation is also called to the universal redemption. This will help the large Christian community to develop a sense of universal fraternity with the world of nature (creation) that will eventually enhance its mitigation. The self-understanding of the Church as New Creation will develop among people the awareness of the mission in environmental care and renewing the face of the earth. The 'dominion over nature' that God gave human beings has to be understood in the sense of a mission for human beings, with their intellectual and spiritual abilities, to care for God's creation as good stewards.

Bibliography

Oral Informants

Abraham, Bernadette, Mtiya

Banda, Jester, Ludzi

Chamatambe, Catechist, Mtengowanthenga parish

Chandanda, Devison, Mwale, Bisai, Kaphamtengo, Killiness, Zimba, Maria, Madisi

Chimvalenji, Michael, assistant priest, Namitete parish

Chimwaye, Mayamiko, Chairman of the parish youth, Madisi

Chinkhandwe, Bridget, Catholic Women Organization member, Ngooko

Chitsulo, Gabriel, Kanengo, and Oscar Phiri, Chigoneka parish

Chiudzu, Grace, and Chiudzu, Hastings, ME Regional Couple, Central Region, Lilongwe

Chiwandira, Christopher, JTI technician, Madisi

Damaseke, Francis, Mlale parish

Dambuleni, Mzira and Mr. Chidzaye, Mndinga

Daniel, Selina, Kalumo-Ntchisi

Densani, Sr. Bernadette, Ludzi

Diliwo, Emmanuel, Mchinji deanery secretary, Kachebere parish

Divaison, Dofa, Prisca Jester, Panganani, Sophret, and Kazula, Veronica, Chakhaza

Evetarita Kalulu, and Maxwell Kalulu, ME Facility Couple, Lilongwe

Griffin Kachitsa, Silumba, and Pemphero Khisi, Chiwembe

James, Amina, eco-women member, Mtemeiti

Joseph Phiri, Mkanda Trading Centre

Jossam, Agness, Chiweza (Kalumo)

Kachitsa, Griffin, Silumba, and Lameki, Kingsley, Malenga

Kachiwala, Agnes, CWO vice chairlady, Natola

Kalimanjira, Matthews, eco-committee member, Msumba

Kaliu, Anita, Lilongwe Archdiocesan Chairlady, Catholic Women Organization, Bwaila - Lilongwe

Kambwembwe, Crispin, Chair of St. Philomena SCC, Mphalawe, Madisi parish

Kamdabweni, Benedict, parish priest, Chilinde Parish, Lilongwe

Kanyambo, Deusdedit, and Kamude, Akleo, Guilleme – Mchinji
Kaphamtengo, Killiness, Malufu
Kapinda, Ezekiel, catechist, Mponela parish
Kaponda, Vincent, Mkangu
Kasiya, Thomas, Youth Chaplain, Archdiocese of Lilongwe, Likuni
Kaziputa, Katalina, Mwadyanji, and Chigwenje, Mercy, Bowe
Lekaleka, Francis, the Lilongwe Archdiocesan Chaplain for CWO
Lockie, Rosaline, and Lockie, Davie, ME leaders, St. Patrick's Circle, Area 12, Lilongwe
Lozo, Ester, and Lozo, Harry, ME regional treasury couple, Area 23, Lilongwe
Machemba, Sr. Jennifer, Mkanda parish
Magalasi, Angella and Magalasi, John, St. Paul SCC leaders, Maula Parish, Lilongwe
Makola, John, Mtima-woyera Parish, Lilongwe
Mapulanga, Juliet, Kalumo
Matemba, Steven, micro-project field officer of the Eco-schools programme, Katakungwa
Mkwezalamba, James, Salima
Mnjowe, Adam, Chika
Moyo, Evance, Mkanda, and Kapachika, Linely, Ntchisi
Mtamila, Andreas, Jesuit priest, Kasungu
Mthumba, Martin, Mtima-woyera parish
Mtonza, Noel, Coordinator, Catholic Commission for Justice and Peace, Likuni
Mwakhwawa, Vincent, Acting Coordinator, ECM Pastoral Directorate, Area 11 - Lilongwe
Ndau, Michael, Pietermaritzburg – Kwa Zulu Natal Province, South Africa
Ngala, Gaudencia, and Ngala, Robert, ME leaders for Nkhotakota Circle, Dwangwa
Nkhoma, George, CADECOM Coordinator, Mponela
Notisi, George, Mbingwa
Paskazio, Mercy, Kabulungo - Dzoole
Phiri, Jonas, Father, pastoral coordinator, Archdiocese of Lusaka, Lusaka, Zambia
Piringu, Raphael, priest, Guilleme
Potani, Matthews, curate, Mkanda

Raphael, Damiano, Chaponda

Sadzu, Cathereen, Malomo, Banda, Victor, Chiwembe II, and Phiri, Martha, Makuka-Kabudula

Salatiyere, Laurent, Sungeni

Sambakunsi, Klara, and Sambakunsi, Peter, Pro-life Movement members, Madisi

Sambo, Dalitso, chairperson of the Catholic Men Organization, St. Patrick's Parish, Area 18-Lilongwe

Samson, Alberto, Mpherere

Sitolo, Matthews, and Ngalande, Francis, Mpherere

Soko, Klara, Mtanila, Madisi

Zikomankhani, Alphaeus, diocesan director, Pro-Life Movement, Likuni

Zimba, Maria, Chinkhwiri

Church Documents

Acta Synodalia Sacrosancti Concilii Oecumenici Vaticano, Roma: Typist Ployglottis Vaticanis.

Archdiocese of Lilongwe, Buku La Nyimbo ndi Mapemphero, Lilongwe: Likuni, 1989.

Archdiocese of Lilongwe, Catholic Directory, Lilongwe: Likuni, 2010.

Benedict XIV, Africa's Commitment: Post-synodal Apostolic Exhortation (Africae Munus), Nairobi: Paulines, 2011.

Benedict XVI, Caritas in Veritate, (no. 38), 2009.

Benedict XVI, Post-Synodal Apostolic Exhortation Africae Munus, 2011.

Diocese of Lilongwe, Youth Constitution, Lilongwe: Likuni, 2011.

Episcopal Conference of Malawi, Social Development Directorate, Kusamalira Dziko Lapansi limene Likutisunga Moyo Tonsefe, Lilongwe: ECM, 2016.

German Bishops' Conference (Translated by Stephen Wentworth), The Church's Confession of Faith: A Catholic Catechism for Adults, San Francisco: Ignatius, 1985.

John Paul II, (December 8, 1989), World Day for Peace message of 1990.

John Paul II, Encyclical Redemptoris Missio on the Church's missionary mandate, 1990.

John Paul II, Ecclesia in Africa: Post-Synodal Apostolic Exhortation of the Holy Father John Paul II to the Church in Africa in its Evangelizing Mission towards the year 2000, Nairobi: Paulines, 1995.

John Paul II, Inter Sanctos (Apostolic Letter AAS 71), 1979.
John Paul II, Post-Synodal Apostolic Exhortation, Familiaris Consortio, 1981.
John Paul II, Post-Synodal Apostolic Exhortation: Christifideles Laici, 1989.
John Paul II, Sollicitudo Rei Socialis, Vatican: Libreria Editrice Vaticana, 1987.
John Paul II, The Catechism of the Catholic Church, Nairobi: Paulines, 1994.
Kalilombe, Patrick A., Mpingo Ndife Tonse: The Lilongwe Mini-Synod, Lilongwe: Likuni, 1975.
Pastoral Secretariat of the Diocese of Lilongwe, Maudindo mu Mphakati ndinso Msonkhano wa Bungwe, Lilongwe: Likuni, 1978.
Paul IV, Evangelii Nuntiandi: An Encyclical on the proclamation of the Gospel, 1975.
Paul VI, Apostolica Sollicitudo, 1965.
Pontifical Council for Justice and Peace, The Compendium of the Social Teaching of the Church, Vatican: Libreria Editrice Vaticana, 2004.
Pope Francis, Laudato Si: On the Care of Our Common Home, Nairobi: Paulines, 2015.
The Archdiocese of Lilongwe, Catholic Directory, Lilongwe: Likuni, 2010.
The Episcopal Conference of Malawi, Caring for Our Families: Pastoral Letter to the Catholic Faithful in celebration of the International Year of the Family, Balaka: Montfort Media, 1994.
The Episcopal Conference of Malawi, Malawi Catholic Directory 2011, Balaka: Montfort Media, 2011.
The Episcopal Conference of Malawi, Social Development Directorate: Kusamalira Dziko Lapansi limene likutisunga Moyo tonsefe, Balaka: Montfort Media, 2016.
Thomas Aquinas, Summa Theologica, 1a, pp. 44-45.
Vatican II, Decree on the Apostolate of the Laity, Apostolicam Actuositatem, 1965.
Vatican II, Decree on the Church's Missionary Activity: Ad gentes divinitus, 1965.
Vatican II, Decree on the Up-to-date Renewal of Religious Life, Perfectae Caritatis, 1965.
Vatican II, Dogmatic Constitution on the Church: Lumen Gentium, 1964.
Vatican II, Pastoral Constitution on the Church in the Modern World: Gaudium et Spes, 1964.

Unpublished

Appiah-Kubi, Francis, "The Church, Family of God: Relevance and Pastoral Challenges of a Metaphor from an African Perspective," Catholic University of Leuven, PhD in Systematic Theology with specialization in Ecclesiology, Leuven-Belgium, 2012.

Khisi, Maximian, "A Pastoral Approach to the Chewa Youth Rites of Passage in Madisi Deanery of the Diocese of Lilongwe, Malawi," Catholic University of Eastern Africa (CUEA-Nairobi-Kenya), MTh with specialization in Pastoral Theology, 2010.

Longwe, Molly, "A Paradox in a Theology of Freedom and Equality: The Experiences of Pastors' Wives (Amayi Busa) in the Baptist Convention of Malawi (BACOMA)," University of KwaZulu-Natal, PhD in Gender and Religion, 2012.

Mwakhwawa, Vincent, "Improving Participation of the Laity in Small Christian Communities/A Pastoral Challenge in the Archdiocese of Lilongwe, Malawi," Catholic University of Eastern Africa (CUEA-Nairobi-Kenya), Master of Theology with specialization in Pastoral Theology, 2012.

Published Sources

Afagbegee, Gabriel SVD, *Building Small Christian Communities: Foundation and Step-by-Step Approach to Building SCCs*, Germiston: Lumko, 2007.

Armellini, Fernando, *Celebrating the Word: Year A Commentary on the Readings*, Nairobi: Paulines, 1992.

Bahemuka, Judith Mbula, *Status and Role of Women in African Societies: Suffering and Hope, in Africa the Kairos of a Synod: Symposium on Africa*, Rome: Sedos, 1994.

Baur, John, *2000 Years of Christianity in Africa*, Nairobi: Paulines, 2009.

Biko, Steve, *I Write what I like*, Chicago: UCP, 1978.

Boff, Leonardo, *Ecology and Liberation: A New Paradigm*, New York: Orbis, 1995.

Bokenkotter, Thomas, *A Concise History of the Catholic Church*, New York: Image, 1979.

Bonhoeffer, Dietrich, *Sanctorum Communio: A Dogmatic Inquiry into the Sociology of the Church*, London: Collins, 1967.

Borruso, Silvano (Trans.), *The Confessions of St. Augustine*, Nairobi: Paulines, 2014.

Brown, Raymond et al, (eds), *The New Jerome Biblical Commentary*, London: Geoffrey Chapman, 1990.

Capucao, Dave D., *Religion and Ethnocentrism: An Empirical-theological Study*, Leiden: Brill, 2010.

Chakanza, Joseph, "A Concern for Creation: Ecological Crisis in Malawi," in *Christianity and the Environment: Care for what you have been Given*, Zomba: Kachere, 2002.

Chakanza, Joseph, *Wisdom of the People: 2000 Chinyanja Proverbs*, Zomba: Kachere, 2000.

Cheza, M, *Le Synode Africain: Historie et textes*, Paris: Karthala, 1996.

Chimole, Matthias, *Maudindo mu Mphakati*, Lilongwe: Likuni, 1989.

Cobb, John B., *Is it too late? A Theology of Ecology*, Beverly Hills: Bruce, 1972.

Cone, James H., *God of the Oppressed*, New York: Seabury, 1975.

Delespesse, Max, *The Church Community: Leaven & Life-Style*, Notre Dame: Ave Maria, 1973.

Dicks, Ian D., *An African Worldview: The Muslim Amacinga Yawo of Southern Malawi*, Zomba: Kachere, 2012.

Donahue, Bernard F., "Political Ecclesiology," in *Theological Studies 33*, Santa Clara: Santa Clara University, 1972.

Donders, Joseph G., *Non-Bourgeois Theology: An African Experience of Jesus*, New York: Orbis, 1985.

Doyle, Dennis M., *The Church Emerging from the Vatican II: A Popular Approach to Contemporary Catholicism*, Connecticut: XXIII, 1992.

Dulles SJ, Avery, *Models of the Church: A Critical Assessment of the Church in all its Aspects*, New York: Image, 1976.

Dulles, Avery, *Models of Mission*, New York: Doubleday, 1978.

Fiorenza, Elizabeth Schüssler (ed.), *The Power of Naming: A Concilium Reader in Feminist Liberation*, New York: Fortress, 1985.

Friedrich, Gerhard, *Ökologie und Bibel*, Stuttgart: Kohlhammer, 1982.

Fries, Henrich, *Aspects of the Church*, Dublin: Gill and Sons, 1965.

Granfield, Patrick, "Ecclesial Cybernetics: Communication in the Church," in *Theological Studies 29*, Santa Clara: SCUP, 1968.

Gwengwe, John W., *Kukula ndi Mwambo*, Blantyre: Dzuka, 1965.

Hamer, Jerome, *The Church is a Communion*, London: Geoffrey Chapman, 1964.

Hastings, Adrian, *African Catholicism: Essays in Discovery*, London: SCM, 1989.

Hastings, Adrian, *Mission and Ministry*, London: Sheed and Ward, 1971.

Hayes, Zachary OFM, *The Cosmos, a Symbol of the Divine, In Franciscan Theology of the Environment: An Introductory Reader*, edited by Dawn M. Nothwehr, Illinois: Franciscan, 2003.

Healey, Joseph and Hinton, Jean (eds.), *Small Christian Communities Today: Capturing the New Moment*, Nairobi: Paulines, 2006.

Healey, Joseph, *Building the Church as Family of God: Evaluation of Small Christian Communities in Eastern Africa*, Nairobi: CUEA, 2012.

Idowu, Bolaji, *God in Yoruba Beliefs*, London: Oxford University Press, 1962.

Infield, Louis (tr.), *Lectures on Ethics*, New York: Harper & Row, 1963.

Joseph SJ, Fr. P.T., *Pastoral Leadership Styles and Emotional Intelligence*, Mumbai: St. Paul's, 2010.

Kalilombe, Patrick A., *Doing Theology at the Grassroots: Theological Essays from Malawi*, Mzuzu: Luviri Press, 2018.

Kalilombe, Patrick A., *Mabvu Adamvana Kuti Aning'e Pamimba*, Lilongwe: Likuni, 1973.

Kalilombe, Patrick A., *Mpingo Ndife Tonse*, Lilongwe: Likuni, 1975.

Kanyoro, Musumbi R.A., "The Challenge of Feminist Theologies," in Musumbi R.A. Kanyoro, *In Search of a Round Table: Gender, Theology and Church Leadership*, Genève: WCC, 1997, pp. 176-183.

Karotemprel, Sebastian (ed.), *Following Christ in Mission: A Fundamental Course in Missiology*, Nairobi: Paulines, 1996.

Kay, Ariel Salleh, "Epistemology and metaphor of production: An eco-feminist reading of critical theory," in *Studies in Humanities*, Special issue on "feminism, ecology, and the future of the humanities," Patrick Murphy (ed.), vol. 15 (2), 2009.

Kirchhoffer, David, *Saving Our World: Approaches to Ecology*, Germiston: Lumko, 2002.

Knox, Peter, "Theology, Ecology, and Africa: No longer Strange Bedfellows," in Agbonkhianmeghe E. Orobator SJ (ed.), *Reconciliation, Justice, and Peace: The Second African Synod*, Nairobi: Acton, 2011.

Kohak, Erazim, *The Ambers and the Stars: A Philosophical Inquiry into the Moral Sense of Nature*, Chicago: UCP, 1984.

Likupe, Raymond, "God in Creation: Towards an African Theology of Creation," in *Religion in Malawi*, November 2010-November 2011, no. 16, Zomba: Kachere, 2011.

Magesa, Laurent, *Anatomy of Inculturation: Transforming the Church in Africa*, Nairobi: Paulines, 2004.

Magesa, Laurenti, *African Religion: The Moral Traditions of Abundant Life*, New York: Orbis, 1997.

Malawi Government (Ministry of Natural Resources, Energy and Environment), *Malawi State of the Environment Report and Outlook Report: Environment for Sustainable Economic Growth 2010*, Lilongwe: Environmental Affairs Department, 2010.

Marias, Julian, *History of Philosophy*, New York: Dover, 1967.

Marins, J., *Latin America in Small Christian Communities: Vision and Practicalities*, Dublin: The Columba, 2002.

Mbiti, John S., *African Religions and Philosophy*, Nairobi: Heinemann, 1969.

Mbiti, John S., *Introduction to African Religion*, Nairobi: East African Educational, 1975.

McDonagh, Sean, *To Care for the Earth*, London: Geoffrey Chapman, 1986.

Merchant, Carolyn, *Radical Ecology: The Search for a Livable World*, New York: Rutledge, 1992.

Merchant, Carolyn, *The Death of Nature: Women, Ecology and Scientific Revolution*, San Francisco: Harper and Row, 1980.

Merrigan, Terrence, *Theological Models in the Thought of Avery Dulles: An Analysis and Evaluation*, Bijdragen: Tijdschrift voor Filosofie en Theologie, 1993.

Merrigan, Terrence, *Theology in an Ecumenical Context: On Catholic Attitudes to the Decision of the General Synod of the Church of England*, Leuven: Katholieke Universiteit Leuven Press, 1993.

Mitchem, Stephanie Y., *Introducing Womanist Theology*, Maryknoll: Orbis, 2002.

Mkhori, Felix, *Lilongwe Mini-Synod: Let us March together in Spreading the Good News of our Lord*, Lilongwe: Likuni, 2006.

Moemeka, Andrew, *Communication and Culture: An African Perspective*, Nairobi: African Church Service, 1989.

Moltmann, Jürgen, *God in Creation: A New Theology of Creation and the Spirit of God*, Minneapolis: Fortress, 1993.

Moyo, Fulata and Ott, Martin (eds.), *Christianity and the Environment: Care for what you have been given*, Zomba: Kachere, 2002.

Mugambi, J.N.K., and Laurenti Magesa (eds.), *The Church in African Christianity: Innovative Essays in Ecclesiology*, Nairobi: Initiatives, 1990.

Mvula, Herman Yokoniah, "Back to the Basics: Caring for Nature is Caring for ourselves," in *Religion & Culture: A Journal of Religious and Cultural Studies*, Mzuzu University, Issue 2 (April 2015), Mzuzu: Mzuni, 2015.

Nothwehr, Dawn OSF, *The Earth is the Lord's: Catholic Theology of Creation, Ecology and the Environment*, Collegeville: Liturgical, 2012.

Okafor, Festus, *Africa at Crossroads*, New York: Vantage, 1974.

Okure, Teresa, "Church-Family of God: The place of God's Reconciliation, Justice, and Peace," in Agbonkhianmeghe E. Orobator (ed.), *Reconciliation, Justice, and Peace*, Nairobi: Acton, 2011.

O'Meara OP, Thomas Franklin quoting D. R. Wall, "Church Architecture," in *New Catholic Encyclopedia 3*, New York: McGraw-Hill, 1967.

O'Meara OP, Thomas Franklin, "Philosophical Models in Ecclesiology," in *Theological Studies 39*, Santa Clara, CA, 1978.

Opongo, Elias Omondi, "The Mission of the Church in the Public Sphere," in Orobator SJ, Agbonkhianmeghe E. (ed.), *Reconciliation, Justice, and Peace: The Second African Synod*, Nairobi: Acton, 2011.

Orobator SJ, Agbonkhianmeghe E. (ed.), *The Church We Want: Foundations, Theology and Mission of the Church in Africa*, Nairobi: Paulines, 2015.

Orobator, Agbonkhianmeghe, *The Church as Family: African Ecclesiology in Its Social Context*, Nairobi: Paulines, 2000.

Ott, Martin, *African Theology in Images*, Zomba: Kachere, 1999.

Peschke, Karl H., *Christian Ethics: Morality in the Light of Vatican II*, Alcester: Goodliffe Neale, 1997.

Pickett, William, *A Concise Guide to Pastoral Planning*, Notre Dame: Ave Maria, 2007.

Preston, Geoffrey, *Faces of the Church*, Edinburgh: T & T Clark, 1997.

Rahner, Karl & Ratzinger, Joseph, *The Episcopate and the Primacy*, London: Burns & Oates, 1962.

Ruether, Rosemary, *New Woman/New Earth: Sexist Ideologies and Human Liberation*, New York: Seabury, 1975.

Ruwaichi, Jude Thaddeus, "The Newness and Pastoral Implications of the Church as a Family," in Cecil Mac Garry et al (eds), *New Strategies for a New Evangelization in Africa*, Nairobi: Paulines, 2002.

Ryan, John, *Science and Spirituality*, Mzuzu: Mzuni Press, 2011.

Schade, Leah D., *Creation-Crisis Preaching: Ecology, Theology and the Pulpit*, New York: Chalice, 2015.

Schillebeeckx, Edward, *World and Church*, London: Sheed & Ward, 1971.

Schofield, Rodney, *Jesus – the Man for others,* Mzuzu: Luviri Press, 2018

Sebastian, Karambai, *Structures of Decision – Making in the Local Church,* Bangalore: Theological Publications in India, 1995.

Shiva, Maria and Vandana, *Ecofeminism,* Halifax N.S: Fernwood, 1993.

Shorter, Aylward and Edwin Onyancha, *Secularism in Africa: A Case Study of Nairobi City,* Nairobi: Paulines 1997.

Shorter, Aylward, "Inculturation: Win or Lose the Future, the Rising of a New Ecclesiology," in Walter von Holzen and Sean Fagan (eds.), *Africa: The Kairos of a Synod: Symposium on Africa,* Rome: Sedos, 1994.

Shorter, Aylward, *African Christian Theology,* London: Geoffrey Chapman, 1975.

Tanye, Gerald K., *The Church-as-Family and Ethnocentrism in Sub-Saharan Africa (*Tübingen Prospects on Pastoral Theology and Religious Pedagogics), Berlin: LIT Verlag, 2010.

The Archdiocese of Lilongwe, *Catholic Directory,* Lilongwe: Likuni, 2010.

Turner, Denys (ed.), *The Church in the Modern World,* Dublin: Scepter, 1968.

Waliggo, John Mary, "The African Clan as the True Model of the African Church," in J.N.K. Mugambi, and Laurenti Magesa (eds.), *The Church in African Christianity: Innovative Essays in Ecclesiology,* Nairobi: Acton, 1990.

Walsh, Gerald G. et al (transl.), *St. Augustine: The City of God,* New York: Image, 1958.

Warren, Karen J. (eds.), *Environmental Philosophy: From Animal Rights to Radical Ecology,* New Jersey: Prentice-Hall, 1993.

Watkins, Clare, "Organizing the People of God: Social Science theories of Organization in Ecclesiology," in *Theological Studies 52,* Santa Clara, 1991.

Watson, Natalie K., *Introducing Feminist Ecclesiology,* Sheffield: Sheffield Academic, 2002.

Web Sources

http://en.wikipedia.org/wiki/Roman_Catechism/
http://en.wikipedia.org/wiki/Roman_Catechism/
https://en.wikipedia.org/wiki/Behavioural_sciences/
www.academia.edu/11802976/
www.academia.edu/The_Second_Vatican_Council/
www.adoremus.org/the-ecclesiology-of-communion/

www.africafiles.org/articles.asp?ID=20359/
www.afrikaworld.net/afrel/community.htm/
www.afrikaworld.net/synod/
www.appleseeds.org/canticle.htm/
www.beingchurchin21stc.wordpress.com/pt2025/1-overview/classic-framework-dulles-models-of-church/
www.blog.spu.edu/lectio/pauls-vision-of-the-new-creation/
www.brill.com/religion-and-ethnocentrism/
www.catholic.org/news/europe/story/
www.catholicworldreport.com/ievangelii_nuntiandi/the_greatest_pastoral_document_that_has_ever_been_written.aspx/
www.christian
www.definition/stward/Merriam-Webster/dictionary/
www.ejournals.bc.edu/ojs/index.php/ctsa/article/viewFile/3020/2639/
www.emeka.at/africa_cultural_values/
www.emeka.at/africa_cultural_values/
www.en.wikipedia.org/wiki/Francis_of_Assisi/
www.en.wikipedia.org/wiki/Johann_Adam_Mohler/
www.en.wikipedia.org/wiki/Johann_Adam_Mohler/
www.en.wikipedia.org/wiki/new-creation-theology/
www.en.wikipedia.org/wiki/Pierre_Teilhard_de_Chardin/
www.en.wikipedia.org/wiki/Priesthood_(Catholic_Church/
www.everyculture.com/
www.jstor.org/stable/1387707/
www.knight of Columbus/domestic-church
www.msue.anr.msu.edu/news/ubuntu_a_south_african_philosophy/
www.mtholyoke.edu/-abdul20j/classweb/politics_116/AWIP.html/
www.mwnation.com/marriage-encounter-clocks-30-yrs-in-malawi/
www.ncronline.org/news/vatican/ghanaian/bishop/palmer/
www.newadvent.org/catholicencyclopedia/Bellarmine/
www.news.va/va/news/vatican-the-first-synod-of-africa/
www.news.va/va/news/Vatican-the-first-synod-of-africa/
www.nsomalawi.mw/2008-population-and-housing-census/
www.nsomalawi.mw/2008-population-and-housing-census/

www.ntcanon.org/Carthage.canon.shtml/
www.osv.com/artMID/articleID/the-ordinary-vocation-of-the-domestic-church/
www.ppja.org/english/countires/malawi/catholic-commission-for-justice-and-peace/
www.state.gov/s/gwi/rls/rem/2012/201503.html/
www.thegreefuse.org/ecofem/
www.theodora.com/encyclopedia/synods-of-Carthage/
www.unitedhumanrights.org/genocide/rwanda/
www.uvm.edu/-gflomenh/ENV-NGO-PA395/articles/Lynn-white/
www.uvm.edu/-gflomenh/ENV-NGO-PA395/articles/Lynn-white/
www.vatican.va/archive/documents/
www.vatican.va/archive/documents/
www.vatican.va/roman_curia/synod/documents/rc_synod_documents/
www.w2.vatican.va/encyclicals/documents
www.w2.vatican.va/peace/documents/
www.wikipedia.org/wiki/Androcentrism/
www.wikipedia/wiki/Duns_Scotus/
www.wikipedia/wiki/Ecofeminism/
www.wikipedia/wiki/ethnocentrism/
www.wikipedia/wiki/First_Vatican_Council/
www.wikipedia/wiki/nominalism/
www.wikipedia/wiki/social_science/
www.wwme.org/
www.zenit.org/articles/pope-the-universality-of-the-church/

Index

Adaptation 81
Administration 10, 28, 43f, 67, 130, 153, 217
Afagbegee, Gabriel SVD 31, 57, 83, 93
Africae munus 51-55, 233
African Synod 6, 10, 17, 43, 45f, 48, 51f, 54f, 68, 70, 76, 119, 123, 127
Aggiornamento 34
Alangizi (counselors) 116, 208, 222
Androcentrism 139-141, 145
Androcracy 99
Anthropocentrism 137, 145, 188, 240f, 255
Apostolic associations 119-121, 132
Apostolic exhortation 6, 10, 39, 41, 46, 51, 53, 60f, 75, 79, 110, 119
Appiah-Kubi, Francis 6, 33, 59
Aquinas, Thomas 20, 173
Aristotelianism 21
Assembly 10, 12f, 43, 46f, 51-53, 59, 71, 75, 77, 96, 111, 122, 130
Association of Consecrated Women in Eastern and Central Africa 220
Association of Diocesan Catholic Clergy of Lilongwe (ADCCOL) 119f, 193, 213-215, 221, 230

Association of Diocesan Clergy in Malawi (ADCOM) 214, 220f
Association of Member Episcopal Conferences in Eastern Africa (AMECEA) 58-61, 114, 220
Association of Men Religious in Malawi (AMRIM) 119f, 193, 213, 218f
Association of Religious Institutes in Malawi (ARIMA) 193, 218, 221, 230
Association of Women Religious in Malawi (AWRIM) 119f, 193, 213, 218f, 221
Augustine of Hippo 30, 156
Authority 23, 31, 45, 94, 96, 99, 106, 140, 150, 159, 186, 189, 202, 246
Bahemuka, Judith Mbula 144
Banda, Joyce 101
Baptism 6, 39, 72, 74, 111, 114, 128f, 202, 207, 251f
Benedict of Nursia 172
Benedict XVI, Pope 51-54, 124, 127, 135
Biko, Steve 89, 92
Body of Christ 12, 14, 20, 25, 29, 33, 36, 126
Bonaventure 159, 173-175
Bride of Christ 14f, 29, 77
Canon 44
Carthage 36, 42-44

Catechism 13, 15, 21f, 30f, 40, 66, 75, 152f, 181, 184f, 243, 247, 262
Catechism of Trent 31
Catechists 52, 118, 122, 129, 196, 222
Catholic Commission for Justice and Peace (CCJP) 128, 193, 197
Catholic Development Commission (CADECOM) 128, 193f, 230
Catholic Men Organization (CMO) 119f, 193, 199, 206f, 230
Catholic Women Organization (CWO) 67, 119f, 142, 193, 199-204, 206, 229f
Catholicism 6, 11, 34f, 56, 72, 75, 109
CCAP 201
Chakanza, Joseph C. 83, 90
Chigwenje, Mercy 196
Chimole, Matthias 117, 128, 223, 225, 228
Chimwaye, Mayamiko 209
Chiwandira, Christopher 194
Christian Family Movement 120, 193, 223, 228, 230
City of God 30f, 167
Clericalization 26
Climate change 7, 188, 195, 197, 238f, 254, 264
Community 7, 9, 13f, 16, 18, 23, 25f, 28f, 34-39, 41, 53, 58, 60, 63, 65-68, 71-79, 82-86, 88-97, 102, 104-106, 109-112, 116, 121, 125f, 128, 131, 135, 140, 163f, 193, 196, 201, 206, 208, 216f, 219, 224, 227, 235, 242, 249, 257f, 263f
Congar, Yves 20
Congregation for Institutes of Consecrated Life and Societies of Apostolic Life (CICLSAL) 220
Cosmic eschatology 162f, 165, 256
Cosmos 154, 164-167, 176, 184, 241, 248
Council 21, 30-33, 35-37, 41f, 44, 55f, 68, 78, 109, 121-123, 127, 153, 185, 187, 192, 199, 203, 207f, 214, 217, 230, 234, 236f, 240, 246f
Council of Trent 23, 30f, 68
Covenant 15, 70f, 74, 160f, 178, 182, 235, 243
Creatio continua 157, 174
Creatio ex-nihilo 8, 149
Curia 46
Data 15
De Chardin, Pierre Teilhard 175
Dean 27
Deanery 27, 63, 115, 118, 122-124, 201, 203, 209, 258
Decolonization 30, 55f, 68, 104, 109

Deforestation 7, 188, 194-197, 209f, 254
Degradation, Environmental 7, 108, 195, 230, 238, 242
Dialogue 26, 34, 48, 50, 55, 95, 134, 148, 220, 224f, 233f, 242, 255
Dignity 28, 38, 41, 56, 90, 110, 125, 146, 162, 172, 195, 243f
Diocese of Lilongwe Council for Catholic Youth (DLCCY) 193, 199, 207
Domination 99, 142-147, 165
Dominion 8, 142, 149, 159, 179f, 184, 189, 191, 243, 264
Donders, Joseph 105, 130
Doyle, Dennis 11, 34, 72
Dulles, Avery 16f, 78
Ecclesia in Africa 6, 10, 46-48, 50, 54f, 75, 95, 113, 119f
Ecclesiological restructuring 62
Ecclesiology 6, 8, 10, 18-24, 26, 28, 30-32, 35, 37, 42, 44f, 47-49, 54-57, 59f, 62, 66, 68, 70, 78, 95, 103, 106, 108f, 121, 123f, 131-133, 135, 138f, 141, 145, 147f, 192, 199f, 208, 214-216, 223, 230-233, 237, 245-258, 260, 263f
Ecclesiology, African 55, 70, 131, 192

Ecology 9, 143, 145-147, 162, 171, 173, 189, 193, 195, 230, 241f, 244, 257
Eco-schools 193, 196f, 230
Ecosystem 242
Ecumenical council 33f, 78
Ecumenism 134, 148, 255
Energy saving 195f, 198, 204, 207
Environmental protection 187, 193
Environmental salvation 150f, 162, 230
Episcopal Conference of Malawi (ECM) 189, 220, 223, 229
Ethical considerations 242
Ethnocentrism 48, 99, 102-104, 107, 255
Evangelii Nuntiandi 39, 60, 109f, 127
Evangelization 21, 46-48, 50-52, 54, 56, 58, 60, 103, 108, 110, 113, 127, 129, 163, 165f, 168, 200, 203, 216
Familia Dei 6, 149
Family of God 6, 8, 30, 33, 35f, 38, 40f, 47-52, 54f, 57-62, 66, 70, 72, 75-78, 82, 95, 103, 108f, 114, 121, 123, 125, 127, 132, 134, 137, 139, 148, 192, 199f, 208, 213, 215f, 223, 229, 231f, 236f, 240, 246, 255, 262
Family planning 199, 207, 210

Fellowship 7, 63, 66, 80, 111, 120, 160, 233
Feminism 143
Flock of God 13, 28
Francis of Assisi 168-170, 172f, 238
Fraternity 7f, 17, 50, 63, 66, 68f, 125-127, 155, 169f, 172, 190f, 200, 208f, 213, 215, 230f, 234, 245f, 257, 264
Gaudium et Spes 16f, 39-41, 127, 129, 185, 234, 236, 246f
Gilman, Charlotte Perkins 140
Globalization 81, 91, 97f, 127, 188, 239f
God's immanence 172, 184
God's transcendence 142, 184
Grassroots 27, 48, 55f, 59, 62f, 102, 111f, 114, 123f, 128, 131f, 148f, 194-196, 229f
Gwengwe, John W. 89
Healey, Joseph 6, 57f, 61, 114
Herald 15f, 29
Hierarchy 19-23, 32, 36, 53, 56, 117, 121, 131
Historicity 19, 23f, 26, 30, 46f, 103, 109, 143, 147, 163, 232f, 236, 262
Hoa Nguyen-Van Hien, Simon 33
Human life 7, 17, 87, 105, 130, 149, 155, 158, 164, 166, 190, 229, 231f, 234, 238f, 241

Images 11-15, 18, 30, 35f, 41, 70, 76f, 106, 108
Imago Dei 8, 149, 190
Incarnation 73f, 124, 163, 174, 184, 248
Inculturation 46-48, 113, 129
Individualism 77, 82, 92, 105, 125
Infallibility 32
Inferiorization 70, 141, 145, 147-150, 254
Institution 10, 15f, 18, 25, 29f, 32, 34-38, 44, 68, 93, 95, 98, 109, 115, 121, 131, 133-135, 193, 229, 260
Institutional-hierarchical nature 30, 32, 68
Interconnectedness 116, 124, 164, 257
International Union of Superiors General (IUSG) 220
Intrinsic goodness 155, 190, 260
John Paul II, Pope 6, 10, 13, 15, 21f, 40f, 45-48, 50f, 55, 60f, 75, 79, 95, 113, 119, 120, 125f, 129, 152f, 171f, 181, 184f, 240, 243, 247
John XXIII, Pope 33f, 78
Johnson, Sirleaf 101
Justice 17, 46, 48, 51-55, 76, 99, 120, 125, 127f, 133, 180, 187, 193, 197, 222, 230, 240f, 261

Kachiwala, Agness 204
Kalilombe, Patrick Augustine 59, 61f, 65, 114f, 118
Kalimanjira, Matthews 198
Kaliu, Anita 202
Kamuzu Banda, Hastings 62, 64, 114
Kasiya, Thomas 209
Kay, Ariel Salleh 143
Killiness, Kaphantengo 204f
Kinship 83, 85-87, 92, 96, 106, 139
Kirchhoffer, David 9, 257
Koinonia 34, 36, 78
Laudato Si 8, 176, 188, 220, 238-240, 242, 244f, 255, 263
Liberation theology 263
Lilongwe Archdiocese 112, 120, 124, 131, 200, 230
Local Church 6, 27, 36, 55-57, 59f, 108-113, 115, 117-120, 129-132, 149, 186, 200, 213, 230, 233, 237, 258, 261
Lumen Gentium 6, 13f, 16, 32, 36-38, 192, 234
Lumko 9, 31, 57, 67, 83, 93, 257
Machemba, Jennifer 218, 225
Magalasi, John 65, 227
Magesa, Laurenti 78, 131
Marriage Encounter (ME) 120, 193, 223-228, 230
Matemba, Steve 197f
Mbiti, John S. 80f, 83-86, 88, 93f

Merchant, Carolyn 145
Metaphor 6, 10-12, 15, 33, 35, 41f, 50, 59, 70, 78, 95, 97f, 121, 128, 133-135, 142f, 148, 192
Methodology 142
Mini-synod 61, 65f, 200
Miphakati 6, 61f, 123, 125
Missionary Church 113, 131f
Mitigation 7f, 192, 230, 232, 246, 264
Mkhori, Felix 65f
Mnjowe, Adamson 196, 207
Models 10-12, 15-19, 21-24, 78
Models of Church 15
Moderation 185-187, 259, 261
Modernization 81, 91, 97f
Moemeka, Andrew 83
Moltmann, Jürgen 163f
Moyol, Fulata 210
Mpakati, Attati 62
Mthumba, Martin 215
Mvula, Herman Yokoniah 151
Mystery 11f, 14, 16, 26, 35f, 39, 48, 73, 138, 153, 161, 165, 247, 252
Mystical communion 29, 134
Natural environment 7f, 118, 154, 158-161, 168f, 175, 177, 179f, 182f, 233, 239, 246, 254f, 260-262
Nature 7f, 10, 12-16, 21-24, 26, 28, 32-34, 48-50, 54, 66, 72-74, 77, 79, 82, 90, 92, 96,

98, 103, 108f, 136-139, 141-147, 149, 159, 161-163, 165, 167-171, 173-177, 179-189, 191-193, 222, 231, 234-238, 240f, 243, 245-249, 251, 253-261, 263f
Ndau, Michael 85
Neoplatonism 19f
Nepotism 102f, 118
New creation 9, 77, 136, 163, 176, 183, 246, 248-256, 258, 261, 263
Ngala, Gaudencia 224
Ngala, Robert 224
Ngalande, Francis 215
Nkhoma, George 194
Nominalism 22
Nova creatio 8, 232, 245f
Obiefuna, Archbishop Albert K. 49
Okafor, Festus 89f
O'Meara, Thomas Franklin 18f, 21-24
Orobator, Agbonkhianmeghe E. 17, 54, 76, 131
Ott, Martin 11
Outstations 58, 63, 123, 208
Over-population 199, 205
Papal primacy 32
Parishes 27, 58, 63, 65f, 109, 117f, 123, 130, 141, 194, 196f, 206-208, 211, 214f, 221, 227f, 261
Participation 7, 26f, 35, 45, 56, 60, 66f, 84, 86, 91, 93, 96,
100-102, 112, 115f, 122, 130f, 141, 143, 148, 172, 190, 195, 203, 206, 252
Particularism 48, 104, 255
Patriarchy 98, 101, 140
Paul VI, Pope 34, 39, 44f, 60f, 78, 111, 127
People of God 12-14, 28, 36-38, 66, 68, 71f, 76, 82, 96, 115, 118, 122-124, 135, 199, 214, 220, 264
Peschke, Karl H. 159, 177, 182, 187, 189f
Phenomenological historicism 11, 19, 24
Philosophy 18-23, 29, 80f, 83f, 93f, 105, 144, 146, 173
Phiri, Jonas 61
Pius IX, Pope 41
Plotinus 19
Pollution 7, 187, 210, 238f, 254, 260
Priests 20f, 46, 52, 56, 71f, 75, 94, 114, 116, 118, 121-124, 129, 132, 201, 213-215, 217, 220, 224-226, 230
Pseudo-Dionysius 19
Rahner, Karl 26
Recapitulation 165
Reconciliation 17, 48, 51-55, 59, 76, 128, 166, 169, 183f, 249, 255, 263
Reformation 22, 31, 252
Religion 7, 23, 85f, 88, 93f, 102f, 106, 130f, 134f, 138,

140, 142, 145, 151f, 242, 245
Restrictivism 136f
Ruether, Rosemary 144, 146
Sacrament 15f, 23, 29, 35, 65, 127, 207
Sanon, Archbishop A.T. 49
Scala natura 8, 149, 171
Scotus, John Duns 174f
Secularization 81, 97
Self-control 179, 186f, 259
Self-limitation 185f, 259, 261
Self-ministering 62, 115-117, 123
Self-propagating 62, 115-117, 123
Self-supporting 115, 117, 123
Servant 15, 17, 23, 28f, 55, 76, 127f, 132, 178f, 258
Small Christian Community (SCC) 6, 27, 30f, 48, 57-63, 65-68, 83, 93, 109, 113-116, 118-121, 123, 125-127, 130f, 193, 195-197, 200-203, 206, 208f, 224, 230, 258
Sociality 26
Socio-anthropological foundations 70, 78
Solidarity 7, 10, 37, 41, 48-50, 55f, 63, 66, 77, 83, 90f, 96, 103, 106, 124-126, 132, 149, 183, 213-215, 219, 236f, 241

Spiritual movements 118-121, 132
Stewardship 150, 152, 177f, 190, 243, 262
Synod 44-50, 52-56, 66, 68, 95, 119, 127, 144
Theology 6f, 10f, 18f, 21, 29, 33, 35, 48, 55, 57, 59, 61, 91, 95, 103, 105, 108f, 115, 118, 124, 129f, 134, 137, 142, 145, 147, 150, 164-166, 168, 173-177, 180, 182f, 186f, 189, 191, 200, 237, 245, 249f, 256f, 263f
Traditionalism 81
Tribalism 102
Trinity 72, 74
Ubuntu philosophy 105
Universal Church 26, 30, 43-45, 47, 52, 60, 110, 112, 116, 120
Universal redemption 159, 166, 264
Urbanization 80f, 91
Vatican Council II 6, 11, 13f, 16f, 23, 26, 30, 32-38, 41, 45, 48, 56f, 59, 68, 72, 95, 109, 111, 115, 122, 127, 129, 159, 177, 182, 187, 189f, 200, 215, 218, 223
Worldviews 8, 142, 146
Zuma, Dlamini 101